2 Cents of Reason

A DEEP DIVE INTO WHAT SHAPES US

Donnell Harris

Title: 2 Cents of Reason
Author: Donnell Harris
Copyright ©2025 by Donnell Harris
All rights reserved.
No part of this book may be reproduced, distributed, or transmitted in any form or by any means, including photocopying, recording, or other electronic or mechanical methods, without the prior written permission of the publisher, except in the case of brief quotations embodied in critical reviews and certain other noncommercial uses permitted by copyright law. For permission requests, write to the publisher at the address below.

Published by Pine Tree Press

www.pinetreepress.com
Printed in USA

DEDICATION

To my father, Francis E. Harris, who on Saturday, August 24, 2024, urged me to rise to this challenge and see it through. My dad is special—not because he is perfect, but because he, like all of us, carries the fine print of human challenges and growth. When I was a kid, he often shared this poem by Sam Walter Foss:

> Let me live in a house by the side of the road,
> Where the race of men go by;
> The men who are good and the men who are bad,
> As good and as bad as I.
> I would not sit in the scorner's seat,
> Or hurl the cynic's ban;
> Let me live in a house by the side of the road
> And be a friend to man.
>
> I see from my house by the side of the road,
> By the side of the highway of life,
> The men who press with the ardor of hope,
> The men who are faint with the strife.
> But I turn not away from their smiles nor their tears
> Both parts of an infinite plan;
> Let me live in my house by the side of the road
> And be a friend to man.
>
> Let me live in my house by the side of the road
> Where the race of men go by;
> They are good, they are bad, they are weak,
> They are strong,
> Wise, foolish— so am I.
> Then why should I sit in the scorner's seat
> Or hurl the cynic's ban? —
> Let me live in my house by the side of the road
> And be a friend to man.

I appreciate my dad's unwavering support. I also dedicate this work to the many librarians and library staff who tirelessly protect and preserve the written word. Locally, they have been my anchor. In recent years, many of these unsung heroes have faced immense challenges, made sacrifices, and provided me with a sanctuary to create these pages. To them, I offer my deepest gratitude. Blessings to all who champion the sacred spaces of learning.

TABLE OF CONTENTS

Introduction To "2 Cents Of Reason" 8

Section I: My Introduction & Personal Evolution

This section offers a backstage pass to my personal journey an unfiltered look at the experiences and challenges that shaped my perspectives. Through the trials and triumphs of my life, I have forged my own '2 cents of reason.' My story matters. My insights hold weight.

My Letter to You 10
The Shortest Reason 12
My Back Story 13
There exists a well 46
Lost But Found: 50
Life: The Great Professor 56

Section II: The Well of Reason

In this section, I invite you to walk alongside me as I explore the philosophical path, experiences, and discoveries that have shaped my inner thoughts—insights I believe will leave a lasting impact.

The Labyrinth of Life 63
The Bubble Effect 75
Let's Talk About Culture 125
Cultural Incarceration and Cultural Confinement 155
Let's Rethink Poverty: 180
Perspective Thinking 186
The Difference Between a Lie and Perspective 224
Man In Population 230
The Powers of Imagination 242
The Reactive Mind 254

Section III: Personal Control & Human Potential

This section dives into the boundless potential within us, the power we hold, and the profound responsibility that comes with it. It's a call to awaken, to rise, and to own the impact we can make.

Myth Conceptions 261
Energies in Motion 293
Paying It Forward 306
A Modern Understanding / Opening New Doors 312
Breaking Free from the Joneses 315
A Reason to Live Out Loud 328

Section IV: A Pause & Call to Action

This section offers a moment of deep reflection before igniting a rallying cry for freedom, bold action, and unstoppable progress.

I've Seen a Lot 334
Keep Up the Fight 339
2 More Cents 342
A Bonus 2 Cents of Reasoning 374
One Last Call 393
Cultural Illiteracy: The Controlled Supremacy of Taste 397
Cultural Literacy: The Power to See, Feel, and Navigate Difference 417

ACKNOWLEDGEMENTS

This book is not mine alone—it belongs to every voice that struggles, questions, hopes, and dares to dream of a better world. I owe thanks to those who challenged me, those who encouraged me, and those who gave me silence to think. To my community, near and far—you are the reason these words exist.

I write with gratitude to all who carry the weight of social challenges, yet still choose to seek peace. May these pages meet you where you are and remind you that your voice, too, matters.

A special thanks goes to **Linda Harris**, who, though more than a thousand miles away, patiently read and critiqued each chapter as I wrote it. Her dedication, insight, and steady encouragement helped give shape and clarity to this work.

Finally, I thank the unseen—those ancestors, mentors, and everyday people who poured wisdom into me without ever knowing where their influence would travel. You are present here, line by line.

INTRODUCTION TO "2 CENTS OF REASON"

Here's my take: I've been around. I've worn out my share of expensive shoes, walking paths that taught me life's lessons, some easy and others hard-earned. These lessons, gathered over more than 60 years, are what I'm sharing with you now.

First, let me say this: I hope you purchased this book. Not because I'm counting pennies, but because I want you to invest in its ideas. Better yet, buy another copy or two and share them with your friends. Sit down together. Discuss the concepts within these pages. Let's start conversations that will spark growth, challenge assumptions, and inspire change.

This book is not a lecture; it's an invitation. We live in a world that is both fragile and resilient, flawed yet full of potential. Picture humanity as a fabric. Some parts are stained, some worn thin, and others scorched by the fires of history. Yet this is the only fabric we have, and it is ours to mend, preserve, and strengthen. We, the billions of people on this planet, are the fibers that weave its stories, carry its histories, and lay the foundation for the generations yet to come.

Through this book, I'm sharing ideas born from my experiences and shaped by moments of joy, pain, triumph, and failure. These ideas include *The Labyrinth*, my personal lens on navigating life's complexities, and *The Bubble Effect*, an exploration of the barriers we create around ourselves and how they confine us. I'll discuss *Cultural Incarceration* and *Cultural Confinement*, shedding light on the ways culture can both define and limit us, and why reducing a person's identity to the color of their skin or other superficial markers does more harm than good.

Then, I'll introduce you to someone extraordinary: a little boy who taught me a lesson I call *Perspective Thinking*. Through him, I learned the humbling truth that the balance in my "intellectual bank account" was insufficiently funded. From there, I'll take you on a journey to *The Bubble Theory* and *The Rubber-Band Effect*, concepts that challenge us to stretch beyond our limits and explore the kinetic potential we unleash when we break free of societal constraints.

Throughout this exploration, my goal is simple: to show you the exponential strength we gain when we stand together—not in uniformity, but in unity. Humanity thrives when our collective will is directed toward building a future that uplifts everyone, a trajectory that is eternally upward bound.

Finally, let me leave you with a story about "keeping up with the Joneses." I've met the Joneses. I've eaten their food, sipped their wine, sat on their fine furniture, and even slept in their beds. But as a poor kid from Parole, I reached a startling conclusion—one I'll share with you in these pages.

When you finish this book, ask yourself, "Did I get it?" If the answer is no, don't worry. The book is in your hands. Read it again. Find a friend, start a reading circle, and explore these ideas together. Every discussion tightens the fabric of our shared humanity, making it stronger and more enduring.

The ideas in this book shouldn't stop with me. They're meant to be shared, adapted, and carried forward. Because together, we can mend what's torn, strengthen what's weak, and weave a world that's better for all.

Let's begin.

MY LETTER TO YOU

Dear Reader,

Again, I want to express my deepest gratitude for your picking up this book and spending your valuable time with me and the words that follow. I know I can sometimes come across as complex—okay, I own it. But I've also been told that I've been inspirational, that I give people hope. The truth is, I have never, and will never, give people hope. Hope is a positive force that we all cultivate within ourselves, at our own pace and in our own way. My role, at best, is to assist you in discovering the hope that is already a part of you—a gift you give to yourself as you maneuver the challenges of life.

From time to time, we all find ourselves under dark clouds of doubt, resentment, and second thoughts. Yet, for most of us, there are also moments when the sun breaks through, casting beams of positivity and light into our lives. Here's what I want you to know: we are alive. If you are reading this, you know that. I'm referring to the energy that you and I have on whatever level. And because we are alive, it is our time to truly live. It is time to be our better selves. We have the power to collectively push back against the cloud of malaise that too often shrouds our nation and much of our world.

I have stood on my often-lonely soapbox since my youth, speaking truths that many did not want to hear. But now, my time has come to break free from the confines of doubt and hesitation. This is my moment to step into the light, to let my voice resonate with the clarity and power that has been building inside me all these years.

No longer will I be constrained by fear or uncertainty. Instead, I embrace the strength that comes from knowing my own worth and the potential within me. It's time to turn my words into actions, to transform dreams into reality, and to inspire others to find their own voices. I invite you to stand.

Consider my intent as you read. My goal is not to make you think like me but to urge you to breathe deeply—then exhale. Take a moment to reason—not just react.

Reason with the full depth of your breath, with the weight of awareness, and with an appreciation for the shared challenges of life. **We are all bound together, a global body, a family—*not by choice, but by existence itself.***

No one selects the labyrinth they must navigate. No one chooses the circumstances into which they are born. Some are stamped "**FORTUNATE**," others "**UNFORTUNATE**." Yet, we are all here—**alive in this moment.**

We must confront **the Bubble**—the unseen walls that shape our perceptions. We must grasp **Perspective**—the lens molded by experience, environment, and inherited thought. These forces either imprison us or set us free.

My **solemn intent** is to awaken a deeper level of reasoning—one that doesn't just serve the self but uplifts **humanity as a whole.** Because the highest freedom is not in what we possess, but in **how we think.**

Let us rise together, fueled by the passion and conviction that we can change the world for the better. Together, we can embrace the light and create a future filled with possibility and hope.

With warmth and appreciation,

Donnell

THE SHORTEST REASON

A reason for our commonality

Unless some groundbreaking life science has been unleashed while I wasn't looking, every single one of us—every grand thinker, every humble laborer, every saint, and every sinner—owes their existence to one undeniable fact: we are the product of a sperm and egg merger.

That's right, folks. No matter how high we climb or how lofty our ambitions, every one of us started as a microscopic collaboration project. An egg and a sperm walked into a cellular bar, and the rest, as they say, is history.

Think about that the next time someone gets too big for their britches. We all share this hilariously humbling origin story. From the most celebrated minds in science to the person who argues about pineapple on pizza, we're all here because two cells decided to get together and make magic—or at least a very elaborate and interesting science experiment.

So, the next time someone questions your worth, remind them that without a little wiggle and a lot of luck, they wouldn't be here either.

And there you have it—the shortest reason, and perhaps the most sobering reminder of our undeniable connection.

MY BACK STORY

Allow me to introduce myself to some and reintroduce myself to others who may be learning about me for the first time. As the developer of **"The 10 Commandments of Peace**,*"* I've embarked on an incredible journey filled with profound discoveries and life lessons. I invite you to join me as I share the story of where I've been, what I've learned, and where I am now. Let's dive into a remarkable journey that bridges culture, faith, and the transformative power of self-discovery.

Picture this: it's a chilly Friday evening, and we're nestled into a cozy, dimly lit living room. The aroma of hot cocoa swirls in the air as we sip and settle in. I want to take you back to my childhood—a time rooted in the doctrines of the Seventh-day Adventist faith. Growing up within this faith wasn't a simple inheritance; it was a culture of deep, intentional indoctrination. My upbringing wasn't about fostering independent thought but about instilling obedience and the rhythms of tradition, much like the comforting but predictable cadence of those Friday evenings.

As we sit together, wrapped in warmth, I'll share something important: I'm not here to persuade you religiously or spiritually. This book isn't about conversion but understanding—a pathway to share how I arrived at my own conclusions.

Within the Adventist community, many of the older members around me were childless couples who, despite their lack of firsthand experience, often shared guidance on parenting and personal character. Their reference? The writings of a woman who passed away in 1915—a figure renowned for her visions and devotion. Her teachings, immortalized in *Child Guidance*, emphasized purity, honesty, self-control, and reverence. It was a framework for living and child-rearing that shaped my upbringing in ways I am still unraveling today.

The goal was straightforward: followers were encouraged to adopt these teachings, likely as a means to instill values seen as "winning" qualities. Yet, there was a twist. Many of the individuals who championed these values had only limited literacy. Some could read at an elementary level; others relied on the rhythms of spoken words without fully understanding the complex ideas embedded within them. The difference between sounding out words and comprehending them runs deep. But there they stood, guiding others with conviction.

How, then, did they share such rich information if they could barely read it themselves? The answer lies in a centuries-old tool of human connection—oral tradition.

Oral tradition holds a significant place in the history of human culture. It's the vessel through which knowledge, values, and cultural identity flow, passed down verbally from generation to generation. Oral traditions transcend literacy, conveying wisdom and values through folktales, songs, chants, and stories. In communities across the world, where literacy wasn't the norm, oral tradition carried the essence of knowledge, preserving beliefs, literature, laws, and other understandings.

In my community, this tradition wasn't just a means of sharing religious beliefs; it became a foundation upon which our entire worldview rested.

As a child, I couldn't fully grasp the impact of oral tradition or the unfiltered, sometimes unfounded knowledge it conveyed. The adults in my life weren't bad people; they were simply sharing what they had learned, passing on wisdom that, while sacred to them, was often unverified, unscientific, and occasionally misleading. As a child, I assumed they knew what they were talking about—after all, they were the adults in the room, the keepers of tradition and knowledge. Like my friends who grew up in similar communities, I trusted these teachings as solid and true.

Each Friday evening, we followed a weekly ritual to welcome the Sabbath—from sunset Friday to sunset Saturday, what we called 'God's holy day.' I'm grateful we didn't live in Northern Alaska, or our "holy day" would have stretched on far too long! To welcome the Sabbath, we sang hymns, recited memorized Bible verses, and closed with a prayer, gathering warmth from the ritual and each other. I vividly remember one particular Friday evening in our small four-room house. The space was snug, filled with the distinct, familiar smells of well-scrubbed floors, thanks to an overused bottle of Breath-O-Pine, mingling with the aromas of our Sabbath meals and the pungent scent of kerosene from the old Duotherm space heater we simply called "the stove." The stove stood as our defense against the cold that crept through cracks in the doors and windows, offering us a comforting shield from the outside chill.

After the Sabbath welcome, we'd settle down for a simple evening meal, one that still evokes memories of that era. One of my favorites was Great Northern beans with sliced hotdogs. Momma would make cornbread too—not the homemade kind but from the light blue Jiffy Corn Muffin mix. She'd blend it with milk and an egg, then bake it in a sheet pan. When it was done, she'd peel back the paper on a stick of oleo-margarine and rub it over the top until the cornbread gleamed under the dim kitchen light. I still remember that warm glow cast over our modest home as if it were a rare treasure, that cornbread shining golden, a simple pleasure in a humble home.

Sitting there, soaking in the warmth and aroma, I had my first inklings of what it meant to live within the framework of a capitalist society. We didn't have much, but those Friday nights felt abundant. It was during those times, however, that I began noticing our place on the margins—aware of what others had and what we did not, realizing how society often defined people by material means. Our house was small, and our resources limited. Daddy worked two jobs, and Momma cleaned other people's houses—never for "colored" families, she'd say, though her reasons eluded me then. With time, I started to understand her sentiments, realizing the intricate cultural dynamics that shaped the way we viewed ourselves and our place in the world.

One Friday night stands out so vividly, cursed with the kind of bitter cold that bit at your skin, tickled your nose, and chilled a young boy's bones. Yet, in our little house, we were safe and warm. After dinner, Momma would gather me and my two younger brothers, and we'd settle on the floor at her feet while she took her place on the bench in front of the piano. Yes, a full-size, black upright piano sat in our small house—a strange luxury amid our modest belongings. My brothers and I might tinker with it now and then, but it was Momma and my oldest sister who could truly make it sing.

These moments—this blend of music, ritual, warmth, and scarcity—were more than routine. They were shaping me, planting seeds of understanding that would grow in unexpected ways. They taught me that even in the smallest spaces, we can nurture something grand, something that transcends circumstances and the limitations imposed by society. These evenings and memories became the backbone of my journey to comprehend, question, and finally reconcile the layers of my heritage with the values I would ultimately choose to carry forward.

Music was woven into the fabric of our home. My dad would strum away on a Sears Signature guitar that I used to think was called the "Alan Francis Guitar." It wasn't until later that I realized the name was a nod to my cousin Alan Francis—my dad's brother's son—from whom the guitar was borrowed. My next-to-oldest sister played the violin, and I was handed a clarinet, though I'm not sure anyone would say I actually played it. My two younger brothers took up the cellos, adding their deep, rich notes to our family's symphony.

It was in those moments, surrounded by music and the warmth of our small house, that I felt a sense of connection—something more profound than just family, something that spoke to the rhythms of life itself. Those were the moments that made everything else fade away, leaving only the sound of our shared melodies and the feeling of being part of something larger than ourselves.

Just a note, as you journey through this book, I want you to be right here with me. My hope is that, as we move forward together, you're finding a sense of comfort—getting to know the me that makes me, me.

Two doors down from our house lived my school's music teacher, Mrs. Irene Richardson. Back then, we studied real subjects in school, and she had an eye for potential. She noticed something in me, even when I was just five years old. I remember being on stage at a PTA meeting one night, playing my little xylophone. I'd learned to play it well enough to perform, and it felt like a big deal at the time.

One day, while I was playing outside, Mrs. Richardson called me over to her house. She only lived a couple of doors down from the Harrises on either side of the road. "Donny," she asked, "would you like to play the piano?" My heart leaped with excitement, but even at that young age, I knew everything came with a cost. Before I could say anything, she assured me that she wouldn't charge me a thing—she wanted to teach me for free. She just needed me to ask my daddy if he'd mind. I rushed home, bubbling with excitement, and presented the idea to Daddy.

"Daddy, Mrs. Richardson wants to teach me how to play the piano. She said she would do it for free," I said, full of hope and excitement. But before I could finish, my father's face darkened with anger. He erupted, his voice booming in a way that sent shockwaves through me. "I'm not going to have my son playing the piano. That's for girls, and you are not a girl!"

I stood there, stunned and confused, trying to understand how my innocent request had triggered such an intense reaction. "But she said it would be free," I stammered, still clinging to the idea that maybe the cost-free offer would change his mind.

In that moment, I didn't realize it, but something deeper was unfolding. Looking back now, I see it clearly—a conservative python was raising its head, often slithering through our home. It was a cultural snake, coiled in the shadows, ready to strike whenever I dared to step outside the rigid boundaries it imposed. That strange shadow, I now recognize, was the dark art of stereotyping—a force that would follow me, whispering limitations and feeding fears throughout the experiences of my life.

This strange episode went on, "I don't care! And don't ask me that again." As a child, I did not understand what was going on. I don't think the word stereotyping had even reached my vocabulary.

As a child, I just felt bad. I did not know the words then but I was learning the feel of being humiliated and rejected. I've got to go back and tell the music teacher no. Dady said, "NO". I had no idea how to produce reasonable argument. I was a child. Daddy would talk about old piano players like Cab Calloway, Ray Charles, Nat King Cole (whom I confused with Old King Cole. They both had soul. One just had a merry old one), and many others. He liked their music even though the Cult was teaching that their music came from the devil. But daddy had another reason for his one of many outbursts. My eyes had reached the dawn of opening. The house of cards was beginning to get taller but a breeze was in the distance.

The child in me retreated, silenced by my father's anger and left with a sense of lingering confusion. His reaction hung over me like an unspoken rule—a reminder that in our home, there were invisible lines that I hadn't even realized existed. The simplicity of my request to learn the piano had stirred something much larger than I could understand as a young boy. All I knew was that an invisible wall had come up, dividing what was acceptable from what was not, and the piano had landed squarely on the "not" side.

As time went on, I began to notice other walls—small, subtle barriers that shaped not only my actions but also the way I perceived myself. It wasn't just the piano that I was forbidden to touch. It was any expression that seemed to step outside the narrow expectations laid out for me, any interest that didn't fit into the mold of what was deemed "appropriate" for an SDA Christian boy. The world around me, though modest, seemed to be made of concrete rules that kept our feet planted on familiar ground, discouraging even the slightest curiosity about the unknown. We were the world. We were the small world.

That sense of cultural confinement was woven into many aspects of our lives, and I wasn't the only one who felt it. Each member of my family had their own lines they couldn't cross, their own silent battles with the expectations set by tradition, society, and, most powerfully, by family. Even my sister, whose nimble fingers danced over violin strings, wasn't immune to these invisible boundaries. Her talent was acknowledged, encouraged even, but only within certain contexts, certain confines. Beyond that, anything too expressive, too bold, seemed to step into territory that was best left unexplored.

As I grew, I started to understand this invisible force for what it was—stereotyping. It was an unspoken language, a silent teacher, teaching us to stay within the boundaries set long before we were born. This was more than mere tradition; it was a force that told me who I could be and, just as importantly, who I could not be. I learned quickly that stereotypes weren't just labels but anchors, keeping us tethered to a version of ourselves that often didn't feel complete or true.

Reflecting now, I can see how the rigid structure of my upbringing left its mark, but it also sparked something equally powerful: a quiet rebellion, a desire to see beyond the walls that had been set up for me. I began questioning those boundaries, asking myself why certain paths were closed off, why certain dreams were considered wrong, even if they didn't harm anyone. These questions simmered inside me, slowly cooking up a need for understanding that would follow me throughout my life.

That moment with Mrs. Richardson, my father, and the forbidden piano became a cornerstone in my journey toward self-awareness. It marked the beginning of a quest—not just for skill or education but for the freedom to define myself on my terms, to break free from the expectations that had tried to keep me within their grasp.

Let's pause for a moment. Picture Momma reading us a Sabbath School lesson from the "Our Little Friend" weekly magazine. It was our SDA version of the Sunday School lesson for kids. On that one special night, something was about to ignite my personal fuse of change. Momma was reading to my two younger brothers and me. As I recall, I heard a story about a guy named Solomon. The way I remember it, the story was rewritten for young children, not truly accurate to the Bible.

As I get older and more studied, I realize many of the stories and images we were shown lacked Biblical accuracy. For example, we were told the story of Moses and the burning bush, but the Bible says the bush wasn't actually burning. Over time, I learned these lessons were designed to keep us under control and feed the economically hungry mouths of those at the denominational top teaching them. This story was no different.

So, let's get back to Momma on the bench at the piano. She's diligently following the pattern she was given, reading to us the story of Solomon. In the story, Solomon had a conversation with God, who gave him the honor of asking for anything he desired. This moment marked one of the many turning points in my life. In short God says, "Hey guy. I've been paying attention to you". Now this is my short version.

I'm telling the story as I understood probably a citizen of the first or second grade. "Guy, 'What would you like to have?" Wow wouldn't I like to have that question given to me from the master of the universe and beyond. "What would you like?" In other words, "What do you want?"

Solomon's response was simple. With all the things that he could ask for, Ol' Solo said, he wanted WISDOM AND KNOWLEDGE. So, God responded by approving his request. However, because he asked and received this approval, God gave him so many other things as well. The focus in this story was that God gave this dude riches and power. This guy was a King like his daddy. King David, we called him.

The young child in me, the curtains were beginning to open on a growing stage. I realized we (our family) had many challenges. I was a kid learning the art of comparison. The neighborhood had families that had more. We were more than often coming up short. Sure, we had the typical responses I learned later to the question, "Daddy, can we get some McDonald's?" Daddy would respond, "No! When we get home your mother will make you some McDonald's." I was just beginning to learn how poor we were. I was observing living in the broke house. We had a pump that was not properly pumping well water. The toilet didn't flush well. The bathroom became no more than an indoor outhouse with a bathtub. The car often needed repairs. The water heater didn't keep up with heating. I had to share a bed with other family members who often had issues with nocturnal incontinence. From time to time that great big Duotherm space heater that took up way too much space in the living room would give up on heating when the ground outside was freezy-cold and white.

We had challenges, but this was the night to change my life. I listened to that story as well as I could. The sentence of my cultural incarceration had been read off in the courtroom of circumstances. I had learned what was right and what was wrong. I found out years later that it was the court order of the empirical spiritual judiciary that was shackling me; binding me in leg irons. As the bailiff of cultural belief was taking me away. "We are right" those who do not see or believe things that we are sentenced to believe and follow are evil. They are "Heathens" and "Philistines" they are spawns of the DEVIL. We had a private way of understanding the broken outside world. We were God's people; and God kept us broke and on the margins of failure to help us to develop and become His righteous minions to carry out His last days work. His last days work is to make others believe as we do. We were called to be Missionaries to the weak. We were distrustful of those who had materialistically more.

We were taught that it was a sin to become successful and selfish. Our money belonged to God. And … God makes limited attempts to share his wealth. By the time I hit elementary school, my head was already being filled with what I see now as nonsense goo. It was the sentence I was to be imprisoned with; seemingly for life. We used the old slave personas that identified the prominent white-man as "Sir" and the colored neighbor as his last name. The community was filled with people of little or no value unless they were friends of my dad.

We were to be suspicious of everyone. Everybody had ill intent. They could not be trusted. We would hand out a little tract that was titled, "Your Friends the Adventists". We were taught to be bait. Be nice to others so that we can at least get them on the hook. We can hold the catch until "Revival" or the "Evangelism" season would come. At that time, it was the pastor's job to convince others that they were destined for hell if they did not think as we did.

Those other people. Those other people. Those shameful, wicked, vile, deranged, dirty other people. Don't play with them. They may corrupt you. Being with any of them is a direct ticket to hell. The ground is about to open and swallow us all if we had any conversation about sex or any other taboo subject. Don't ask questions. Just be obedient. Do God's will and never, never ask for pay. God needs our money to hasten the rapid return of Jesus. Basically, I learned God has cattle on a thousand hills, but his wealth doesn't transfer well against the American dollar.

Now my mother was a little different. She was more patient and accepting. While my dad was an over-the-top SDA guy and the first one in his family, momma was a third generation Seventh Day Adventist. She was a little more laid back. Her heart was an open door to most excluding that witch and that little old man across the street. That was the other plague we had to live through in our home. We couldn't celebrate any holiday but the old man's birthday. That would be my granddaddy because his birthday was the fourth of July. America celebrated Grandaddy's birthday. But momma had ongoing Issues with her In-laws. They would argue fuss and fight often through my father. Daddy would not only lay down the law in our house, he would also fight energetically to lay down his parent's law in our house. His parents knew how we were to live. So, between the parents, the grandparents, and the church, I was worn out before taking on my new, and always continuing to grow, venture – school. There was an odd and growing legalism that was rapidly becoming the wallpaper of my life.

Life was packed with a lot of well wrapped boxes. Oh my God, the gifts the promises. The dreams pushed away in boxes stored with IOU cards and announcements. When the selective box of promise was opened, it was usually found to be empty. If a note would be written it would remind us of Jesus promise of golden streets and a land flowing with milk and honey. Interestingly, a good and powerful natural enema is produced with milk and honey. Maybe, that's why I now find many of those early entrapments full of – well I'll let you the reader figure that out. (Thanks for taking the time to read)

Life was something else. Joy was a sin. Anything that cost money was a sin. And no, momma could not make McDonald's at home (parents – Please don't tell your children that). Vegan meat made from pecans, oatmeal, cottage cheese, or home-made gluten, won't replace the smell of McDonald's fries and grilled onion aromas concentrated in the air of the fast-food giant that has served billions of sandwiches. We were taught to believe our gifts; our rewards are coming to us only when Jesus comes back. That's why the church needed both my savings and my hustling for endless offerings.

So here we are, back from the tangential train. I promise you, with the many stories that developed my viewpoints that I cherish today this reading train may run off the track a few times, but ride with me as long as you can. I promise I won't bite.

Where was I? Oh yeah. Momma on the bench at the piano. As she read, I was captivated by the simplicity of Solomon's request. He asked for wisdom and knowledge. Because he asked for these two items, God blessed him with an abundance of the many things that people refer to as wealth. This dude had everything followers of the world would want. By Biblical standards, He had it all. He had money in the bank. People brought him money – lots and lots of money. He built a great temple. They donated to him special items and exotic woods for construction. He had the sports car; camel fur and horsepower galore. I believe he had the golf course. He had tickets to the game. Whoa! Wait! He was the game. The dude had wives – hundreds of wives. He had girlfriends – Muchos Muchos buku buckets ~ storage units of girlfriends. A polygamist was to be our example, but that would not be shared in the storyline my mother shared.

That Friday night story at the piano bench was a sanitized version of the gameshow "Ask God". Ask him the right way and you will win the lottery. This is the careless teaching that has imprisoned so-many in a culture that should flow with freedom and curiosity, innovation and invention, new ideas that drive a more positive evolution of humanity. No, I was not taught as a child the realities of life. I was forced to drink the poison that has stifled and became a finishing line for so many. I was in a fix. Something was wrong. I needed a way out. I needed some security. I needed stability. I needed to pray. I decided that night as momma read that one story, life was going to change. She didn't know it, but I was fixated on a plan. I don't know for sure; I believe I was 5, 6, maybe 7 years old – and I had a secret plan.

Bedtime couldn't come fast enough. You see we had a ritual. As sinful as rituals are as Seventh Day Adventists, we damn sure had a lot of rituals. They started out as innocent rituals. Our ritual was to wash our face and hands and put on pajamas. Then when we were ready to go to bed, we had to kneel and say the same prayer each and every night.

"Now I lay me down to sleep, I pray oh Lord my soul to keep. God bless everybody. Make me a nice little boy. Thank you, God, for everything. God forgive me for what I did wrong today."

Then, in our prayers, we would pile on the accessories. You can imagine – the "Bless daddy" the "Bless mammas". Bless the church and the things that they told us were important. You get it – "Thanks for the food" and stuff like that. However, at my young age, that night, I made a decision. It was my secret. When the lights were out, I decided to have my own prayer. It was going to be by myself. I was going to design my own words and challenges to God. I knew that night from the piano bench to the bed what I needed to pray for. I was lacking something. That kid in me found out what it was. I couldn't get it from Wonder bread – that at that time *"helped build a body 12 ways"*. I wasn't going to get it from One-A-Day vitamins. Popeye's spinach was no match for what I decided to do that night.

We were dressed in our pajamas and sent to bed. We were inspected by my mother. Did I wash behind my ears? That was one of the big nightly interview questions. When we met up with the list of measurements, we were signed off on the approval to go to bed. There was one thing left to do, we had to go through the nightly ritual of prayer. We said our prayer and slid under the covers. She turned off the lights. It was usually quiet on Friday nights at that point. Unlike the other nights during the week, God didn't allow much during the hours of Sabbath observance. God didn't allow TV or any other form of entertainment.

I pretended to drift off. As soon as I believed everybody had gone to sleep, I got off my bottom bunk and hit the floor on bended knees. I spiritually headed off to God in prayer. "God" I thought, "we ain't got much. Please give me wisdom and knowledge. Thanks." That was good enough.

I've been praying that prayer for a long time—more than five decades, in fact. I've been asking for that same special request, but King Solomon's receipts must have gotten lost in the mail. Instead, I've received more challenge, confusion, pain, and disappointment than I ever imagined. I've seen the fog of humanity and the tornadic dance of trouble spiraling out of control. I've been discredited and mocked by many, including my own family, but despite it all, I had and continue to have a goal.

In my quest for wisdom, I discovered that the challenges I faced held unique stories and life lessons that resonate universally. I identified consistencies—a thread of reality weaving the fabric of the human family together. Despite our differences, often shaped by the billions of bubbles defining our cultural observances and actions, we share common experiences. We all breathe, our hearts beat, and some rely on artificial means, but we all move consistently through the life cycle, the time code, and life experience.

While I am not comparing myself to King Solomon, I often look back at his story and see a richness that goes beyond his reported wealth. His story is filled with errors in judgment that landed him in tight spots, forcing him to think quickly and come up with common solutions to uncommon challenges. We call Solomon wise, but let's not forget this man-whore and ladies' man had some residual issues from his adulterous dad, King David. We could say he had a hard time keeping it zipped up, but the zipper wasn't invented until the early 1890s. I guess he had some serious costume, robing, and disrobing issues.

Like Solomon's life, many things, odd things, occurred in the times of his life and the many centuries of life since those moments. I got up from my knees. I got in bed and went to sleep. I woke up the next day waiting for my wisdom. I waited for my knowledge. I wanted understanding. I wanted the things that the rich people have. I wanted a home that eight people could fit in comfortably. I wanted the dining room that some of my friends had. I wanted to see our China closet even though I had no clue as to what China was. I wanted to drink from something other than an old jelly or mayonnaise jar. I wanted the things that a child imagined Solomon to have because he pleased God when he asked for wisdom and knowledge.

For years, it has been like searching under a Christmas tree that didn't exist. There were no wrapped gifts to be ripped open with excitement. I would go to school and get beat up. I would go out on the playground and, as children would choose other kids to be on their kickball teams, I would have to wait for the teacher to encourage the other students to pick me. When they would not choose me to be on their side or teams, the teachers would often assign me to a team. This many times upset some students that showed their rage of having me on their teams. I was always losing value in myself that I never requested in the first place.

In grade six, daddy took the denominational bait. He sent my two younger brothers and me off to church school. The only thing I guess he knew or believed was that we were going to receive a good Christian education. Really? He sent three of his youngest sons off to a Christian Nationalist, YT assimilating reformatory school long before the title Christian Nationalist was coined. This was a group of many white kids that came from traditionally conservative backgrounds. Often, they were nasty. Now please don't get me wrong. Spencerville Jr. Academy had some wonderful loving kids as well. A couple of kids actually looked out for me more than often.

Most of the time I spent worried about how my younger brothers were being treated. Sure, I would here the things like the traditional, "You need to go back to where you people come from." When I hear that today, it sounds no different being said to someone else, someone's child, someone's brother or sister, a grandparent, a grandchild, as it did to that young six grader.

We would commute daily on a bus with other kids who attended that so-called church school. To get there from Annapolis, Maryland, we had to travel through Bowie and Crofton. We picked up some students there. We would cut through Ft. Mead and pick up some students there. We would travel through Laurel and Beltsville on our way to Spencerville. One day, we were returning from school. Traffic was at a standstill. I believe we were almost at the Red Barn near the intersection where we would cross over Beltsville Road. Traffic was not moving. There was a huge crowd at the Laurel Shopping Center. There were police and all sorts of flashing lights. Something happened that we could not see from the school bus windows.

Seeds were being planted. Many years we stood by and watch the slow growing reach of a strange plant. I was getting a front row seat and did not realize it. Life would go on and we would return to public school. That was because my grandfather, who would at times cross the fence of leadership and power that was governing our home, he got involved. I personally sought granddaddy's influence. I knew we had to get away from that school. It may have been good for some black kids that grew up there and was used to things being the way they were but, it was not good for us. It was a poor slow elixir of social bile that had a potential influence. Seeds were being planted.

I've had many experiences in my life between that time and the moment that I'm writing these words. The experiences, almost in totality, delivered an obvious impact on my life. Slowly the curtain would sway in the breezes of circumstances. Something was happening. Seeds were being planted.

I completed middle school, or as some would say in some school districts Jr. High School. I went to the same old Annapolis high school that my oldest brother and sister graduated from. The second year of high school, I attended South River high school. I then returned to the new Annapolis high school that I graduated from. I then ran off to college. I was back with the Seventh Day Adventist again. I was mentored by a great leader in that denomination, Edward Earl Cleveland.

Cleveland was an author that I had the honor of meeting before I arrived at what was then Oakwood College. In my freshman year, Dr. Cleveland had taken notice of a rare ability I had developed in talking with people. Even though he was a professor at the school, he was also the head of Student Missions. He and I would talk from time to time. He recruited me to be a Student Missionary. Under his leadership, I was sent to Japan where I served until my time was completed in the following year. Trust me, seeds were being planted.

Oh boy! Don't I have stories. I don't want to run the risk of boring you or losing you at this time. My life was splattered with experiences. But, isn't that every life that exist? The case that I am making is that many of my experiences were super extraordinary. I spent some time at the Capital Newspaper where I served as a District Manager and contributing editor from time to time. I had very good mentors like Fran Jacques, Tom Marquardt, and Sarah Neely. The most influential one was a former history teacher of mine George Rossiter. They each taught me very special things that changed my perspective in a moment. Their influencing was developing for me different perspectives. Seeds were being planted.

I worked for the Anne Arundel County Board of Education as a Teaching Assistant under Aretha Stubbs, Putt Willet, and Ron Alberico. I spent years there beginning as soon as I returned from Japan. I had the honor of working with students and teachers representing an array of backgrounds. Each one had a sticky note or story attached to them. I often took the time to listen. I remember the students introducing themselves on an occasion when one young man told me, his family was Palestinian and his family had no homeland. Seeds were being planted.

I recall meeting a number of prominent politicians and enjoying the honor of talking with them one on one as just with simple citizens like myself. I recall being invited to sit and talk with Ohio's Congressman Jim Traficant. I remember driving around to give California's Congressman Ron Dellums a tour of Annapolis and listen to his sharing his views on the U.S. and the world. I was extremely interested in his thoughts on South Africa and his Comprehensive Anti-Apartheid Act of 1986 that called for the divestments of American corporations. I will never forget talking with people like Rosa Parks who started our conversation by asking, "Baby, can you help me? I would like something to drink." I think she called me baby because she could not remember my name. The Joy was the care she used to engage me and the honor of having some moments with her.

I remember the people from Georgia like Dr. Bernice King who stopped me at the doors of Mount Olive AME church by saying, "Hold on a minute. I want to talk with you." I had the honor of meeting Congressman Hank Johnson when he served on the DeKalb County Board of Commissioners where I served as a Special Assistant to the Presiding Officer of the Commission Burl Ellis. The realest Georgian I saw standing on the mall by himself. He had participated in a couple of events we had invited him to when I served the community in Annapolis. I said to myself this would be an opportunity to speak with him again.

However, with his fame and recognition he wouldn't remember me. He's a politician. He has been around and knows many influential people. He surely won't remember me. I walked over and said, "Hello Mr. Lewis, I know you may not remember me but," and before I could say anything else social activist, and humanitarian giant Representative John Lewis looked me in the eyes and said, "Of course I remember you Brother Harris." These people were as real as real could be. Some of them shared their flaws as human but only to encourage me for the distance ahead in my life. Seeds were being planted.

When I authored my first book 'One Last Call," I remember the help and support I received with letters from people like New York's Governor Mario Cuomo and Pennsylvania's U.S. Senator Arlen Specter. These guys were able to understand me but more than that, I was able to understand their messages of support and guidance. These guys were not perfect people they were people. For so long, we have been growing more and more to miss that important fact. The celebrity is human. I could have said the political celebrity is human but it goes much further than that. Often, in our quest and sometimes struggle for that personal mount of better, we forget the commonality of human existence.

Yes, there are leaders in politics, sports, the arts, religion, commerce, and so many other venues that erect monumental attractions developing the mask of celebrity that we forget the celebrity was born too. They develop all around our world. They gain much attention. They are often known for their mistakes and failures. So often we build them and look at what we've helped to construct and trash and burn them in the flames of our disappointments, dissatisfactions, and volcanic torrent of oozing vitriol. I was paying attention and I learned some things. Seeds were being planted.

I recall meeting the daughter of Senator Bobby Kennedy. She taught me grace and true humility. I never met her dad, but her dad inspired me with a very simple phrase printed on a paper fan left in that small church I partially developed my spiritual roots in. That statement read, *"Some men see things as they are and ask why. I dream things that are not and ask, why not?"* That one statement has been attached to my story in life for so long. I had seen the Lieutenant Governor on a number of occasions. During those times, I served with the local Central Committee. I met many people. I met people like Josh Cohen that later served as mayor of Annapolis. I met Councilman Carl Snowden who often mentored me not so much politically as he did so much more in helping me to understand my community socially and those intricate things that matter in an evolving world. Through him I had the opportunity to often converse with Baltimore's Congressmen Elijah Cummings, Kweisi Mfume, and so many other real people who did their seemingly best to serve those they represented and those who lived far beyond their voting districts.

Everybody was not a Democrat. I remember a walk I had with Lt. Governor Michael Steele who later became Chairman of the Republican National Committee. As we walked, I recall him saying he needed to talk with me. I listened as he made his pitch to recruit me to the party that he served. I told him I was not interested and why. I saw the party going in a direction that seemed nobody could stop. It reminded me of some of the dark and menacing characters that were part of the community of that special SDA school I once attended. Even then, seeds were being planted. I have great admiration for Mr. Steele. He has shown me grace and strength. He like so many did so by putting his nation above politics. He already stood tall but he stands even taller today.

Standing above the spectacular of so many others was the daughter of Bobby Kennedy, the brother of President John Kennedy. We had an event at the Anne Arundel Community College. American historian icon Taylor Branch and so many others were present at the event. One of the speakers, to my surprise got up and shared some damning thoughts on Kathleen Kennedy Townsend's dad. I was getting frustrated. I wanted so bad to stop the event or to stop the speaker at best. He was raining on the history I had understood. He was very negative and unyielding with a mercy laced with cyanide. Just then, Lt. Governor Kathleen stood to interrupt the speaker. In his response to her, he ordered her with no humane respect to "sit down." He told her she had her time and now he's speaking. I saw all sorts of social grace and consideration flee that auditorium. However, she returned to her seat.

When the event concluded, everybody left for the reception preplanned to follow the event. I remember walking up onto the stage to put the chairs and other equipment away. A lady stayed by to my right when I heard her voice, "I'll help you."

It was the Lt. Governor. She not only offered to help me, she just kicked in and went to work. At one point I stopped her. I asked, "How did that make you feel when that lawyer said those things about your dad?" I went on to tell her I was about to stop him. The guy snapped at her in a very disrespectful way. She said to me, "Donnell, he was right. I had my turn and he was using his time to speak." She explained to me more in her face and attitude a compassion that I had only noticed in very rare moments in the lives of the so many celebrated people. She helped me to understand we all don't hold the same picture of history. People have a right to share their views and understanding of history. The one thing we both believe is that history, no matter how you window dress it, paint it, or anything else done to rewrite the stories, dramas, and theater that history ignites, history – TRUE HISTORY, will always tell the truth. Once the moment passes, history is sealed.

On January 17, 2000, I welcomed my sons Jack and Brandon into the world. I remember it snowing. I also remembered I was invited to an event to introduce the Lt. Governor. I missed the event because of those things associated with dad's welcoming the arrival of his first children. Many of my political colleagues shared their wrath with me for not attending the event. They were then getting used to the energy I was becoming known for to whip up the energy in the room. I'm a much-forgotten man these days sitting on the sidelines; sometimes confused in the shade of life. I stepped off; wandering through the shades and shadows of America. I've had the opportunity to meet and converse with so many wonderful people.

I've sat with leaders and grifters, preachers and poor, I've sat with the dignified and with those who rummage through garbage cans of waste looking for the remains of uneaten cuisine. Thank you, Ms. Kathleen Kennedy-Townsend. So many wonderful people I had the opportunity to meet but none of them told me what you told me when I decided to call you to apologize for my no show. It was a conversation that told me who you really were at heart.

"Lt. Governor," I called her. I didn't understand if she was correcting me or not when she said, "this is Kathleen." I told her why I was a no show for her event and apologized to her. She told me, she knew what had happened. She congratulated me and said she had wanted to call me. She told me that they missed me at the event. Then she changed the weight on my history when she told me not to worry about what others say. She reminded me that I did the right thing by choosing to stay with my wife and the boys. She told me, if I had done anything different, she would have lost respect for me. Please understand, seeds were being planted.

I've been a lot of places in my life and times. I love that song from Brother Ray Charles. As I write, I have entered my Simply Red moment. I'm holding back the years; holding back the tears. I have been so blessed by so many wonderful people of so many backgrounds and challenges. Some stories I will share. Some I will gently put them to sleep.

I remember that one Friday night. When that little boy got off that bottom bunk. I got out of that black steel and black and white complemented bunkbed to pray. That little boy, that chubby little kid, got out of bed to ask for a favor that has yet to materialize. As I wait, I consider the patchwork of fabrics that has been sewn into the tapestries and quilts of my life. I have nothing spectacular to share. My life looks on the surface as an abject failure. I've witnessed more pain than pleasure. But now I understand more why members of the generations before me wanted me to understand a little about agriculture.

Often, I shoveled the shit by myself. I know what the elders meant in the passing cloud of gaseous metabolic waste that filled the air of grifters and snake-oil sellers. When the clouds of con were swept up and moved on by the breeze of time the elders would often use that same word my dad threatened his children not to use; BULL SHIT! I participated in the large hot fields and smaller but large gardens. I've participated in every facet from seed to filling my gut. As I look back, I realize seeds were being planted.

I'm shamed by divorce. I'm shamed within when well-meaning people remind me of where I've been and who I've been. The merry-go-round of life and our misguided understanding of success spun fast. I just wanted off. I wanted to see what others were seeing. I stopped playing music because I had no understanding of what other people were seeing. I just couldn't understand. I stopped a local TV show and radio spots. I was not an entertainer. I was serious and hoped to move things to the better side of the scales. I was undermined by some people, close people, that I trusted the most. I was disappointed but I respected their choices. I know the lies, maneuverings, and manipulations from the scenes and left-over theatrical props behind the moth-eaten curtains. I call this experience. All along, it was believed the game was on me, but seeds were being planted.

I had fun from time to time sitting in with some awesome musicians. I grew up reaching into the swamp water to grab frogs and tadpoles with more than a few. That's what we did as kids. But life evolves and we go our ways. I went my way but I could not forget those moments that paused me long enough to stop by the supply store to grab a few items to construct an answer to a prayer that I still continue to pray.

I was living in a community called Vally Brook Apartments. My brother Emory shared something with me. He told me that I could make money playing music. I told him I could not do that. I did not have the talent, the ability to even get people to believe I could. He told me Davidsonville United Methodist Church was looking for a musician. I told Emory, I wouldn't do it. I was not interested. He told me he had set me up for an interview. He asked me could I do it just to make him look good. Because he had promised he could get me to come in and talk to them. I agreed to do so.

I met with the committee and listened to their pitch. I had no experience doing this and I told them, I was not a musician. The exchange was simple. They responded by saying they understood, but I was then asked would I do it until they found someone? I gave in and decided to help them out. Everybody ran circles around me. Shirlette Boysaw, Lloyd Folks, and yes, my brother Charles Emory were all musicians. They were the catapult for my meeting other singers and musicians. I was playing music for Davidsonville United Methodist church when new pastor Eddy Smith, who replaced Rev. Charles Creek, invited me to play at Wilson UM. Rev. Eddy, as I called my friend, wanted me to go with him on Sundays to finish out his church services.

Let me tell you now, I had no desire to ever play at that church. The musician was Vincent Simms. He had to leave early on Sundays because he was scheduled to play at First Baptist church in Annapolis. This was a thing that many musicians did on Sundays. They would contract to play music for many congregations. I did it as well when I learned that I could earn a living wage from the monies these contracts afforded.

Vincent was different. Vincent came from a musically talented family as well. I Knew them very well. I grew up just on the other side of Dorsey Drive; across the street from his family. His family lived just two doors down from my grandparents. He was a close friend of my oldest sister Vena. He played in the military and was a graduate of the Juilliard Conservatory. He had played for and with the Baltimore Symphony Orchestra, other orchestras, and artistic venues. This guy was phenomenal. I could barely play 'Mary Had a Little Lamb' without making an error. Again, I considered the heart that extended the invitation for my limited talent and services.

While I served this group something else was playing in the background. This church was the family church of the Queen Sisters; a local gospel group. My brother played for them as a bassist and sometimes as a percussionist. The Queen Sisters made a request that I play with them as well. That was it. After a Sunday service. I remember speaking with Betty Queen, I was finally brave enough to let the cat out of the bag. She stopped me after service and asked again would I be willing to play for them? This was my opportunity to set this music thing straight.

"Betty," I nervously started off, "I need you to know something. I am not a musician; I don't know what I'm doing."

She says, "We know." She shocked me. I told her why I was hesitant and why I surely did not want to play behind Vincent. She listened. She finished me off with a "um hum." "Why is it that you guys want me to play?" Betty said, something that sparked a change in me. The story is not always completed through the author. The author is responsible in sharing the story. Other perspectives are important. I don't always understand, but I encourage us all to move closer to understanding. We may not be examining the same values or perspectives. Betty touched my heart when she said, "Donnell, we love your spirit." Decades later, I realize seeds were being planted.

There are so many great memories that come to mind as I take an extended look back over the many years expanding from the night that little boy, now a man, prayed. Of course, there were so many more wonderful and amazing people who helped to furnish my bubble. People like Maryland House Speaker Mike Busch who opened the door welcoming me onto the political scene. There were the people whose names were not shared or forgotten drowned out by the echoes of their energies of love and welcome. Yes, I met the kindness and welcome of a lady from time to time at a television studio on Television Hill in Baltimore; until she was caught up in the draft that swept her out to the windy city where she helped to change the world. In that story, I would show up from time to time under the "WJZ Candelabra Tower" when guest like the 'Family Counselor' was present after the movie was aired 'The Day After.' It was there that I connected with one of Maryland's finest a mayor, later Governor, William Donald Schaefer who helped me in my career as a student of people. She knew then as I do now, in life – seeds are being planted.

There were the ladies from a women's homeless shelter that extended an invitation for me to share Thanksgiving dinner with them. People like Purley, a young kid and member of the Blackfeet Nation who lived in Pendleton, Oregon. One day there was a knock at my door. It was Purley and his siblings who came by to sing on my doorsteps. Other names like sisters-in-law Dorothy and Margurite two elderly ladies who in their youth were runaways from an orphanage they left to chart out a new life in California. The list of luminaries and instructors of my personal life university is vast and growing. As I consider the impacts and implications of both major and minor events that helped to shape every case study that helped to produce the philosophical angles that will be presented in this book are born of the fact that seeds were being planted.

So here I am, my friend. I'm back. I've made it through a lot—personal issues, divorce, and even Covid-19. I remember working in government, writing legislation, and lobbying to win political leaders' support. I recall being called to the hospital to visit with a mother and father, a grandmother, and an aunt as they grieved in the emergency room of a public hospital the death of a 7-year-old girl. I've not seen all. I've only seen a fraction of a fraction. It was a tale of the giants that lured me into the shadows when I thought I reached for light. In the shadows the evenings ushered in darkness, but in the darkness, I found light. In the situations of life, seeds are being planted. It is the rooting and cultivation of a kid's quest, an adult's journey for a destination he may never reach. Seeds are being planted.

I may not be much to those around me now, but I've lived through moments that have shaped me in ways I never could have imagined. I was there with that young mother and her father when she brought twins into this world—only to lose one of them too soon. I remember cradling that tiny, lifeless body in my arms, while the mother and grandfather fought to hold back their tears. In that moment, I saw life in all its extremes: the highest joys and the deepest sorrows.

I have often found myself rewinding and replaying through the episodes of time, remembering a little boy praying beside his bed, unaware that wisdom is born from living through life's trials; and so often life's trash. As I share my story with you, I'll take you through the experiences that shaped my understanding and led me to land on certain ideas, beliefs, truths, and philosophies. You may now see, conclusions are funny things—they rush us to the end of the story, but they also complete the journey of a creative mind. Conclusions put a stop to the endless spinning of ideas, but they also equip us with the tools of comfort and survival that we pass on to the labyrinths of generations to come.

Certainly, life has taken me on quite an adventure. I have been exploring new horizons, learning valuable lessons, and gathering insights from my experiences. The stewing well of flubs and blunders, challenges and wins are now page ready to be shared with you. Over the past few years, I have delved deeper into understanding what brings true peace and fulfillment in our lives. My experiences have been varied and rich, from traveling to new places and meeting incredible people, to facing challenges that tested my resolve and taught me resilience. Through it all, I have continued my quest for knowledge and personal growth.

I am excited to share my findings. Pay close attention, I said *"findings"* not *'conclusions.'* It has become my belief that true intellect is not absolute. Thus, it cannot be totally conclusive.

I've noticed that one odd trait in the communities of fundamentalism. They often portray themselves as absolutists. They have come to the correct conclusions but a million different ways. Each group yelling, "Do it our way and you will live! Do it their way and you'll die!"

In these pages I attempt to expose my concepts; not my conclusions. The journey of life goes on with or without me. This is my book report sharing what I've gained from my unique life experiences so far. I believe that the lessons I've learned can offer valuable perspectives and practical advice for anyone looking to enhance their own journey towards something higher on the mountain of challenge.

Thank you for being a part of my journey. Your support means the world to me, and I look forward to continuing to share this portion of the path with you.

Stay tuned for more updates and insights!

What a Wild Ride

What a ride. What a wild ride! It's been bumpy, and the weather has rarely worked in my favor. I seem to drift in and out of arenas where the odds are stacked against me. Share this journey of recalculation as we discover pivotal moments when random signals of hope pierced through the multiverse, breaking through the gloom imposed by well-meaning but intellectually lacking influences. These folks, despite their good hearts and commendable intentions, often feel to me as useful as a wet sack of used Depends. Yet, even those could nurture vibrant flowers with an opposing fragrance. Planted seeds take root producing stems, budding plants, producing fruits and fragrances of perspectives that may differ as much as the fingerprint.

2 CENTS OF REASON   A DEEP DIVE INTO WHAT SHAPES US

This is my story, raw and unfiltered. I invite you to join me as I share my testimony. You're reading and sharing my journey helps me to face and understand this moment of reality. This dude—who is still me—had to get woke fast. It just took me decades to do it. And I promise you, this volume will share my unique understandings.

THERE EXISTS A WELL

There exists a well—a deep and timeless source brimming with wisdom and understanding, overflowing with the nutrients that have nourished our world's development across the ages. This well has not only enriched wealth and industry but has also cultivated the character of those aligned with the higher energies of love, compassion, and decency.

Yet, we often find ourselves stumbling through darkness, led by figures of low character. These are not true leaders but charlatans—mere actors, crafting deceptive personas for selfish gain. While they may acknowledge the existence of this well, they spend their time building shallow, illusory pools, convincing others of their supposed magic. But their waters are devoid of substance, leaving those who follow them parched and wanting. These figures are menaces, cankers, worms gnawing at the very threads that bind our world together in its potential greatness.

Make no mistake: the world is great because it simply is. But humanity has often been strangled by tyrants and zealots, their grip so tight that entire cultures and societies have been choked out of existence. Bad things happen, and that is undeniably terrifying, especially for those caught in their wake. Yet, for every shadow, there exists the possibility of light. The potential for things to go right is just as real as the potential for things to go wrong.

We have been misled into believing that darkness must not be fought. If you were to face it with the crude weaponry of human power and military might, I would agree. No society, no matter how armed, has ever truly vanquished darkness this way. Such battles may appear victorious at first, but darkness has a way of creeping back, like a fire that smolders beneath the ashes. A brief respite, a temporary joy—these are but flickers, like a turn signal that changes direction at the last moment, leaving the driver—and the rest of us—wondering where to go.

The real battle against darkness is won with the overpowering force of light. From the dawn of time, light has been the true power over darkness, representing all that is good, all that is just. It is the goodness within us, often hesitant and scared, that ultimately pushes back the darkness. This is not merely a battle of force but a battle of knowledge, of correct understanding. The evolution of human consciousness is our beacon; it shows that the light always returns, stronger than before.

There is a well. Often, we wait for those who claim to know the way, those who present themselves as wise. Yet the truly wise have no need to tell you of their intelligence. You will see it in the way they live their lives, the wisdom that emerges from their actions, the lessons learned not just from triumphs but from mistakes and missteps. It is not the cunning mind that liberates the imprisoned soul; it is the condemned, redeemed by his own reason, who learns to be truly free and inspires freedom in those who still think themselves unchained but are bound by the prison of their own ignorance.

This well exists, though so few ever find it. It is a well with a cosmic magnetism, a metaphysical invitation that draws the willing, the seeking, to drink deeply from its waters. This is no ordinary fount; it quenches the thirst of those who dare to separate themselves from the arid deserts of exhausted reasoning. It charts the uncharted, presenting new construction projects of forward-thinking and vision.

Yes, there is a well, my friend.

It stands ready, waiting for those with the courage to seek it, for those willing to break free from the illusion of limitation and drink deeply from the waters of true wisdom and understanding. **Where is it, you ask?** The power lies not in the well's location, but in the relentless pursuit to find it. For those who dare to search, the well has already nourished the minds that have shaped and continue to elevate the civilized world.

Our world needs more well-seekers. Isn't it astonishing that it's not always the teacher, but the vigilant, hyper-aware student—ever observant—who births the groundbreaking ideas and revolutionary thoughts that propel us forward? The well is the sustenance of the creative mind. It fuels the spark that ignites innovative thinking, transforming dreams into realities, and crafting the blueprints of a brighter tomorrow.

We must demand more from every system that educates, every institution that shapes minds—whether they train students, workers, artists, or artisans. They must not fear encouraging those in their charge to seek out the well. For in each era, the echoes of visionary voices declare, **"Amazing! You've seen nothing yet."** There is always more to discover, more to create, more to become. Technology alone stands as a testament to the power of this well, showing us time and again that every positive change, every breakthrough, pries open the door to new possibilities, revealing ever-greater human potential.

Each generation strengthens the next. It is our duty to inspire the coming wave of thinkers, dreamers, and doers to seek the well—to be unafraid, to be relentless, to be filled with the promise of what's possible.

There is a well. And the world is waiting for those brave enough to find it.

LOST BUT FOUND:

A journey through time, discovery, and learning from both personal experience and the collective human condition

When the world does not know you, get to know the world

Every now and then, I run into old friends or acquaintances people from various walks of life, yet somehow connected by an invisible thread. It feels as though they all graduated from the same school of thought or shared wisdom from the same mentor. Their greetings are almost scripted, something you might have heard before or even said yourself. With a smile and a knowing look, they ask, *"Hey stranger, where have you been?"*

Well, let me tell you. I've been here all along. But more than just existing, I've been on a journey—one of deep observation, reflection, and growth. This journey wasn't something I planned; it found me, like a path unfolding before my feet. In these pages, I invite you to walk beside me, as I share the lessons I've discovered along the way. These insights have not only shaped my understanding but continue to guide me as I move forward.

I served my community in the realm of politics. I hosted a weekly local TV show called *"Your Schools, Your Community, and You,"* where I provided political commentary and conducted interviews on several stations. Alongside my media work, I collaborated with various local churches that sought my guidance. But of all my roles, what made me most proud was being a father and watching my sons thrive and enjoy life. I also had a passion for gardening—growing both food and flowers brought me joy.

After facing some rapid and unbelievable life challenges, I made the decision to walk away from it all. I wasn't entirely sure what I was walking into, but I knew I had to move forward. At times, it felt as if I had fallen through the looking glass, like Alice in Lewis Carroll's *Alice in Wonderland*. It almost seemed like a strange payback for my exploration into metaphysics. I've ventured into many places and had dreams that led me to meet countless people. Through them, I learned invaluable lessons, and for that, I am deeply grateful.

When life was going well, it was learning season. But when dark clouds gathered and disaster struck with typhoon force, I came to understand that this, too, was a season for learning. From time to time, I returned to school, whether for another degree or certification. Let's face it, when the world doesn't know you, they often trust that piece of paper—a document that opens doors but can also close many.

Some years ago, I earned one such document. My sister Jackie, who had dropped out of middle school with my father's encouragement, was deeply moved by my educational achievements. In my family, education wasn't highly valued, especially in my generation. At times, resentment toward my accomplishments was hard to miss, bubbling up as jealousy and, in some cases, manifesting as hurtful behavior.

It seemed like I was expected to hold back, to not pursue the education I was proud of, just to keep the peace or to preserve others' sense of honor in their own imagined ways. But that's neither fair nor right. Why should I resist my potential just because others choose not to, or feel they can't, reach higher?

When I graduated, Jackie made a big deal of my achievements, so much so that I decided to give her my diplomas. She had never shown that level of enthusiasm for herself. As I handed them over to her, I said, *"Jackie, I want you to remember this: The man makes the paper, but the paper does not make the man."*

From time to time, Jackie will tell others about my scholastic accomplishments. She'll even let me know when she's shown my diplomas to someone. I've consistently asked her not to do that. There's something I've understood for a very long time: when people know you only through those pieces of paper, they begin to speak to the image they've created of you. That image can overshadow who you really are. I wouldn't be able to see the true, raw, and honest person standing before me.

I want people to know me as Donnell—not as a set of credentials, but as a human being. I want them to recognize the qualities I have, qualities that aren't all that different from anyone else's. We all possess qualities worth exposing, worth nurturing.

Everyone has qualities. Some of them may be questionable, of limited value, or even harmful (which is why we have a judicial system to help navigate such issues). But others are of the highest order, offering benefits to the whole of humanity. The one undeniable truth that connects us all is that we share this human condition together. We will continue to share it until the day our hearts stop beating, and our brains lose the ability to think.

If you missed that, perhaps René Descartes wouldn't have. It was Descartes who famously declared, *"Cogito, ergo sum,"* which in English translates to *"I think, therefore I am."*

What this means to me is that the very act of doubting my

existence proves that I must exist. I exist because, as part of this human journey, I am one of nearly nine billion thinking entities—each a bubble within a bubble, as you'll soon see responsible for contemplating the very nature of existence. Descartes gave us a universal axiom, a foundational truth of reason: even when everything else might seem unclear or uncertain, the fact that I am thinking is evidence of my existence. Simply put, because I think, I am.

From that past moment until this present moment, when I told her, 'The man makes the paper, but the paper does not make the man,' I have never wavered from that statement. Every now and then, when she starts boasting about my status, I ask her, 'Do you remember what I said about those papers?'

I believe it's reasonable to suggest that, despite our enormous advances in every aspect of life, we often overlook the essentials that breathe life into our human, social, environmental, and technological existence. We have become so reliant on document-driven status that we may fail to recognize the genius that could live next door. We may not pay attention to that peculiar kid who taps into their creativity, finding practical solutions to complex problems.

Our focus is often on the status of those paraded before us, but in doing so, we may neglect cultivating the innovative minds of children whose natural curiosity and problem-solving abilities flourish with vibrancy. Encouraging critical thinking in young minds can profoundly impact health, technology, safety, and the well-being of our communities.

When we nurture and uplift rather than mock, we become part of the creative engine that fuels progress. Creative minds stir the waters of reason, leading to innovation and invention. This is where new ideas and products are born. We can build team spirit in uncertain times and promote unity by supporting common needs. Encouragement fosters mental health, helps to combat depression, and even reduces the risk of suicide. Promoting civility strengthens families, which, in turn, nurtures personal faith, respect, and responsibility.

I have traveled across many parts of our nation, sampling cultures far different from the one I grew up in. I wasn't on these journeys for the typical tourist thrills. Instead, I was a simple, ordinary citizen, experiencing life alongside people from all walks of life. From the shorelines of the Atlantic to the coastlands of the Pacific, I've seen it all—a cross-sectional view of America. I've witnessed a tarp sheltering a homeless person, just feet away from bustling commerce, and I've stood on the marbled floors of mansions filled with indifference to the struggles of the middle class and poor.

I've listened to words filled with contempt, hidden behind the polished facades of self-constructed images. From Skid Row in Portland, Oregon, to Wall Street in New York City, I've observed a wide spectrum of life in America.

As an observer, I noticed patterns that connect us all as we navigate the challenges of life. When these insights hit me, it felt like the answer to a question I'd been asking for years. It was all right in front of me: the missing persons, the hidden stories, the people behind the prestigious titles and documents. I saw selfishness, shallowness, and an ability to answer questions without ever addressing the real issues that affect far too many.

Along my journey, I've fallen victim to scammers and encountered countless challenges. But I've also learned from great men, women, and even children—people who've taught me invaluable lessons and inspired me to share the insights you are about to read. They opened my eyes to deeper realities, teaching me that failures often disguise victories. I've witnessed love in action, a force powerful enough to push back the delusions and destruction of hate. At the same time, I've observed a lack of humanity, something I can only hope is rooted in ignorance and selfishness—the invisible eyes of hate.

Throughout it all, I've learned so much, yet I'm fully aware that I've only scratched the surface of life's vastness. I've realized that the distasteful things that happened to me are not unique, even though they uniquely impacted me. Darkness touches us all at some point. It has happened, is happening, or will happen, simply because we are part of life's ebb and flow. My hope is that through this writing, I can bring greater awareness, broaden perspectives, and inspire a rapid movement toward the better aspects of humanity.

This is not about the paper; it's about the person behind these pages. I invite you to join me on this life-driven journey of discovery. Explore the thoughts I share and empower yourself to become an active part of the story—the story that will define our moment in the human saga, striving for the best we can be.

LIFE: THE GREAT PROFESSOR

We all have a journey. Whether we realize it or not, from the moment we were born, we were thrust into it. Dropped off at the depot of our birth, we didn't purchase the tickets for this ride, but we must pay the price for it along the way. Some journeys are filled with joy and laughter, while others are marked by sadness, fear, or self-inflicted isolation. No matter the route, some journeys are transformative.

Take this hiker, for instance. He was alone, navigating a narrow, high path when he lost his footing. Gravity took hold, pulling him downward like a magnet. As he fell, time seemed to slow, his heart racing as fragments of his life flashed before his eyes. The unknown awaited below. Then, with a jolt, everything stopped.

He hit the rocks, losing a tooth and briefly consciousness. When he came to, he was wracked with pain—his head pounding, his body bruised. But as he opened his eyes, he noticed a flicker, a strange glimmer in the distance. A streak of yellow light caught his attention, blinking on and off like it was calling his name. Slowly, that flicker became a sparkle, and his curiosity ignited.

Despite his injuries, he crawled closer. What he thought was maybe a chunk of iron pyrite seemed to beckon him. It was as if the rock was winking at him. Through the pain, he reached for it, over and over. Finally, he grabbed the small, shining object. It was not the pyrite many call fool's gold. It was gold. It was real; it was honest gold. Real, solid gold. And in that moment, he realized something profound: even in his fall, he had found something of immense value.

Life is like that. It has a way of giving us 'bullshit'—and I mean that literally. Fertilizer, born from waste, has nourished billions of tons of vegetation, extending the survival of humanity. Crap helps things grow. And so do the challenges we face.

I've seen my fair share of crap. I've taken my bumps, bruises, and breaks along the way. But through it all, I've learned. Life, that great professor, taught me invaluable lessons, often when I least expected it. My journey wasn't always easy—some experiences demanded an uncomfortable high and often excruciating price. But through these challenges, I've come to understand that you can't have change without struggle. In other words, you can't have change without challenge.

I remember discovering the works of Napoleon Hill in my teens. He wrote, "Every adversity, every failure, every heartache carries with it the seed of an equal or greater benefit." At that time, I didn't fully grasp the depth of this idea. But as life piled on its darkness, I began to see the light, just as that hiker did. I learned to ask "Why?"—not out of confusion, but to seek deeper truths. And these truths, as I've learned, are often universal.

The more I reflect, the more I see that much of society is trapped in a cultural penal colony, bound by invisible bars. Many of us don't even realize we're prisoners, unable to comprehend what true freedom means. We're confined by the Bubble Effect—our limited perspective. Trying to rearrange the contents of someone else's bubble without understanding our own leads to disaster. I've witnessed it countless times in the lives of others and in my own experience.

Then there's the Rubber Band Effect—that moment when someone recognizes their confinement and strives to break free. Contrary to what we've been taught, escaping isn't as hard as we think. The prison doors aren't locked. But tradition and fundamental thinking keep us in place, warning of disaster if we dare open our eyes to the truth. This, I suspect, is what some call being 'woke.'

There are always those who benefit from keeping us confined—leaders, governments, corporations. They instill fear, create laws, and manipulate reality to keep the masses under control. Why do the winners so often stand on the backs of the humble and meek? The CEOs, the heads of state—they may donate millions to charity, but when it comes to paying a living wage, they balk. It's as if they're content to let the rest of us cling to lifeboats on ships that are long past scraping against and being ripped open by the iceberg.

Why is this? I've seen enough to know that the key to freedom is within us. The bars of cultural imprisonment aren't real. The only true prison is in our minds, and those in power know this. They depend on our mental surrender. It happens in politics, in religion, in industry—it's all fear-based control, manipulating the imagination and producing results for those who care little about the least of us.

In this book, as I share my journey with you— I hope to convey to you what I've learned, what I've seen, and how I've navigated the highs and lows. Along the way, I've unearthed some startling truths and scratched the surface of realities we rarely question. But every conversation must start somewhere, and this is where we begin. One of the greatest discoveries I made long ago is this: **the prison bars have no locks. The only key is deeply located in our minds.** *Follow my story and stories.*

I set a personal deadline for myself on the last day of December 2023. I had already resigned from the Elders Board of my local church, giving the leadership ample time to prove my open and honest observations wrong. Yet, nothing changed. During this time, I was under the weather, struggling with my health. The past couple of years had been filled with surgeries—four of them in total. The wear and tear of it all had taken a toll on me, physically and emotionally. But what happened next was entirely unexpected.

I visited my specialist, who prescribed a new medication. We had a heated exchange when I admitted I often stopped medications if I didn't see results quickly. The doctor chastised me, but I pushed back—**it's my body, after all.** I firmly believe no one, not politicians, not religious institutions, nor any authority should dictate personal medical decisions. Those are sacred choices, ones that belong solely to the individual under the guidance of trusted medical advisors.

Still, I promised my specialist I would try this new prescription for 30 days, no interruptions. I filled it, took it as directed, and for 27 days, things seemed fine. But on day 28, I started to feel terribly ill. I made an emergency appointment with my Primary Care doctor, who suspected I was having a severe allergic reaction to the medication. I was bleeding, growing weaker by the hour. My Primary Care doctor told me to stop the medication immediately, but I was determined to fulfill my 30-day agreement. I barely made it to day 29.

When I returned to my specialist, I was met with apologies and a new prescription. Yet, on my way home, I collapsed and ended up in the hospital. The next three days were spent under intense medical supervision as they worked to stop the internal bleeding. I was sent home to recuperate, still weak and grappling with the physical toll of this ordeal.

During those slow, quiet weekends in bed, thanks to the COVID-19 pandemic, I began watching my church

services online. What I noticed shook me to my core.

Sometimes, clarity comes when we're forced to step back, when life pushes us off our usual paths, and we find ourselves free-falling from the heights of familiarity. In those quiet moments, replaying my experiences like a slow-motion film, I began to see things I had missed before.

In church, it's easy to get swept up in groupthink. There's an unspoken game we play, much like the children's game of **"Follow the Leader."** We create bubbles of comfort, encased in early, unquestioned beliefs handed down and forced fed to us. The child is taught to remember certain things, yet has no awareness of opposing views, no position from which to mount a challenge. Survival, both physical and social, often hinges on conformity. But sustenance—true sustenance for survival—should nourish the body, the mind, and the spirit in ways that allow for growth, not an unsigned certification for control.

I began to notice a disturbing pattern, a consistency that stretched across the vast expanse of westernized Christianity. The message we were always exhorted to share, "We love everybody." I'd heard that phrase from my earliest days of paying attention, indoctrinated to believe it was the Christ-like way. The church would burst into affirmations of agreement, a public display of self-righteousness, patting ourselves on the back for being good Christians, good followers of Jesus.

But as I lay there, reflecting, I began to hear something that was deeply offbeat, out of harmony with the words we proclaimed. In church, we said we loved everybody, but in the same breath, we condemned those who were different. Week after week, I would hear members, and leaders of the so-called

Christian organization I grew up with, get up and denounce various groups—those who didn't fit into their narrow view, and rancid representation of righteousness. **I even heard that being 'woke' was a sin.**

How ironic, isn't it? **Is it not the very mission of Christianity to awaken the world to the light of Christ?** To bring awareness, to flip on the lights of love, compassion, and understanding? Yet, here we were, condemning awareness, demonizing the very act of waking up.

This realization was a turning point. The church I had dedicated so much of my life to, the beliefs I had held so dear, were suddenly exposed in their contradictions. And it was in this space—this uncomfortable, unsettling space—that I began to truly learn, not from the pulpit, but from the great professor we call **Life.**

Life, with its highs and lows, its unexpected twists and painful truths, taught me more than any sermon ever could. It is in the raw, unfiltered experiences that we find wisdom. And it is in the acknowledgment of our flaws, both personal and communal, that we begin to grow.

So, if you take nothing else from this chapter, remember this: **Life is a well-qualified professor. Pay attention. Observe Life. If you are searching, you will find the well, my friend. It's there for those who seek, for those willing to break free from the illusion of limitation and drink deeply from the waters of understanding.**

Seek it, question everything, and never be afraid to let go of the beliefs that no longer serve you. **Because the well is real, and it's waiting for those brave enough to find it. Life may teach you experience, through experience, to experience** the Great Positioning System. Surprisingly, it has been around a long time.

Life can often be "The Great Professor."

2 CENTS OF REASON

A DEEP DIVE INTO WHAT SHAPES US

THE LABYRINTH OF LIFE

Let's open with a tangential history lesson. One hundred years and five months before my birth, Clara Barton could be seen on the streets of Annapolis, Maryland. Clarissa Harlowe Barton, was her name. She is one of the more honored women in American history. Barton risked her life to bring supplies and support to soldiers in the field during the Civil War. She founded the American Red Cross in 1881. Help save a life. Donate some blood today.

Back to the story – Barton's fame was a little different for the locals of my birthplace home, Annapolis. This town was once the Capital of the United States. It continues to be the home of the U.S. Naval Academy which makes up a significant part of my history. It was in that place that the famed Barton opened the Missing Soldiers Office. This location came to be known as Camp Parole. The camp was established during the American Civil War to accept Union prisoners of war until they could be exchanged for Confederate prisoners of war confined in the south.

In 1966, I began my first big step in the world beyond the walls of my home, my family, and small community. I began kindergarten right in that section of Annapolis that was once called Camp Parole. My first formal public education challenge was delivered to me at the Parole Elementary School (*known today as* **Walter S. Mills-Parole Elementary**). I was excited when I was driven away from home first by my mother and later by a yellow school bus.

It was at Parole that I met my new line of constantly changing best friends. I needed every one of them from Billy to Bruce, from Anne to Gail and an alumnus of so many others. I needed the teachers, the principals, the custodial staff, and librarians that were assisting me in the development of a new and expanding life. I needed the food service workers that fed me when I lied and said I forgot my lunch because I felt to embarrassed to bring out my smelly tuna fish or pungent egg salad sandwich that I later found my hard-working parents had invested so much of their hard-earned wealth into. Yes, my outside life, beyond my close-knit culture of church and neighborhood friends began on the campus of Parole.

Cookies and milk, finger-painting and naptime were the early winners that my older siblings used to excite me with eye-popping expectations. New people, new things, new sounds, and a community of new smells were expanding at a rapid rate under the sky of education. One of the most powerful memories that helped to shape the later portion of my life began in a classroom at the Parole Elementary School.

One morning in the first grade, the teacher walked into the classroom with a stack of fresh mimeographed papers. I, like most of my classmates, could not wait to be given mine. This was my introduction to addictions. I had taken on the peer influence to sniff the soon to dry ink from the copy machine. Later, the photo copier forced me to stop my huffing addiction cold turkey. Of course, there were other smells like that kindergarten Tempera Paint that required us getting dressed up in daddy's old dress shirt to stand at an easel to get high. However, with all the new smells, new colors, and new highs, I found another love. I developed a special appreciation for what was often printed with that mind-blowing wet ink. On that ink and paper production was one of my favorite things that became a guide for me in trying to understand life and its myriads of challenges today.

That early experience at Parole Elementary marked both the end of one chapter and the thrilling beginning of another in the book of my life. I discovered my love for mazes—those winding, twisting puzzles that seemed to pop up everywhere in my young world. They were on the pages of the *Weekly Reader*, on cereal boxes, even on grocery bags. Mazes were everywhere, a constant reminder of the excitement, uncertainty, and curiosity I felt stepping into the world for the first time.

Looking back, I realize I had already entered a maze—a labyrinth of life—without even knowing it. My first day at Parole Elementary was that pivotal moment when I stepped into my earliest memories of life's twists and turns, surrounded by unfamiliar paths and intriguing characters. Each one brought clues or distractions, shaping my journey in ways I could never have imagined.

In this chapter, I invite you to join me as we explore this labyrinth together, following the paths that have led me to a deeper understanding of life.

When I first encountered a maze, it was a simple, one-dimensional diagram printed on paper, with a clear entrance and an elusive exit. The maze was a network of pathways, each filled with roadblocks and dead ends, challenging me to find that single, unbroken route to the goal. It was more than just a pastime—it was a tool for developing critical thinking and problem-solving skills, a miniature test of patience and persistence. Each maze presented itself as a new challenge, a puzzle to solve without any prior understanding of its twists and turns.

Many people think of the word 'maze' as synonymous with 'labyrinth.' On a basic level, this comparison holds true. However, a labyrinth is a more sophisticated, multidimensional version, rooted in ancient history, and far more complex than the one-dimensional puzzles presented to the child version of myself. Unlike a simple maze, a labyrinth is a network of intricate passageways, blind corridors, and confusing alleys—an experience that can be truly mind-bending and challenging to navigate.

It is the labyrinth that I've chosen as the metaphor for my ongoing journey through life. We can measure and examine yesterday because it is in the past. Our understanding of today is constantly evolving, limited by the partial knowledge of the present. As for the future, it balances precariously on a sea of uncertainties, shaped by both what we know and what we have yet to discover. While hope springs from what is possible, it is often tempered by the unknown territories of probability. Each future step is birthed from the converging paths of our past and present experiences, demanding the problem-solving skills we've honed along the way to navigate what remains mysterious and unseen.

The Construction Zone

Let's start at the draftsman's table, where all projects begin as an idea or a fleeting thought. Such thoughts often arise unexpectedly, appearing like gifts that must be seized in the moment—a 'do it now' impulse. In that instant, many variables of value and judgment are pushed forward, driven by a mix of urgency, panic, and self-interest. The constant refrain of 'do it now' often echoes at the entryway of the labyrinth, shaping its initial course. Alongside this urgency, there is an underlying current of excited energy, an invisible force that subtly guides the deliberate design and construction of the labyrinth ahead. These pre-existing conditions serve as the early influencers, forming the initial corridors and evolving chambers of the maze.

I've come to see the Labyrinth as the true maze of life—an ever-expanding landscape that defies confinement to any single dimension, or even three. It's a multi-dimensional tapestry, woven with threads of interconnected experiences. It includes the tangible—the feel of touch, the resonance of sounds that spark memories of triumphs and failures, the spectacle of life's dramas and comedies, the tastes and scents that linger in the recesses of our minds. Yet, beyond all this, I sense an ethereal substance—a force that binds the visible with the invisible, the known with the unknown. This is the energy that shapes our reality, the mysterious undercurrent that guides the hand of creation. Together, these elements—seen and unseen—lay the groundwork for constructing, shaping, and navigating the intricate complexities of the labyrinth.

Looking back, I realize how far I've come. I see the labyrinth of life as a spiritual journey, shaped and guided by the experiences I've encountered along the way. It now feels more navigable when those ethereal elements—the unseen forces that guide us—help diminish the fears and uncertainties of the unknown. In this openness, the human experience finds a purpose that aligns with the full measure of its journey.

The labyrinth begins as a simple, one-dimensional design on a drafter's table, but quickly expands into a multi-dimensional reality—hallways and chambers stretching from short to long, at times spacious and at others oppressively narrow. Temperatures shift unpredictably, from the biting cold of a bone-chilling winter to the sweltering humidity of a midsummer's day. Brief moments of comfort can swiftly turn into discomfort without warning. Tension runs through every passage, shaped by the labyrinth's structure and the unknown length of time it takes to traverse.

Reaching the end of one corridor is like completing a chapter in the book of experience. But new questions immediately arise: Do we go forward, turn left, or choose the right path? What if we press on, only to collide with a wall or find the floor missing beneath us? The senses become heightened—strange smells fill the air; insects may be lurking. The walls could be smooth, bumpy, or rough under our touch, and the floor might be pristine or filthy. Overhead, a roof seals the interior, confining our journey. The lanterns and flashlights of our youth no longer provide illumination. Faint sounds, whether real or imagined, echo through the labyrinth, adding to the unease. It's often a lonely place, where the whispers of the distant night bring forth a zoo of creatures—mere shadows of the past.

There are exits scattered along the journey, but many lead only to disaster and destruction. The guiding force that propels us forward is the relentless push of time, constantly shortening the distance to some ever-elusive, ever-changing vision of utopia.

The labyrinth often represents a collision course where the familiar stumble of hope meets the looming shadow of fear. It's here that the unexpected awakens us from the fog of complacency, where moments of joy can, without warning, transform into deep wells of sorrow. These are the recognizable fortunes and misfortunes woven into the fabric of the labyrinth of life. At its entrance, a life is born and a journey begins; in its winding middle, a path unfolds—marked by lessons learned and unlearned, and the endless repetition of challenges. At the exit, we find the summation of a life lived. This is why I see life as a labyrinth—a complex journey filled with mysteries that define and shape us.

A License to Drive

I've often wondered, who's really driving here? This question feels pretty crucial when it comes to navigating life's maze. Sure, we might think we're in control, but the real motivator is time itself. You can decide to sit still, but time? Oh, time keeps moving—no pit stops allowed!

We start our journey with parents or guardians at the wheel, those trusted chauffeurs navigating us through the early twists and turns of life's streets and avenues within. They eventually hand over the keys, or at least share the road, with teachers, mentors, and other helpful copilots who point out signs, steer us clear of potholes, and offer a bit of guidance on this wild ride through the labyrinth.

But then comes the age of accountability—the moment our personalities are pretty much molded, and we start itching for the driver's seat. And oh, the tension kicks in! It's natural; the passenger wants to become the driver. Suddenly, it's unclear who's in charge. The driver feels a tug on the wheel, the former passenger grabs at it, and now we're in a bit of a backseat-driver situation.

Things can get a little awkward—maybe even lonely for a while. The once happily chauffeured passenger might just find themselves hoofing it solo for a stretch, navigating their way, with nothing but the open road ahead and a whole lot of growing up to do.

Lessons I've Learned (So Far) from the Labyrinth

As I sit here, trapped in the imagination of a fire crackling softly, I find myself thinking about the labyrinth of life and why it holds such importance. You, I can imagine as reader, asked me that very question, and I'm grateful you did. Because in reflecting on it, I've come to see that the labyrinth represents one of the few places where we, as humans, can find a delicate balance—where civil values and natural instincts meet.

The labyrinth gave me pause and made me realize that my life story, with all its twists and turns, could be told through its winding paths. As I made this association, I saw the common ground we all share as human beings—those moments of joy and sorrow, the victories, the wounds, the fleeting sunshine, and the deep shadows that each of us encounters. We're all driven by time, moving through the hidden course of our personal labyrinths.

But here's what I've learned: while we share the journey, we are not the same. Our commonality isn't found in the details of our stories but in the courageous enterprise of life itself—the solitary exploration each of us must undertake in those hidden corridors. What I realize now, in this second chapter of my life, is this: "Don't complicate life—LIVE IT!"

I've been shaped by my own path through the labyrinth. There were times when fear overwhelmed my courage, until I saw the delicate balance that humanity has grappled with for centuries—our shared struggle to find meaning on this communal ground we call Earth. I'm reminded of the steady voice of Walter Cronkite on the CBS Evening News, who would end with, "And that's the way it is." In those words, I find a simple truth: life is what happens, in all its unpredictability, and we are all carried forward by the relentless flow of time. We are drawn to what we seek, shaped by the past and driven by our hopes for the future.

My father once encouraged me to write this book—perhaps to channel my constant stream of words into something that could be shared. "You are an author," he said. "There's an audience that needs your story." He's lived over a century, outliving most of his peers, yet he has also witnessed unimaginable loss—the burning remains of a grandson who chose to end his own journey. A young man with a tender heart, who felt overlooked and misunderstood by a world that failed to recognize his worth. His struggle reminds me of how hard it is to truly understand another's labyrinth, how often we judge without knowing the full measure of another's path.

My dad has lived a long life, but it's not a life fully lived until this very moment. He's seen both the beauty of longevity and the tragedy of lives cut short, like my brother's young son, a giant in our family's story, whose journey ended far too soon. And yet, even in loss, there is a lesson: that the labyrinth is not just a place of confusion and fear, but also of discovery and hope, where every step, every turn, holds the potential for new understanding.

So, my dear friend, this is why the labyrinth of life matters. It's where we find ourselves, lose ourselves, and, if we're lucky, learn to cherish the path—every step, every stumble, every twist, and turn. If it is completed, then that is simply the way it was — a reality that can often feel cold and harsh. I've learned that my history is the truth I have lived. Every breath I've taken, every event that has shaped my life, is now past. Even the moment you began reading these words has already become a part of your own history. All my tomorrows are constructed from dreams I hold and expectations I hope for. But am I left only with lessons wrapped in 'If I had'? 'If I had turned right.' 'If I had gone along.' 'If I had invested.'

The 'If I' is often synonymous with the second-guessing of 'Had I.' 'Had I taken that trip.' 'Had I stayed.' 'Had I moved.'

'Had I been born in a different place — in a small town, a bustling city, or a world beyond my knowing.' These reflections form a maze of possibilities, paths not taken, and the endless yearning for the roads that might have been.

These are the self-imposed trials borne of personal expectations—the existential dilemmas that we, as conscious agents, encounter on our unique voyages. We fancy ourselves as the sovereign commanders of our destinies, captains of our metaphysical ships, and yet, we are bound by the finitude of our mortal faculties. One may unfurl the sails of ambition, but we lack the power to summon the winds that propel them. Some adeptly harness the gusts of fortune; others, paralyzed by uncertainty, dare not raise their sails at all.

Within the cloistered pathways of the labyrinthine life, a few possess the audacity to navigate the turns that might lead them closer to self-actualization. To these, we give our admiration. Yet, the very same twists can also hasten others into unforeseen catastrophe. There are those who, in despair, opt for the nearest exit, abandoning the quest prematurely. Meanwhile, others learn to savor the journey, aligning themselves with the ineffable joys that speak to the deeper rhythms of human existence. They attune themselves to that ancient, almost mythical guidance system—the timeless compass that has steered human aspiration towards innovation, construction, and transcendence. This is the shared human condition, the experience that transcends borders, nations, and all arbitrary divisions.

This lived experience is a natural endowment, an inherent right that opens both heart and intellect to the creative possibilities of existence. It is the generative potential that forges the keys to understanding, which, when applied to the right locks, unveils the doors that usher all of humanity forward. It builds upon both positive and negative encounters, synthesizing the sum total of all lived moments into blueprints, foundations upon which the kinetic force of our will lays another brick in the edifice of tomorrow.

What we share is this: every human being traverses their own labyrinth. Some traverse it with the measured pace of contemplation; others with the frantic sprint of urgency. Ultimately, it is time, not speed or distance, that propels us. Time inexorably ushers us toward that enigmatic final door, the inevitable exit we know as death—a constant that has reigned unchallenged since the dawn of existence. Our lives, in their fullest expanse, remain beyond complete apprehension. We are, at once, both historians and narrators, tasked with responding to the legacies of our own pasts. The labyrinth itself stands as the fundamental commonality of the human race. To understand this is to see beyond the walls that divide us, enabling us to honor the boundaries of others while working towards a more harmonious world.

This is our moment to grasp the profundity of existence. Time, not spatial distance, is the true measure of our lives. In each fleeting moment, we must ask: What have we done? What are we doing now? What will be the enduring legacy of our time? These are the questions I pose to myself continually."

As I've journeyed through my own labyrinth, I've picked up a few insights, theories, and principles that I think might just be universal. Let me share a few thoughts about culture. It's easy to overlook how deeply culture shapes who we are and how we see the world. But when we pause to notice, we see that each of us moves to the rhythm of our own culture—a rhythm that guides our choices, seasons our tastes, launches our reactions, and even how we make sense of life. And somewhere in all this, there's a beautiful dance, a chance to find balance and connection across all the different beats. The labyrinth is the unique fingerprint of every soul—a path each of us is born into and, through the relentless push of time, must navigate empowered by the ever-developing influence of memory.

THE BUBBLE EFFECT

The Invisible Framework that I call "The Bubble Theory"

Across all of humanity, there exists a singular, inescapable reality—one that transcends race, gender, education, and economic status. It has shaped our perceptions since the moment we took our first breath, dictating what we accept as truth and what we reject as foreign. It is the unseen force that governs our choices, our beliefs, and our limitations—yet, most never recognize its presence.

What is this silent architect of our reality? It is neither fate nor intellect, yet it determines both. It is the reason two people can witness the same event and tell two completely different stories. It is why cultures remain locked in cycles of tradition, belief, and bias, even when the world around them demands change. It is the unseen enclosure of perception—the *Bubble*.

Like an invisible boundary, the *Bubble* surrounds us, defining what is familiar and what is *other*. It determines not just how we see the world, but how we engage with it. Some bubbles are reinforced by privilege; others are reinforced by struggle. Some provide a window to expansion, while others act as a prison of thought. This is where *Cultural Confinement* takes root—within the very structures that shape our understanding of who we are and what is possible.

But here is the truth: the *Bubble* is not an impenetrable barrier. It is a construct—one that can be examined, stretched, and even broken. To recognize it is to take the first step toward true freedom of thought.

The Universal Constant of Human Experience

Across all of humanity, there exists a singular, inescapable consistency—one that transcends race, gender, education, and socioeconomic status. It is present from the moment of conception, persists through every stage of existence, and remains with us until we draw our final breath. This commonality is not bound by geography, wealth, or any external measure of identity, yet it is so deeply ingrained in the human condition that many remain unaware of its profound influence.

What is this unifying feature of intelligent life? It is neither a mystery nor an abstraction, yet it governs our responses, our assertiveness, our silence, and our expression. It is the unseen framework through which we interpret reality. It shapes perception, dictates reaction, and defines the boundaries of what we believe to be possible. It is as present in the instinctual behaviors of the animal kingdom as it is in the complexities of human civilization.

This fundamental construct is the seat of the self, the home base of individual and collective understanding. **It is the *Bubble*** —the unseen yet ever-present enclosure of perception that defines and confines our reality. And it is here that our exploration begins.

Let's continue with this narrative:

"I simply can't believe that," she spat, her face twisting in utter disgust. She looked as if she'd just tasted something rancid. "He should be ashamed—no, his whole family, his community, everyone who ever taught him anything should be ashamed that this idiot is out here representing them."

With a dramatic flourish, she shot up from her chair, rolling her eyes so hard I thought they'd get stuck. I quietly handed her the sweater she had draped over the back of her seat. She snatched it from my hand, still fuming, still triggered by every word he'd just unleashed. **His opinions? Offensive, racist, misogynistic, and flat-out rude**—as she so bluntly put it while storming off.

"He's too young to be this idiotic," she muttered, her voice trailing off as she stomped away.

Meanwhile, he sat there, still in the circle, surrounded by a silence so thick you could cut it with a knife. The few remaining souls hadn't fled, but they sat like statues, unsure of what to do next.

He wore a look of slow amazement, like someone who had just witnessed an alien spaceship land right in front of him, only to see the little green figures vanish into thin air.

Damn! That was the headline written all over his face. He was the so-called "born genius," the one who thought he knew better than anyone in the room, only to find himself bewildered when his brilliance wasn't applauded but rejected. If you could read his mind at that moment, it would scream just one word: **DAMN!**

Over decades of working with various clients, I've developed a theory I call "The Bubble Effect." This theory emerged from my ongoing observations and the introspection that followed. I began to notice a recurring pattern: the behaviors and thought processes I observed in others closely mirrored what I discovered within myself. At the heart of these behaviors lies a common thread.

In essence, I refer to this phenomenon as the Bubble Effect, an outgrowth of what I understand as Perspective Thinking. It delves into how we form our perspectives and how easily those perspectives can be manipulated. A skilled con artist, for instance, can distort our reasoning by exploiting our imaginations, making us see a reality they've crafted for their own gain.

Our safe zone is the bubble—An ethereal protective space where we house our mental and emotional furnishings. However, when we allow others to infiltrate this space and rearrange our internal landscape, we risk partnering with them in the gradual destruction of our inner selves.

This theory encapsulates my concept of personal bubbles or echo chambers, where individuals surround themselves with like-minded people and ideas. This, in turn, can lead to limited perspectives and a narrowing of understanding. Through the Bubble Effect, I aim to explore the importance of diversity, open-mindedness, and the need for meaningful dialogue across differing viewpoints.

The Bubble is fundamentally reactive, mirroring the same behavioral patterns identified in B.F. Skinner's operant conditioning and Ivan Pavlov's classical conditioning experiments. These experiments were pivotal in revealing the 'Condition/Response' primitive deeply embedded within each of us. Much like the subjects in Skinner's box, who were conditioned to push a lever in response to stimuli, or Pavlov's dogs, who salivated at the sound of a bell, individuals within their personal Bubbles are often triggered by external cues that reinforce existing beliefs and biases. This reactivity is not just a social phenomenon but a conditioned reflex, one that is hardwired through repeated exposure and reinforcement within their socio-cultural environments.

In this sense, the Bubble functions like an invisible Skinner Box, where people are rewarded with social approval or punished with disapproval based on their conformity to shared beliefs. Similarly, like Pavlov's dogs, they respond automatically to the 'bells' of their environment—be it social media, religious doctrine, or cultural narratives—without conscious awareness. The Bubble, therefore, is not merely a metaphor for insular thinking; it is a psychological reality grounded in the conditioned responses that shape human behavior. To break free from the Bubble is to recognize these patterns, question the stimuli that control us, and seek the well of true wisdom beyond the automatic, conditioned reactions.

So, What's The Bubble?

The Bubble is my way of describing the self—the individual as they exist in their own mental and emotional world. Think of each of us as a bubble: I'm a bubble, you're a bubble, and the world is filled with countless others floating around in their unique spheres.

The Bubble represents the inner self, shaped by a lifetime of experiences, thoughts, and beliefs. It is inherently self-centered, focused on self-preservation, self-interest, and self-protection. Within the Bubble are the internal "furnishings" of our minds—the accumulated ideas, perceptions, and assumptions we've gathered over time. These form the framework of how we see the world and how we interact with it.

Just as a bubble floats within its own fragile boundaries, the self is surrounded by the limits of its understanding, yet always influenced by the fizz and suds of life around it. Recognizing this Bubble is the first step in understanding ourselves—and in seeing beyond it.

Let's break this down. When I was born, the global population was about 3.12 billion people. Now, before we go any further, let's talk about that word "billion." We hear it a lot—especially when talking about money. Some people know what it really means, but honestly, a lot of good and well-meaning people don't.

We're often curious and/or interested in the subject concerning who is a billionaire, putting them up on a pedestal, like they're something special. But a billion is a massive number, and it's not just about money. Scientists even use it to describe the distance between stars, saying some are a billion light years apart—that's mind-blowingly far!

But what exactly is a billion? Picture this: think about how many grains of sand there are on the beaches and beneath the oceans. That's the kind of huge number we're talking about.

Let's Break This Down

When I was born, the global population was about 3.12 billion people. Let's pause here to really understand what "billion" means. We hear it often—usually about money or scientific distances—but the sheer size of this number can be hard to grasp.

A billion is 1,000 million—that's 1,000,000,000. Imagine trying to count to a billion. If you counted one number per second without stopping, it would take you over 31 years to reach a billion! That's a mind-boggling number. Scientists even use "billion" to describe the distance between stars—some are billions of light-years apart, meaning the number isn't just big, it's astronomical.

Now, when I was born, the world had around 3.12 billion people. Fast forward sixty-two years, and that number has more than doubled to over 8.16 billion today. Think about that—the number of people on Earth has more than doubled in my lifetime.

Despite these billions of individuals, we all share one fundamental truth: our humanity. To put it another way, imagine each person as a bubble floating in the vast sea of the human population. Each bubble is unique—shaped by experiences, thoughts, and perspectives—but together, we form the collective fizz and suds; the foam of life on Earth.

When we zoom out and see this big picture, it's a reminder that we're all part of something much larger than ourselves—a global body of individuals, connected by our shared existence.

Understanding the Bubble

The Bubble represents each of us—our unique identity. Just as no two fingerprints among the 8.16 billion people on Earth are alike, no two bubbles are the same. From the moment our brains start forming thoughts, our bubble begins to take shape and expand.

In the early stages of life, this expansion happens naturally, guided largely by caregivers. As we grow, it's influenced by our environment and the choices we make. For some, the bubble expands quickly; for others, it grows more slowly, depending on factors like upbringing, culture, and life circumstances.

Negative influences, such as neglect, abuse, or a harmful environment, can hinder the bubble's growth. Challenges like illness or poverty can also slow its expansion. On the other hand, positive influences—like supportive communities, access to education, and opportunities for personal and spiritual growth—can help the bubble grow in healthier ways.

It's important to note that spiritual growth doesn't necessarily mean being part of a religious group. It refers to personal development that helps us find meaning, purpose, and connection. These positive influences can guide the bubble into a second stage, where its expansion depends more on personal decisions and commitments.

Independence is another factor in shaping our bubble. The more autonomy we have, the more we can choose how to grow and furnish the inside of our bubble. And that's a critical point: the furnishings inside the bubble are what shape how we perceive and interact with the world around us.

These furnishings—our beliefs, experiences, and values—are influenced by the layers of the world outside. Culture, education, relationships, and even the broader society seep through the protective shell of our bubble and leave their mark. These elements ultimately determine how we interact with other bubbles in the vast fizz of humanity.

The Aspects of the Bubble: Does It Burst?

Let's explore the nature of the bubble—our self. You might be wondering: *Does the bubble ever burst?* The short answer is no. The bubble only ceases to exist when life itself ends. As long as we're alive, the bubble persists, evolving, growing, and adapting in ways unique to each of us.

The bubble begins forming early—right alongside our brain's development. Just like fingerprints, each bubble is one-of-a-kind. Its expansion never truly stops. At times, it might slow down, speed up, or even seem stuck. Yet, it remains influenced by everything we encounter: our environment, experiences, and even the tiniest, fleeting moments. A bird landing nearby, a sudden smile from a stranger, or a single falling leaf—all these seemingly insignificant details add depth to the bubble's growth.

But no matter what life throws at it—aging, trauma, heartbreak, or addiction—the bubble doesn't burst. These experiences might dent it, stretch it, or alter its shape, but they can't erase it. The bubble reflects our existence; it holds our thoughts, memories, hopes, and fears. It endures as long as we do, constantly expanding and adapting, a testament to our ongoing journey in life.

Each of us is a bubble, part of the billions of others who share the common thread of existence. Some bubbles may shine brighter; others might carry scars. Yet all are unbroken as long as life persists.

What truly makes each bubble remarkable is what lies within it. This is where our individuality lives—our beliefs, memories, dreams, and even our vulnerabilities. This space inside the bubble belongs entirely to us. It's a living, breathing archive of everything that makes us who we are.

It's also our responsibility. No one else can manage or nurture this inner space for us. How we furnish it—what we choose to keep, discard, or embrace—shapes how we interact with the world outside. The bubble isn't just a container; it's a dynamic force, holding our essence and guiding our path through life.

In the larger scheme of things, the bubble reminds us that while we may be just one in billions, each of us holds a universe within.

Let's take a look inside. This is what I call the "furnishing" of the bubble.

Earlier, I shared my fascination with psychology, particularly the Psychology of Religion. But it doesn't stop there—the Psychology of Politics, Economics, Neighborhoods, and more could all be cousins in this expanding family. Each domain represents a unique lens through which we understand human behavior and thought.

Psychology, at its core, is the scientific or systematic study of the mind and behavior. Yet, I propose that our individual bubbles—our personal spaces—are just as worthy of exploration. Each bubble is like a small, dynamic universe reflecting how we relate to the world around us. It's not just about what we think or feel; it's about how our inner world interacts with our outer world. Understanding this requires a deeper, more nuanced approach—almost like diving into a rabbit hole where the exploration is endless.

This journey began for me in high school, during a moment that would become foundational to my thinking. I remember sitting in science class, captivated by a model of the solar system. It was nothing extraordinary—just a large yellow ball for the sun with colorful smaller balls attached to metal arms, representing the planets. Then, I noticed something else: the textbook illustration of an atom. The nucleus, like the sun, sat at the center, with electrons orbiting around it. The similarities were uncanny. Both systems had a core, and both had things orbiting around that core.

Whenever one concept seemed out of reach, I'd use the other to make sense of it. If the atom felt too abstract, I thought of the solar system. If the solar system's scale was overwhelming, I zoomed into the atom. This simple practice became my personal mantra: *"If you can't understand the micro, consider the macro."* It was a mental pivot that helped me solve puzzles in science, but it didn't stop there.

I began to see this pattern everywhere. Everything seemed to have a center—whether it was a family, a community, or even my own thoughts. Just like the planets and electrons, our personal spaces—our bubbles—are influenced by forces that orbit around them. And just like the atom or the solar system, each bubble contains its own rules, its own rhythms, and its own story.

This idea of the bubble as a dynamic, evolving space fascinated me, especially as I reflected on how our bubbles are "furnished" with experiences, ideas, and influences from the moment of our existence.

Life in the Bubble: A Universe of Our Own Making

We all live in bubbles. These aren't the fragile, soapy spheres that drift and pop in a moment's time; these are far more resilient, more complex. Each bubble is a world unto itself, shaped by the forces of culture, experience, and individuality. Our bubbles are alive, growing and shifting as we move through life.

But what is a bubble, really? At its core, it's a boundary—a membrane that separates the self from the vastness of the outside world. It defines us, but it also confines us. Inside, our thoughts and beliefs swirl around, furnishing the space with meaning. It's cozy, familiar, and often comforting. But like any home, a bubble can be cluttered, cramped, or even isolating.

The Building Blocks of the Bubble

Where do these bubbles come from? Imagine a newborn, entering the world as a blank canvas. From their very first moments, their bubble begins to form. Parents, caregivers, and culture set the foundation, layering the bubble with stories, beliefs, and norms. "This is who you are," they say, directly or indirectly.

As we grow, we continue to furnish our bubbles. Education adds shelves of knowledge. Friends and peers bring in furniture—some of it stylish, some of it uncomfortable. Media and technology install windows, but they're often tinted or distorted, framing the outside world in ways that reflect someone else's agenda.

By adulthood, our bubbles are fully furnished, but they're far from static. Every experience, every relationship, every piece of information we encounter adds something new or rearranges what's already there.

Bubble Life and the Illusion of Transparency

Here's the catch: bubbles aren't entirely opaque or transparent. We think we see the world clearly through our bubble, but in truth, we see the world as our bubble *allows* us to see it. The colors of the glass, the thickness of the walls—these distortions are invisible to us because they're all we've ever known.

Take my high school realization about atoms and solar systems. It opened my eyes to the idea that perspective is everything. Just as I learned to use the macro to understand the micro, I realized that we can also use others' bubbles to understand our own. When we dare to step outside of ourselves—or even just peek through the cracks in our bubble's walls—we begin to see the limits of our perspective.

The Comfort and the Challenge

Living in a bubble isn't inherently bad. In fact, it's necessary. Without our bubbles, we'd be overwhelmed by the chaos of the world. They give us structure, identity, and a sense of control. But they also come with a price: the risk of stagnation, of mistaking our bubble's furnishings for universal truths.

Think about the last time you disagreed with someone. Did you try to understand their perspective, or did you retreat further into your bubble, reinforcing its walls? It's a natural response, but it's also a limiting one.

The challenge, then, is to make our bubbles more flexible, more porous. To let light and air in, even if it disrupts our carefully curated interior. It's not about abandoning our bubbles—it's about expanding them.

Bursting or Growing: The Choice is Ours

Some bubbles burst under pressure. A life-changing event—a loss, a revelation, a moment of profound connection—can shatter the walls we thought were indestructible. When that happens, we're left exposed, vulnerable, and unsure of who we are without the boundaries we once relied on. We simply die, or in other words surrender. We give up and often get out of the control of the self; letting the energies of passing bubbles control us.

But bursting isn't the only option. We can also choose to grow. To stretch our bubbles outward, embracing the discomfort of new ideas and experiences. It's a slower process, but it's one that leads to greater understanding, empathy, and responsible connection to the world around us.

A Universe of Bubbles

Picture a room filled with bubbles of every size and color, each one unique, yet all part of the same vast tapestry. That's humanity. Each of us live in our own bubble, but we're also part of a larger collective. The way our bubbles interact—whether they collide, merge, or repel—shapes the course of our lives and may influence world we share.

This is the essence of bubble life: a delicate balance between the self and the other, the individual and the collective, the known and the unknown. It's a life of constant evolution, where growth comes not from bursting bubbles, but from expanding them.

Okay, Let's Break It Down Further

Let's peek again inside the bubble and see how it's furnished. The bubble is filled with all kinds of experiences and influences that shape how a person sees themselves and relates to the world. It all starts in the womb. Science shows us that the environment surrounding the mother—the sights, sounds, vibrations, and even her emotional responses—begin to impact the unborn child long before that first independent breath. The mother's fears, her calm, her choices, her moods—they all become the first layers of the bubble's furnishings, laying down the blueprint for a life to come.

I once believed that a baby arrived in this world as a blank slate, but I've come to see it differently. The bubble theory suggests that this child isn't starting from zero; they're already learning, already building survival instincts in that natural classroom of the womb. The moment they're born, they're ready—seeking connection, recognizing safety, sensing the world's welcome or its cold shoulder. That first cry, that first grip of a finger—it's all about survival. And from that moment, the furnishings start taking shape: recognition, anxiety, fear, comfort. The bubble grows, influenced by everything it encounters, from birth to the very end of life.

This is just the first glimpse into the bubble, from the outside looking in. We can never fully grasp the entirety of human thought—it's confined within each of our bubbles. It's reactive, always responding to what's happening inside and out. And it's only through living, sharing, and experiencing that we catch a glimpse of what lies within each person's bubble. The bubble is the keeper of our unique stories, our personal trials, and triumphs. It's who we are, and it's expanding every single day.

The Clash of the Bubbles

Determination is an untapped powerhouse within the intimate architecture of the bubble—the self. The way we reason, make decisions, and interpret the world are all acts of personal accommodation, guided by the unique furnishings of our bubbles. It is in this deeply personal space that we find the true essence of our identity. The danger comes when outside forces—other bubbles—seek to infiltrate, manipulate, and rearrange the inner sanctum of our being. These invasions, often cloaked in influence, can escalate into outright hostility, demanding conformity and obedience. Whether through subtle persuasion or outright violence, there are always external forces trying to set fire bringing destruction to the sanctity of our bubbles.

But here's the truth: the inner space of the bubble belongs solely to its owner—shared only with the permissions they grant, and safeguarded by the soul's resolve. This is where the micro mirrors the macro, where the personal becomes cosmic.

Many quote the Bible, often carelessly, missing the profound depth of a single word that reveals a truth worth wrestling with: 'Image.' To understand this is to recognize that our self-image is the closest we come to reflecting the grand Image of our ultimate origin—the one that breathed life into every bubble. It's a force that can't be coerced, diluted, or dismissed. It's the sacred balance between the microcosm of the individual and the macrocosm of creation, where every breath, thought, and choice carries the echo of a greater purpose.

Consider the baby, arriving in this world without a mission to hate. A baby's bubble — the space that defines their self — starts out simple, unblemished by the complexities that adults often wrestle with. In those early moments, the baby has no power of reasoning or personal choice; their bubble is an open, vulnerable field, easily furnished with whatever the surrounding community decides to place inside it.

Hate is not inherent; it's an imported item, often thrust into the young bubble by the adult world of guardianship. A baby, unable to distinguish, must barter its trust for survival, absorbing the ideas, fears, and prejudices of those who provide care. It's within these early transactions that the community begins to inflate the bubble with notions that might include hostility, fear, or even outright hate. And so, the hate takes root — often pointed at those outside the bubble, strangers who don't fit the narratives the baby is raised with.

This is why, as we journey across different parts of America, we find some places warm and welcoming to outsiders, while others seem harsh and suspicious of visitors. These contrasting attitudes aren't spontaneous; they're the results of generations of bubbles formed and misinformed. Each new pair of eyes, upon opening, is immediately exposed to cues, both direct and passive, about who is to be trusted and who is to be feared. Thus, the bubble grows — not just with love and curiosity, but also with the furniture of prejudice and hand me down items of thought by previous generations.

The baby grows into a developing agent of hostility, absorbing the biases and fears embedded in their environment. This is how xenophobia takes root. The child, now fixated on 'THOSE PEOPLE,' perceives them as a danger, unable to discern between safe and unsafe influences. Until new, healthier furnishings replace the old, these fear-soaked and fear-stained beliefs remain combustible, ever ready to ignite into harmful actions. Consider figures like Timothy McVeigh, Dylann Roof, or the Unabomber Ted Kaczynski—all once babies, all shaped by the furnishings within their bubbles.

What I'm suggesting is not new, but it's a stark reminder of how easily hatred and fear can be passed down through generations, shaping minds into agents of peril. History is full of such names—individuals who, from a young age, were groomed into a mindset that sought to destroy rather than to understand. Sadly, the dynamics of their behavior often produce frightening headlines heralding their violent clashings with other bubbles in infamous ways.

At its core, selfishness becomes a protective mechanism, a desperate defense against perceived threats. Many adults who cling to hatred also harbor a deep distrust of education, rejecting anything that challenges their beliefs or expands their understanding. They choose to stay confined within the narrow boundaries of their fear-filled bubbles, resisting any expansion that might introduce new ideas or perspectives. It is this refusal to grow that feeds the cycle of hostility and ignorance.

It is remarkable that love, like fear, begins in the same way—with a baby. Conceived, born, and welcomed into the world, the child receives love as a gift, not as something to be bartered or earned. True love is granted freely, unburdened by the expectation of compensation. But for those who grow up bartering for love, the furnishings within their bubble become stale—outdated and musty.

This difference is evident in the lives of artists, musicians, inventors, and all those who stand at the forefront of creativity. These individuals are the carriers of light, offering gifts that bless the world with joy, innovation, and fresh perspectives. Yet, they are often misunderstood or even despised by those whose bubbles remain stunted, unable to expand and thrive. These naysayers resist change, clinging to their narrow views and even calling for external forces, like government interventions, to halt progress.

It is always the roots of optimism that nourish a brave, new, ever-evolving world. Those who embrace love as an unconditional force—those who welcome the furnishings of creativity, curiosity, and open-mindedness—become the architects of the future. In contrast, those who remain trapped in fear, clinging to the past, are left behind as the world moves forward.

There are many items I call 'furnishings' within the bubble. These can be immense, shaping the very core of who we are, or small and fragile, yet still significant. The size of the bubble is not dictated by age but by the breadth and depth of one's experiences. Some might think they understand my concept of the bubble and its furnishings and conclude that the best course of action would be to discard the old and bring in the new. But here's the catch: we can never truly rid ourselves of these furnishings. We can only acquire more. And it is through acquiring new furnishings that we begin to balance, and sometimes even overshadow, those we might wish to discard.

Where have I heard this before? 'Put off the old man and put on the new?' Growing up, I was surrounded by this kind of thinking. In my church, they would baptize so-called believers, and some would even undergo rebaptism multiple times, believing that each plunge would wash away the old self and resurrect a new one. But many of these baptized souls would emerge as part-time Christians, living one way in the light of Sunday and another in the shadows of their daily lives. If you doubt this, try catching them on their days off. If you disagree with them, displease them, or make them believe they have a reason to be angry (because, remember, anger is an act of self-control within the bubble), you'll quickly see their part-time status in full display.

Even those who are baptized still carry the memories of their youthful mischiefs—like tying a flame to a cat's tail and watching it dart into the cornfield—not that I would ever do that, of course. These memories, these experiences, remain part of the bubble's furnishings, shaping the self as much as any new intention or resolve.

There are some who might say, 'Destroy the bubble. Pop it. Do whatever it takes to shatter it.' But understand this: the destruction of the bubble is the end of life, for the bubble represents the self. To destroy the self is to achieve death through self-annihilation. The Bubble Theory, as I propose it, encourages both myself and you, the reader, to be in a constant search for new and enriching experiences that bring positive furnishings—those that carry a constant sight and fragrance of renewal.

It is also essential to cleanse the old. Disinfect the parts that have grown stale or harmful. Rid the bubble of the bedbugs, cockroaches, and spiders—those remnants of a prehistoric past that cling to us like cobwebs, tangling us in outdated legacies and toxic thinking. Remember, the bubble is yours. My bubble is mine. We alone determine the content within our personal space.

Like-minded bubbles attract one another, forming what I call community. This community often reinforces our comfort and contentment within the confines of our bubbles, creating a shared space where growth and transformation can thrive.

Can I say more about the specific furniture contained within the bubble? Absolutely—I'm the author, after all, and this is my concept of the Bubble Theory. So, let's dive in. Each of us is influenced by the furnishings that exist within the confines of our bubble. Few might consciously focus on these contents, but everyone, everywhere, is impacted and shaped by every aspect of the environment inside their bubble. The influence of the parental bubble, along with the surrounding bubbles that make up the accepted community, directly affects the taste and selection of the furnishings that fill our bubbles. The scholastic community—whether public, private, or home-schooled—has profound and often growing influence over what is confined within our bubble.

Consider, for example, phobias. According to the 5th edition of the Diagnostic and Statistical Manual of Mental Disorders (DSM-5), 'a specific phobia is a persistent, irrational fear of a specific object, situation, or person that is disproportionate to the actual danger.' In simpler terms, a phobia is an exaggerated anxiety disorder, defined by an irrational, unrealistic, and excessive fear of an object, person, animal, activity, or situation that poses little or no real danger.

A phobia serves as a prime example of a type of furnishing located within the bubble that directly impacts our relationship with the environment and the surrounding community of bubbles. This piece of 'furniture' dictates how we navigate life, often limiting our movement and understanding based on fears that were installed before we even had the chance to challenge them.

Phobias are real, but they are also learned behaviors shaped by the experiences and impacts exerted on the bubble. Consider a chair as an example. A baby might be held by a guardian sitting in a chair. At first, the baby cares little about the chair itself; the baby's primary concern is survival—nourishment, comfort, and attention provided by the guardian. In this initial stage, the chair is merely part of the environment, unnoticed by the baby.

As the child grows into a toddler, the relationship with the chair begins to change. Now, the chair becomes associated with predictable routines: being fed, read to, or rocked to sleep. The chair takes on new meaning—a place where needs are met and comfort is found. As the child continues to develop, the emotional significance deepens. The chair becomes linked with memories of friends, family, and visitors, creating a web of affiliative connections. Thus, the child begins to build a personal understanding of the chair that will influence them throughout their life. The ease with which the child learns the art of connecting is deeply affected by the experiences tied to this chair.

As an adult, I've encountered many experiences, just as we all have. Each experience represents the furnishings of our lives. When I look back, I think of one of the greatest doctors

I've ever known—my mother, known to the community as Ms. Elaine. I've had many great doctors in my life, but none like the lady who held me on that chair. She had the best medicine for both toothaches and stomachaches alike. I remember being laid across her knees while she rubbed my back—her medicine always soothed my distress. Even when the cause of my discomfort remained, the anxiety that left me wailing would melt away. It was tender love and care that began in a chair I can't even remember clearly.

As the child matures, they learn to select friends and form a community, each contributing to how the chair—and other objects—are perceived. The child develops a sense of value and worth. This stage marks a veering away from the safety of home, guided by principles rooted in those early experiences. Eventually, the child declares, "This is who I am." This stage was being drafted from the womb, shaped by each experience along the way.

The World of Phobias

So, why mention phobias? Because phobias are a key part of the furnishings found within the bubble. Even a person who claims to fear nothing might, under scrutiny, reveal fears rooted in an 'us vs. them' mentality—a common playbook of phobias. I am not a psychiatrist or psychologist, but I do have qualifications in psychotherapy and experience in helping clients navigate challenges through various psychological approaches.

Phobias often originate from early childhood experiences, such as those first encounters with a chair. A phobia can develop through direct exposure to a traumatic event, witnessing someone else's fear, or even hearing about a frightening situation. This is known as classical conditioning, where a neutral stimulus becomes associated with fear. Early on, this type of conditioning becomes the interior designer of the bubble, laying out a life shaped by suggestion and association.

Now, let's explore some of the specific furnishings that lead to irrational and often hazardous outcomes. Phobias are intense personal fears—very real to the person experiencing them. Some phobias are newly introduced or redeveloped, but many are fashioned from the same old designs that have shaped human behavior for decades, if not centuries. These furnishings are real, yet they are also real exaggerations. They are shaped by the influence of 'furniture makers and movers'— those who infiltrate the territory of the bubble and determine its interior design. The bubble's host, influenced by the level of unchecked appreciation or the unexamined quality of the bubble's contents, unconsciously decides what furnishings to accept or reject, based on the values set by these influencers and the accepted community around them.

On this level, we are all the same. This model represents a universal human act that has assigned value—whether perceived as good or bad—since the dawn of humanity. Are the behaviors that emerge from the bubble instinctive or learned? I believe we arrive in the world with an instinct that begins to develop in the mother's womb. Once we are born, however, we are defenseless against the growing number of influencers that shape our lives. In our preverbal stage, we are guided by experiences and shaped by the company of other bubbles whose furnishings leave lasting impressions. Over time, these experiences foster a self-centered and guarded sense of taste—a topic I will explore further in the chapter on 'Cultural Incarceration and Cultural Confinement.'

But let's continue our brief exploration of phobias. I believe a phobia is an adaptive furnishing—a response to a negative stimulus or event that has impacted the bubble in a harmful way. Consider a well-known phobia, like claustrophobia. This fear manifests as an abnormal discomfort or dread of being confined in small spaces with no escape. It can show itself in various forms: fear of elevators, airplanes, subways, crowded buses, traffic jams, or even standing in line at a venue. For the person with claustrophobia, these everyday situations become fraught with anxiety and panic.

Contrast this with another, yet similar fear: agoraphobia, which presents as an ongoing anxiety about being in situations where escape seems difficult or impossible. This fear, too, can trigger panic attacks. While both phobias share a fear of confinement, they differ in their specific triggers and manifestations, yet both remind us of how our internal 'furnishings' can govern our reality, shaping our actions and reactions in profound ways.

Most phobias create a complex web of anxiety that can be incredibly difficult to manage. They can range from arachnophobia, the fear of spiders, to hemophobia, the fear of blood—each carrying its own unique furnishings shaped by personal or cultural experiences. For instance, hemophobia was notably heightened during the AIDS epidemic, when fear of blood became a profound and pervasive furnishing in the collective consciousness. Phobias cover the entire alphabet, from A to Z—extending all the way to zoophobia, the fear of animals. Each of these fears represents a different way the bubble is shaped, influenced, and constrained by the experiences and environments around us.

This leads us to a range of more modern and nuanced

phobias—some seemingly fabricated to excuse acts of hatred, cultural insensitivity, or deep-seated prejudices that are really just old, reupholstered furnishings in the bubble. Take, for instance, the supposed 'Spectascribophobia'—the fear of someone watching you as you write an email—or 'Egochristicolaphobia,' the fear of being associated with the word 'Christian.' While such notions might provoke anxiety in certain contexts, they don't find any legitimate recognition in the DSM-5 as genuine behavioral issues.

Let's pause here to make a meaningful contrast. Consider a declared phobia that could easily be mistaken for a fear-based condition, yet is actually related to an allergic reaction—like anaphylaxis, which is a severe allergic response to an antigen such as bee venom. But then there's 'arachibutyrophobia,' the so-called fear of peanut butter sticking to the roof of your mouth. It's real in the sense that it happens, but it's more about discomfort than a genuine psychological condition. I remember experiencing this as a child. The cure was simple: my best doctor—the woman sitting in the chair, my mother—warned me not to stuff too much of my peanut butter and jelly sandwich in my mouth at once. She told me to drink some milk and swallow carefully. It worked, and I guess I didn't have arachibutyrophobia after all.

I am not dismissing or making light of legitimate matters that develop within the bubble. These psychological conditions truly exist as products of the bubble's confines and control, representing real, measurable distinctions between exaggerated fears and genuine disorders. However, there's a need to address the rise of politicized phobias that are escalating at an alarming rate, resulting in tragic loss of life and ongoing endangerment. These phobias have become troubling furnishings in far too many bubbles.

Consider xenophobia—the fear or distrust of strangers, foreigners, or anything perceived as 'other.' This fear often morphs into outright hatred. Alongside it are its equally dangerous counterparts: transphobia and homophobia. Transphobia, an irrational fear or aversion to transgender individuals, frequently leads to discrimination, violence, and sometimes death. Homophobia similarly entails an irrational fear or aversion to gay people or homosexuality. This over-politicized fear, often rooted in religious communities and perpetuated by certain political leaders, has caused substantial harm and fueled discrimination against the LGBTQ+ community. Like xenophobia and transphobia, it is a reckless contribution to ongoing dangers and death.

I must openly address the role of certain religious and political leaders in promoting these phobias. Their irresponsible rhetoric has also fostered the growth of Islamophobia—a fear or aversion to Islam and those who practice it. Within the bubble, these fears transform the self into a territory wary of anything perceived as foreign or strange. Yet, if we're honest, each of our bubbles contains its own oddities and curiosities—furnishings shaped by our unique experiences and perspectives."

This version sharpens the focus on how politicized phobias are fostered by external influences, while maintaining a balanced tone that acknowledges the complexity of the human experience.

What Triggers the Bubbles?

The word 'trigger' refers to anything that causes the furnishings within a bubble to shift suddenly or violently. This often results in the bubble's owner becoming reactive, manifesting in behaviors that range from microaggressions to intense outbursts and even violence. A trigger is an indicator of how the bubble has been furnished over time, shaped by the owner's life experiences. Some furnishings are like radioactive materials—hidden but harmful. Others resemble volcanoes, dormant until they erupt. And some are like smoldering embers, quiet but capable of igniting wildfires under the right conditions.

These triggers are not confined to individual lives; they manifest in personal relationships, extend into communities, and, at their most extreme, provoke global conflicts and wars. A seemingly small spark can set off a chain reaction, revealing just how volatile and interconnected our inner worlds and outer realities can be.

Now comes the moment of reckoning—the "what we were told" moment. What we were told, when accepted as fact, becomes a powerful tool for welcoming the furniture movers into our lives. It's time to reclaim that often-demonized word: Indoctrination. Think about it: how often do we hear that "they" are the indoctrinated ones, the ones taught to follow the "thems"? Indoctrination is typically wielded as a weapon in descriptions of those we fiercely disagree with—most often heard from communities of faith or in the corridors of political discourse. Yet, the truth is that all bubbles are vulnerable. Furnishings of thought and belief are often slipped under the veil of darkness by those we trust, or worse, by those who seek control for their own gain.

The reality is that we are all indoctrinated in countless ways. Some of us have been indoctrinated to express boundless love. They have been driven by their indoctrination to care deeply for the environment, to fight against global warming, and to ensure everyone has access to safe drinking water. They advocate for good nutrition for all and for housing that is both affordable and fair. They build amusement parks that bring joy and create sanctuaries that protect the animal kingdom. We say they were taught to care. They envision a world, however transitory or utopian, where all things balance out for the greater good. They have been indoctrinated with the furnishings of hope and are often seen bleeding optimism. These are the purveyors who are not afraid to dream big and build when the right resources and materials are available. They take risks—believing in the best that life has to offer, in their one and present moment of time.

In the delicate balance of yin and yang, there lies a stark contrast of indoctrination. On one side, there are those who have been taught to see all lawyers as inherently evil, to trust no politician unless they echo the narrow worldview that shores up their most basic presuppositions. Their understanding of the vast, complex world is shaped by a limited community, an inherited mistrust, and the exaggerated fears that grifters exploit with endless gaslighting. They feed on the frenzy of misinformation like a rabid beast frothing at the mouth of reason. For them, it's easy to follow the path laid by their surroundings, as their tastes in furnishings are relics of dampened hopes and simmering anger—handed-down, moth-eaten, cockroach-infested furniture with broken arms, propped-up legs, and off-track drawers that are accepted because they represent the comfort of their community.

Yet, both of these groups are products of indoctrination. One is bold and venturesome, the other hesitant and withdrawn, but both are molded by the beliefs that have been ingrained in them over time. And both are volatile. The triggers that set them off vary, but they always hinge upon the pressure within the bubble—on the heat and humidity that unsettle the comfort of the self. Triggering occurs in that critical moment when the bubble's owner erupts, declaring, 'I can't take it anymore.

The collision between owned reality and perceived illusions can lead to mental conflict, often resulting in unintended and sometimes irreparable damage. The trigger point occurs when an individual feels the tension between their indoctrinated beliefs and the reality they face. For instance, an individual who was once employed but is now out of work may struggle with the loss of economic stability. A homemaker experiencing the dissolution of a family may find themselves grappling with a distorted sense of love and security. An entrepreneur who fails to achieve their business goals may confront the reality of unmet dreams. Even an environmentalist, who feels their message is falling on deaf ears, must deal with the disheartening reality of unfulfilled advocacy.

Triggers, whether stemming from positive or negative experiences, are inherent to everyone—be they optimists or pessimists. The triggers are a result of the bubbles host feeling its own. The personally guided under the bubble's furnishing as absolute belief of being attacked. These triggers can be intense and challenging, but they can be managed by the individual navigations of their own bubbles.

Can We Refurbish the Bubble?

The short answer is no. To refurbish means to restore something to its original state. But when it comes to our "bubble"—our inner world and experiences—things aren't that simple. We can clean up, repair, or even redecorate, but those efforts are really about adjusting what's already there, not erasing or starting over.

In psychology, we learn that a person's personality is mostly formed by the time they're around 10 to 12 years old. This means the basic "furnishings" of our bubble—the core ideas, beliefs, and behaviors that shape how we see the world—are usually set early on. While we can move things around, paint the walls, or change the flooring, the original pieces will always exist somewhere inside.

However, the good news is that we can always bring in new "furnishings"—new ideas, perspectives, and experiences. If we stay open and willing to consider other viewpoints, our bubble can grow and expand. The older pieces might fade into the background, but they never completely disappear.

Think of it like this: imagine you once saw a unique bird and stored that memory in your mind. Even if years go by, someone might mention it, and suddenly that memory is right back in focus. Similarly, when our bubble feels threatened or under attack, we might find ourselves leaning back on old, familiar ways of thinking and feeling, even if we've adopted new ones over time.

The Resurgence of the Old Man: A Philosophical Reflection

I recently shared my perspective on "the bubble" with a dear friend, a woman in her early 80s. She was struck by my ideology, saying she understood it deeply. Then, she offered her take: "We need to get rid of the old furniture, destroy it, burn it up, and bring in new pieces." Her response was not surprising to me. We both grew up under the teachings of the same Christian denomination, one that often promoted this simplistic vision—out with the old, in with the new.

This mindset is dangerously encouraged by those who exploit faith to uphold their own bigotries or feelings of superiority. We've often heard the call to "put off the old man and put on the new." But I ask: where does this "old man" go? The reality is unsettling: upset the bubble, agitate it, insult it, put it under intense pressure, and you might discover that the "old man" never truly left.

In fact, trigger the bubble, and the old man may return with a vengeance. His presence, once familiar yet repressed, can reclaim the central space of the self. The hostility of the old furniture, even if it's been reupholstered or tucked away, can re-emerge, raw and unyielding. The "old man" isn't just a memory; he is a lingering force, always poised to reappear, and when he does, he can be terrifying or even dangerously unpredictable.

This is what the Bible was revealing in the Gospel of Matthew. In chapter 12, verses 43–45, Jesus speaks of the human spirit and the battle within:

"When an unclean spirit has gone out of a person, it passes through waterless places seeking rest, but finds none. Then it says, 'I will return to

my house from which I came.' And when it comes, it finds the house empty, swept, and put in order. Then it goes and brings with it seven other spirits more evil than itself, and they enter and dwell there; and the last state of that person is worse than the first. So also, will it be with this wicked generation."

Even Jesus understood this principle: that our inner lives—the bubbles we inhabit—are never empty for long. When we clear out old furniture, we must be mindful of what we choose to replace it with, or risk inviting in something even more destructive. Our bubbles, our selves, are always present, always existing in relation to the bubbles around us. Each bubble is uniquely fashioned by the collection of our experiences, choices, and beliefs. These items never leave. Even as we strive to cleanse, to renew, and to change, we must be vigilant, for the battle within is unceasing.

William Ernest Henley captured this struggle in his poem "Invictus," a reflection from deep within his own bubble, a testament to the unconquerable human spirit. This poem, so often recited by Nelson Mandela, speaks to the resilience required to maintain one's inner sanctum against all odds:

> "Out of the night that covers me,
> Black as the Pit from pole to pole,
> I thank whatever gods may be
> For my unconquerable soul.
>
> In the fell clutch of circumstance
> I have not winced nor cried aloud.
> Under the bludgeonings of chance
> My head is bloody, but unbowed.

> Beyond this place of wrath and tears
> Looms but the Horror of the shade,
> And yet the menace of the years
> Finds and shall find me unafraid.
>
> It matters not how strait the gate,
> How charged with punishments the scroll,
> I am the master of my fate,
> I am the captain of my soul.

Henley knew, as Mandela experienced, that life would throw its darkest nights, its fiercest storms. Yet even when the head is "bloody, but unbowed," the human spirit can stand firm. Mandela, who faced unimaginable hardship, held tight to this truth: ***"I am the master of my fate: I am the captain of my soul."***

Our bubbles are fragile but resilient, vulnerable but fortified. They carry the imprints of our past, the echoes of our upbringing, and the whispers of every experience. They are shaped by what we choose to accept and what we choose to discard. Yet, in the end, we are not powerless. As functioning teens, breaking away from the confines of childhood, and adults, we hold within us the ability to decide what furnishings we bring in, what remains, and what must be set aside.

We have the power to master our fate, to captain our souls, and to courageously shape the inner sanctum of our own bubbles. We can face whatever "spirits" come knocking and choose—through faith, wisdom, and resilience—what we allow in. In doing so, we reclaim the authority over our inner worlds, choosing light over darkness, love over fear, and hope over despair.

So, the question remains: What will you let into your bubble? How will you captain your soul? What will be your furnishings and interior design?

We cannot eliminate the bubble or its contents. To rid ourselves of the bubble would mean to end our very existence in this life. The bubble is a part of us, an inseparable companion in our journey. But within its walls, we have a choice—a bold responsibility—to take ownership of what it holds.

Yet, even when we try to silence it, the bubble speaks. In our quietest moments, its echoes persist. Memories, experiences, and emotions reverberate within us, shaped by our interactions with others and the world around us. These are the shared energies of the bubble, spun from its very core, connecting us to every life we touch.

Our bubbles are alive, not only with our choices and beliefs but with the imprints of those we encounter, the stories we share, and the love or pain we pass along. This is the powerful truth: we may not control the existence of our bubble, but we can influence its voice, its tone, and its purpose. In this, we find the freedom to shape our lives and the courage to live authentically.

The Bubble Theory: An Observatory View

There will always be critics, judges, and influencers. The wolf dressed in sheep's clothing still walks among us, and the voice that shakes mountains and stirs seas will continue to echo. These forces rip the earth with tremors, arriving softly, meekly, disguised as fragile. They offer delicate and savory temptations, whispering, "Come closer, trust us." They may mean no harm, but they often form an army, both intentional and unintentional. Together, they are the observers.

I've sat down with them, face to face, to try and make sense of their claims. Consider this my gift to you—a coupon for new furnishings, a chance to examine what truly belongs inside your bubble. Remember, the observer is just an illusion, a phantom echo that seems to control but never truly does. Their voices will penetrate the bubble's walls, selling you new ideas, attempting to reshape your inner space. But you, like me, are the sole proprietors of your bubble's interior. After the age of accountability, there is no ownership beyond the self.

Observers can be allies in times of pressure, helping us expand and connect with like-minded bubbles. Yet, they can also be invaders, igniting the worst in us, sparking our deepest fears. Their presence is external. They only know what you allow them to see. The true construction of the self remains a private matter.

The bubble is you. I am the bubble. Together, we create the suds of community, the fizz of a collective existence. Each bubble sounds its unique chorus—a symphony of pops from those who have lived and who have been shaped by life.

Through "The Bubble Theory," I've shared my vision. I invite you to pause and inspect your own furnishings. Remember, there is always room to expand, but we can never shrink the size of our bubble. Some bubbles expand rapidly, some at the speed of light, exploring the farthest reaches of human potential. Some glow brightly, reflecting the best of humanity, while others drift in darkness, cast in the shadows of fear.

Yet, all bubbles move through their time, floating at the center and the margins of life. The bubble theory invites us to see ourselves clearly and fully, to embrace the opportunity to grow, to love, to connect, and to find our place amid the infinite tapestry of existence.

Will you dare to examine your bubble, to expand its boundaries, to let in more light, and to dance on the edge of what is possible?

The power of choice, as always, and like all bubbles, is yours.

Hate: *The Hidden Element of the Bubble*

Hate is a four-letter word we often see when looking at others who make us feel uncomfortable or challenge our sense of certainty. It is a word laden with history, emotion, and consequence, yet it is rarely acknowledged by those who harbor it. Before I close this section on The Bubble Theory, I feel it's essential to explore my personal understanding of how hate operates within the human experience.

Within the singular human bubble, there exists a mysterious accessory: a box. This box, crafted from ethereal matter, is not immediately visible or consciously acknowledged. It serves as both a container and a mirror, reflecting deeply embedded fears, biases, and assumptions. For many, this box is akin to a modern Pandora's Box—an object both fascinating and forbidden, a repository of destructive potential cloaked in the guise of utility.

A Modern Pandora's Box

The ancient Greek myth of Pandora's Box offers a compelling analogy for understanding hate. As the story goes, Pandora—created by the gods—was gifted with boundless curiosity alongside her beauty and other traits. Her fatal flaw was this curiosity, which led her to open a container she was explicitly warned not to touch. In doing so, she unleashed evils and suffering into the world. The myth serves as a cautionary tale: curiosity, while a vital part of learning and growth, becomes dangerous when left unchecked or misdirected.

Similarly, the box within our bubble functions as a place where unchecked curiosity about others can fester into suspicion, and suspicion can evolve into prejudice. The contents of this box are not inherently evil; rather, they reflect the fears, misunderstandings, and cultural biases that we have absorbed throughout our lives. But unlike Pandora, many of us are unaware of the box's existence—or its influence.

The Box as a False Anchor

For many, this box becomes a crutch. It provides a sense of stability by allowing the owner to declare their superiority, often without realizing it. It acts as a metaphysical talisman, protecting the ego from the discomfort of confronting alternative perspectives. By clinging to the box and its contents, we insulate ourselves from the complexity of others' realities. The box becomes a mechanism for justifying incomplete and narrow views of the world beyond our own bubble.

Ironically, the box is not a protective shield against hate but a generator of it. It fills the imagination with distorted images of "the other," nurturing a soft prejudice that deceives the owner. This subtle form of prejudice rarely announces itself as hate; instead, it manifests as defensiveness, avoidance, or judgment cloaked in rationalizations. The owner of the box, convinced of their fairness and reason, fails to see the ways in which the contents of their box shape their interactions with the world.

The Denial of Hate

One of the strangest and most troubling aspects of hate is its invisibility to the hater. Few will openly admit to hating others; instead, they develop elaborate justifications to mask it. "It's not hate," they might say. "I'm just being cautious." Or, "It's not prejudice—it's common sense." These alibis, born from the box, allow the individual to shift blame onto others while absolving themselves of responsibility. In doing so, they perpetuate cycles of misunderstanding and division.

Confronting the Box Within

To address the hate concealed within our bubbles, we must first acknowledge the existence of the box. This requires courage and self-awareness, as it means confronting the deeply held beliefs and fears we may not even realize we carry. It means questioning the stories we tell ourselves about others and challenging the excuses we use to justify our discomfort or hostility.

In a pluralistic world, where diverse bubbles intersect and collide, the contents of our box can either be a source of division or an opportunity for growth. The choice is ours: will we let the box define us, or will we confront its influence and strive for a deeper understanding of the bubbles around us?

The Subtle Masks of Hate: A Closer Look

To delve deeper into this concept, let's examine real-life examples that highlight the low levels of intolerance often disguised as benign disagreement or cultural preference. These instances, while seemingly minor, reveal the unrecognized or low-level hate simmering beneath the surface. Have you ever heard someone say, **"I don't hate them, I just have a problem with . . ."**? This phrase, in its many forms, often serves as the opening volley in a stealthy and insidious cold war of microaggressions.

Such statements are rarely direct admissions of hatred. Instead, they act as shields, allowing the speaker to maintain a veneer of civility while perpetuating subtle forms of division. Let's explore how these dynamics play out in familiar settings, beginning with the church—a space often viewed as a bastion of moral teaching but one that too frequently serves as the breeding ground for intolerance cloaked in righteousness.

The Church as an Arena of Intolerance

Churches, temples, and other religious institutions are often meticulously designed to educate followers in their interpretations of divine truth. They hold profound influence over how adherents perceive themselves and others. At their best, these institutions inspire unity, compassion, and shared purpose. But too often, they reinforce exclusivity, superiority, and judgment, creating fertile ground for hate to take root under the guise of doctrinal purity.

Take, for instance, the historical tensions between **Catholics and Protestants**. Many Catholics pay little mind to Protestants in their daily lives, and vice versa. However, within both groups, there are deeply embedded doctrines that predetermine the other's eternal destiny. For some Catholics, Protestants are heretics who lack full access to divine grace. For some Protestants, Catholics are idolaters trapped in a tradition-bound system that obscures true salvation. Neither group may openly express hatred, but their judgments about the other's beliefs foster an unspoken disdain that perpetuates division.

This division trickles down into finer doctrinal disputes. Consider the debate between **Baptists** and **Methodists** over the method of baptism. Baptists hold that baptism by full immersion is the only valid fulfillment of God's requirement, while many Methodists believe that sprinkling water over a person suffices. On the surface, this disagreement might seem trivial, but for some, it becomes a point of superiority and exclusion, leading to an "us versus them" mentality.

Broader Religious Intolerance

The divisions do not stop within Christianity. Major Abrahamic faiths—Christianity, Judaism, and Islam—often exhibit dismissive attitudes toward one another, despite their shared roots in the story of Abraham. A Rabbi may critique Christian or Islamic practices as deviations from the Torah's teachings. A Christian might view Judaism as incomplete without the New Testament or see Islam as misguided. Many Muslims, in turn, view Christianity and Judaism as corrupted versions of God's original revelations.

Collectively, these faiths frequently dismiss the religious practices of **Buddhists**, **Hindus**, and other non-Abrahamic traditions as entirely outside the bounds of truth. This dismissiveness often translates into subtle prejudices that ripple through communities, shaping policies, cultural attitudes, and personal interactions.

Micro and Macro Comparisons

On a micro level, these prejudices manifest as subtle but cutting remarks, exclusionary practices, or an unwillingness to engage with those who hold different beliefs. On a macro level, they can fuel systemic discrimination, geopolitical conflicts, and even acts of violence. In both cases, the root is the same:

an inability—or unwillingness—to recognize the validity of another's humanity outside of one's own framework.

A False Sense of Innocence

One of the most dangerous aspects of this phenomenon is the false sense of innocence it engenders. When prejudice is wrapped in religious or cultural doctrine, it becomes easy to justify intolerance as fidelity to one's faith or values. This rationalization allows individuals and institutions to perpetuate harm while maintaining the appearance of moral righteousness.

The Path Forward

Recognizing these dynamics requires a willingness to confront uncomfortable truths about ourselves and the systems we inhabit. It means questioning the judgments we make about others, examining the sources of our beliefs, and challenging the institutions that reinforce division rather than unity.

Hate, in its subtle forms, thrives on ignorance and inaction. To dismantle it, we must commit to deeper understanding, greater empathy, and the courage to bridge divides—whether in the church, the mosque, the synagogue, or the world at large.

Breaking Down Hate with a Dash of Humor

Let's have some fun while unpacking this heavy topic. To make things even more simplistic on a micro level, let me share a slice of my own experience. I grew up in a subculture of the so-called Christian movement. We were commandment-keeping people, steadfast in our beliefs. However, we just thought that the "New Commandment" Jesus gave was okay to dismiss. We couldn't cling to our pearls because jewelry was forbidden by God. This sparked such a battle that the church eventually had to acquiesce to the influence of a younger culture that was less focused on the eternal value of heaven and more enamored with the sparkle of a diamond-set gold ring. Many still refuse to describe it as a ring. For some, it's called a wedding band. Our people don't wear rings. Bad people do.

Rings and Riddles

Another quirky issue in that culture was the age-old debate: **Vegetarian vs. the Meat-eater.** I was so glad when the **Vegan** jumped into the ring, hitting the mat and placing the **Vegetarian** on the cultural ropes. It's like watching a live-action version of *Rocky*—only with tofu and steak instead of gloves and punches. Through these playful yet pointed skirmishes, I learned that many people aren't part of the cult I consider myself to have been raised in. Whether for religious reasons or other culturally designed adherence, these distinctions create micro-level battlegrounds within our bubbles.

The Ethereal Box: Pandora 2.0

The core matter here is that our society, composed of countless bubbles, has a tendency to activate that ethereal box. For some, it's well stored away and never opened, like a secret stash of snacks. For others, it's akin to that "In case of emergency, Break THE GLASS" item—always ready to be triggered by hidden "isms" related not only to religion but also to race, skin color, national origin, sex, age, and the myriad of other "likes" that define our social interactions.

Imagine the box as our personal Pandora's Box, but instead of unleashing plagues and sorrows, it releases microaggressions and subtle prejudices. These aren't overt acts of hatred but rather the quiet, often unintentional jabs that erode understanding and foster division. It's like playing a game of *Jenga*—each small act of intolerance is a block removed from the tower of harmony, inching us closer to collapse.

The Animal Kingdom Parallel

This behavior isn't unique to humans. In the animal kingdom, certain hierarchies and territorial behaviors are instinctual. Yet, as an intelligent species, we have the capacity to recognize these patterns and choose a different path. Instead of succumbing to our primal instincts, we can lean towards acceptance and understanding, embracing those who have the right to exist and express themselves just as we do.

Embracing Acceptance Over Instinct

So, how do we shift from these ingrained behaviors to a more accepting and compassionate society? It starts with awareness and a willingness to challenge our own bubbles. Here are a few playful yet profound steps we can take:

1. **Playfully Question Assumptions** Next time you catch yourself saying, "I don't hate them, I just have a problem with...," pause and ask why. Is it truly a problem, or is it a hidden prejudice trying to disguise itself? Think of it as a *Guess Who?* game—unmask the assumptions behind your statements.

2. **Laugh at the Absurdity** Humor can be a powerful tool in breaking down barriers. Recognize the absurdity in holding onto outdated prejudices. Share a laugh with someone who has a different perspective, and watch as the walls begin to crumble.

3. **Celebrate Diversity with Music** Just as we enjoy a diverse playlist, let's celebrate the diversity of human experiences and cultures. Embrace the idea that every

person brings a unique melody to the symphony of life. *"We Are the World"* (USA for Africa) is a reminder that our collective harmony is richer when every voice is heard.

4. **Engage in Playful Dialogue** Approach conversations with curiosity rather than judgment. Ask questions like, "What's your story?" instead of making assumptions based on superficial differences. It's like having an improv session where every idea is welcome and explored.

Closing the Loop with Harmony

As we navigate our personal labyrinths, let's commit to keeping our ethereal boxes closed—unless they're filled with curiosity and understanding. By doing so, we prevent the insidious spread of low-level hate and foster a culture of acceptance and peace. Think of it as maintaining the perfect harmony in a band, where every instrument plays its part without overshadowing the others.

In the end, it's about turning down the volume on intolerance and turning up the volume on acceptance. Let's create a world where our bubbles don't clash but complement each other, where our differences become the notes that make our collective song beautiful and enduring.

Question: *Is my bubble greater than your bubble?*

This question pulls back the curtain on the illusion of greatness. Greatness, as we often perceive it, is socially constructed—a measurement of external markers like success, power, or influence. But in truth, my bubble is not greater than yours, or anyone else's. Greatness isn't an outward comparison; it's an inward journey.

The real question is: how much have we chosen to expand our own inner territory? The more I expand my bubble, the more room I create for new ideas, relationships, and understandings. This expansion allows me to furnish my inner space with the tools necessary to better comprehend the world around me. And, crucially, it helps me navigate the relationship between my inner world and the broader universe.

Greatness, then, is not a title to be worn or a competition to be won. It's an invitation to grow, to cultivate an ever-evolving space within ourselves.

A) Focus on responding thoughtfully instead of reacting impulsively. This shift in perspective can transform your experience of life.

B) Pause and take a breath. Give yourself that crucial millisecond before reacting.

C) Take an honest, personal assessment of yourself—beyond the confines of conformity. Give yourself a reality check and identify your triggers.

D) Rediscover and replenish your inner energy. Remember, you've got this for the rest of your thinking life.

E) William Shakespeare once said, "The world is a stage and we are the actors." Take control and become the director of your own movie set. If the script isn't working, start slowly but methodically rewriting and redirecting your personal story.

F) If you believe you need help, never hesitate to seek a legitimate, trained, and qualified therapist to help you uncover your true self. Remember, you are not seeking a relationship with the therapist, but rather using their services to guide you in the rediscovery of your authentic self, uniquely endowed by your very existence – a gift of your creator. As you embark on this journey of self-discovery, grant others the freedom to be themselves. They may not understand. They are controlled by the furnishings of their own individual bubbles. The rewards of such a personal exchange of respect are truly invaluable.

Expand your bubble. Give your space a little makeover—move things around, shake it up a bit. But remember, this space is yours. So, what's holding you back? We've gotten so used to the mental walls we've built that we're afraid of the wardens and guards we've imagined. But here's the thing: you can't really escape your bubble; it's like a turtle's shell. Just like a baby turtle, the moment it's born, it carries its home on its back.

"I Am Not an Absolutist, but '*Hoc Credo*' - I Believe This"

This idea struck me as I was reflecting on the reasoning I've shared with you in this chapter. Let me explain the challenge of the Bubble Theory in this way:

When all someone has to rely on are the comforts of their own furnishings, and you don't like how they think, the problem isn't theirs—it's yours. Your issue isn't truly with them either. The problem is that you've spent your energy trying to make them understand using the furnishings familiar to you, not them. Maybe you even called them an idiot?

You could have spent your time more wisely, creating higher-quality mental furniture—ideas, examples, and frameworks—that they would find attractive and compelling. Furnishings so well-made and relatable that they'd want to bring them into their bubble.

The truth is, both of you are navigating the world from the comforts of your own bubbles. The real challenge is in efficiency, not opposition.

Help them. Ignite curiosity, not pain. Replace negative pressure with compassionate understanding. Show them you care.

This is the highest universal principle of love.

Here's two pennies more on the bubble?

Understanding Narcissism: A Reflection on Self-Worth and the Bubble

Before we move on, let's address an important topic that relates closely to the dynamics of the bubble: narcissism. The term "narcissism" is often used casually, but this can lead to misunderstandings that damage relationships and inhibit genuine self-reflection. So, let's explore what narcissism truly entails and how it intersects with our sense of self-worth and perceptions of others.

What Narcissism Really Is

Narcissistic Personality Disorder (NPD) is a clinically diagnosable condition defined in the *Diagnostic and Statistical Manual of Mental Disorders, Fifth Edition* (DSM-5). It is characterized by a pervasive pattern of grandiosity, a lack of empathy, and an excessive need for admiration. This pattern typically begins in early adulthood and is reflected in several key traits:

1. **Grandiosity** – An exaggerated sense of self-importance, often tied to fantasies of success, power, beauty, or idealization.

2. **Need for Admiration** – A craving for excessive admiration and the expectation of being recognized as superior without necessarily earning it.

3. **Lack of Empathy** – Difficulty understanding or valuing others' feelings, often seeing them as weakness.

Other behaviors associated with NPD include entitlement, exploitative tendencies, envy, and arrogance. However, diagnosing narcissism is a complex task best left to trained professionals. It's crucial not to misuse this term as a weapon in casual conversation or conflict.

The Danger of Careless Labeling

It is all too common to label someone as a narcissist when we feel overshadowed or inadequate in their presence. This tendency often stems not from the other person's actions but from our own insecurities. For example, encountering someone with extraordinary achievements—a well-received Ivy League astrophysicist, for instance—may highlight our own perceived shortcomings. Yet, this does not make the accomplished individual a narcissist. It is instead an opportunity for self-reflection:

- Am I reacting out of feelings of inferiority?
- Have I mistaken their success for arrogance, when in reality, they have simply walked a different path?

Labeling someone as narcissistic without evidence can act as a wrecking ball in relationships. It reduces complex human interactions to a simplistic competition of "who is better than whom" and can foster resentment rather than understanding.

Bubbles and Perception

The bubble contains the aroma our perceptions. A person's perception of the external world is an honest and direct reflection of their inner world. Our self-developed / self-driven mental descriptions are mirrors of our evolving social development. The personal bubble establishes limitations on how we view the world around us. Positive or negative, the bubble can be infected.

The truth is, what often appears to be narcissism may simply be the product of someone else's bubble. Each of us views the world through the lens of our personal experiences, values, and cultural furnishings. These perspectives can lead us to impose our own value systems onto others, judging them by our subjective standards rather than objective observation.

This is why it requires tremendous character to approach others' bubbles with objectivity and openness. True understanding comes from a willingness to consider not only the furnishings of our own bubbles but also the labyrinths that others navigate. It involves recognizing that their values and experiences may differ from our own and appreciating that these differences enrich the human experience rather than diminish it.

A Call for Kindness and Perspective

The next time you feel the urge to label someone, pause and reflect. Ask yourself:

- Am I projecting my insecurities onto this person?
- Could I benefit from understanding their perspective instead of judging it?

We all have a sense of self-worth, and when we clash with others, it's often because their bubble challenges the comfort of our own. However, growth comes not from name-calling or assigning blame but from seeking common ground and understanding. It's not about proving who is superior; it's about fostering relationships built on respect and kindness.

The highest principle of humanity is love—a love that sees beyond bubbles and values the unique contributions of each individual. Let's strive to live by this principle, building bridges instead of barriers and offering the gift of understanding to ourselves and others.

LET'S TALK ABOUT CULTURE

What in fact is culture? I define culture as the various ways in which living beings exist and thrive. It's about the habitats and survival strategies that life forms develop. Just like lions and elephants have their unique cultures in the animal kingdom, humans have a learned culture that shapes our way of living.

For humans, culture encompasses arts, beliefs, religious practices, politics, institutions, and so much more. It is a guiding framework for our societal structures. This understanding of culture, along with the intentional and unintentional pressures exerted by a population, shapes societal norms and is usually passed down from one generation to the next. Let me stop here to say, Culture evolves. That is not to say it gets better or worse. I am saying that culture develops. As the human changes, so does the culture.

Culture is often described as "the way of life for an entire society." It encompasses the many aspects of life that define us, including the subtle handprints that shape our manners, customs, and behaviors. Culture influences everything from the way we eat, our dress and fashion, also the ways in which we speak, to the rituals and art forms we cherish.

For me, religion is a unique form of spiritual art that significantly impacts the evolution of culture. It plays a crucial role in shaping our values and beliefs, guiding our behaviors, and adding depth to the cultural tapestry that defines us.

Let's Talk About a Man Named Job

The Bible, whether embraced as a sacred text or regarded as a historical and cultural artifact, contains a story about a man named Job. Interestingly, the book of Job is often regarded by theologians and biblical historians as the oldest book in the Bible. Found in the *Ketuvim* ("Writings") section of the Hebrew Bible and the Old Testament of the Christian Bible, it is widely considered a masterpiece of world literature.

The story of Job portrays profound cultural themes: the experience of suffering, the endurance of faith, and the interplay of wisdom and character formation. What makes Job's tale remarkable is that one need not be a believer in God to engage with its essence—it is a human story of how one man confronted the storms of life.

Job is introduced as a man of great wealth and stature, residing in a place called Uz. His household is extensive, complete with a sizable family and impressive flocks. Within his culture, Job had cultivated a reputation as a man of integrity, someone who strove to live a life free of wrongdoing as defined by the societal norms of his time. Moreover, Job's sense of responsibility extended beyond himself—he habitually offered prayers on behalf of his children; in case they had erred unknowingly.

This type of narrative paints a picture of a man deeply shaped by his cultural context. His values and actions are reflections of the principles and practices he internalized within his community. Yet, while Job developed within this cultural framework, it is important to consider that culture is not monolithic. Each individual interacts with their environment uniquely, forming personal connections to various aspects of their community.

For instance, Job's wife and children were part of the same geographical community, yet the story hints that their cultural inclinations and values might not align entirely with Job's.

Culture influences and impacts individuals differently, depending on their attractions and connections within the larger societal framework.

One compelling aspect of the story is how Job's life and values became so notable that his name arose in a celestial conversation between Satan and God—an exchange Job himself was unaware of. This raises a fascinating question: Who served as the witness to recount this story, ensuring it was preserved and passed down through generations?

When I first heard the story of Job as a child, it was presented as a universal tale, one that seemed to permeate the cultural fabric of my upbringing. It was as though everyone in my community, part of my personal "childhood culture," had also been introduced to this narrative. This ubiquity is a testament to how cultural stories, like Job's, transcend time and space, shaping and being shaped by the communities that carry them forward.

As I grew older and revisited the book of Job—reading it multiple times and in various translations—I began to see the narrative differently. I realized that my community of believers had handed me a story wrapped in cultural expectations, one that I carried without question. It was expected of me to see Job as a "just" and "upright" man, a figure of perfection in every way, undeniably "God's man."

On the other hand, Job's wife was presented as the epitome of disrespect, wickedness, and folly. Her infamous words to Job—"curse God and die"—became the definitive proof of her character in the eyes of my cultural upbringing.

This is where the weight of culture becomes profoundly significant. The story of Job reveals as much, if not more, about the cultural moorings of those interpreting it as it does about Job and his family. In the male-dominated society of my upbringing, I was expected to enter the "believer's courtroom" of criticism and declare Job's wife guilty without ever hearing her case.

With time and a more critical lens, I've revisited this story, aiming to examine the neglected areas that deserve responsible critique.

Let's begin with the loss of Job's children. In Job 1:19, we learn that Job's children were gathered at the eldest brother's house. They were having a party. Job knew his children. He had to know them so well that he prayed for them just in case they did something wrong. My imagination tells me up at the house and as a matter of fact, I would use these words from the great Lionel Richie – they were 'dancing on the ceiling' when a great wind—a natural disaster that sounds like tornadic activity to me, though I'll leave that to the meteorologists—struck the house. This wind "smote the four corners of the house, and it fell upon the young men, and they are dead."

Curiously, while verse 13 makes it clear that Job's sons and daughters were at the gathering, only the young men are mentioned as casualties in verse 19. The daughters—present and partying alongside their brothers—are conspicuously absent from the narrative's fatal tally. This omission is striking. In Job's cultural context, women were not valued enough to merit mention beyond the initial setup of the story.

In the tradition I was raised in, these details were often overlooked. The story's focus remained on Job's suffering and his steadfast faith. Rarely did anyone pause to question the erasure of the women or the cultural biases embedded in the text.

There's more. While we have long acknowledged the tragedy of Job losing his children, we often miss an obvious biological fact: Job did not give birth to any children. Science would suggest that his wife—the same woman who is so harshly judged for her words—was the one who bore the physical and emotional toll of childbirth.

The story as told by my community overlooked these realities, focusing solely on Job's loss and fortitude. Yet, the pain of losing children was not his alone to bear. His wife's grief, though unspoken and unexplored in the narrative, was equally real.

By revisiting this story with fresh eyes, I've come to see how cultural biases shaped not only the interpretation of Job's wife but also the framing of the narrative itself. It compels us to ask: How much of what we believe about this story is shaped by the culture that delivered it to us?

Madam Job had her share of troubles too. Her husband's rotting sores and torn flesh filled her days with the constant stench of decay and despair. She wasn't privy to the cosmic wager that turned their lives upside down, but she bore the consequences nonetheless. When Job lost his business, she lost a significant portion of their family's income. When Job's servants perished, she lost the support and stability they provided. And most painfully, she gave birth to the very children whose lives were sacrificed in the unfolding drama—despite God supposedly standing for the 'sanctity of life.' Those children, her children, were taken in the wager's collateral damage.

The patriarchal culture I come from once taught me to demonize and belittle this woman, to label her as faithless and foolish, all because her patience had reached its end. Her grief, her exhaustion, and her humanity were swept aside in favor of a narrative that praised Job's steadfastness while dismissing her pain.

This story, when viewed through a sharper lens, tells us less about the ancient world and more about how our own culture has historically valued and respected women—or failed to do so. It is a mirror reflecting our biases and blind spots, a tale that reveals as much about our collective values as it does about the supposed history captured in the Bible.

I hope you're thinking a little deeper with me at this point. Let's take a moment to peel back another layer and consider culture on a deeper level. Culture is not just the backdrop of our lives; it is the very fabric that shapes our beliefs, values, and interpretations. It whispers to us about who we are and how we should see the world—even when we don't realize we're listening.

In Job's story, culture is the invisible hand guiding how we judge its characters, how we weigh their virtues, and how we define their faults. It taught me to exalt Job as the paragon of righteousness while casting his wife as a cautionary tale, a symbol of weakness or faithlessness. But as we pull back the veil, the story becomes less about ancient people in an ancient land and more about us—our blind spots, our inherited biases, and the ways we've allowed culture to shape our perceptions without question.

What Is Culture?

Before we go any deeper, let's take a moment to really understand what 'culture' means. Culture is a tricky thing to define, whether you're talking about it casually or in an academic setting. Figuring out what makes up a culture takes serious thought and reflection. A lot of the time, we judge people based on what we see on the surface—their appearance, their actions, or the way they speak. If someone doesn't click with us, it's easy to say, 'That's just their culture,' without really knowing what that even means. Most of the time, this comes from our imagination, not from actual knowledge. We need to remember that people learn their culture through a process of being shaped by their surroundings and experiences, which is why there are so many different cultures in the world.

We use the word *culture* all the time, but do we truly understand what it means? And what about *cult*—a word that often stirs an even stronger reaction? Let's pause for a moment, you and I, and place these two terms under the bright, unflinching spotlight of examination.

Why do these words make some of us uneasy, our shoulders tensing like an athlete at the starting block? Why do others become rigid and defensive, or ready to flee like Olympic sprinters the moment they hear them mentioned? What is it about *culture* and *cult* that provokes such powerful responses?

Before we can understand ourselves or others, we must first understand the language we use to describe each other. Culture is often the label assigned to us, the box we're put in, the explanation offered for our every action and belief. So, let's take a moment to explore how this word functions in our conversations, in our judgments, and in our souls. Let's commit to finding a clearer, deeper understanding—one that transcends the superficial and challenges any lingering ignorance.

Let's Get Real About Stereotypes

Stereotypes are not culture even though vile stereotypes can be born within cultures.

When people talk about "Black culture," they often lean on the ugliest clichés: that Black people are religious fanatics, superstitious by nature. That Black families are fractured, dominated by single mothers or grandmothers left to fend for themselves because the fathers have vanished—deadbeats or deserters; stored away for life in some prison. That their cuisine is limited to chitlins, ribs, black-eyed peas, and collard greens. One Black person might even say these things about another, buying into the lies.

A Black person is often reduced to nothing more than dark skin, a "threat" whose supposed predisposition for violence makes others flinch. When Black people gather in large numbers, particularly in inner cities, the area is labeled a "danger zone," a place of poverty, a no-go for "decent folk." Black people are painted as lazy, aimlessly wandering the streets, moaning for more welfare, incapable of making a meaningful contribution to society. They are deemed loud, vulgar, uncultured, and their music is blamed for their violence and troubles. They are branded as thieves, grifters playing the "race card" whenever possible. In short, the narrative goes: they are the wretched.

This is what so many people hear when they think of Black culture. But let's be clear—this is *not* culture. This is ignorance and a horrendously horrid hatred, masquerading as truth.

The Danger of Misunderstanding Culture

Those who speak within the margins of these stereotypes are often influenced by bigotry and racism, leading the so-called "poorly educated" to consider drastic solutions. If you're struggling to understand this, let's take a step back and visit the oldest AME church in the Southern United States, Emanuel African Methodist Episcopal Church—fondly known as Mother Emanuel. Founded in 1816, it stood as a symbol of faith and resilience for almost 200 years until June 17, 2015, when history took a dark and hauntingly evil turn. Thanks to the hateful misinformation believed by Dylann Roof, this historic church became known as the site of the Charleston church massacre, where nine people were killed and one wounded during a Bible study.

Still not getting it? Let's consider Payton S. Gendron, an 18-year-old from Conklin, New York, who allegedly issued a White supremacist manifesto online. He then traveled nearly 200 miles to a Tops Friendly Markets grocery store in Buffalo, New York, known for its large Black clientele, and livestreamed his attack that murdered ten people and wounded three others. The loss extended beyond those directly affected, touching families, friends, and communities. Like Roof, Gendron had a warped desire to ignite a race war, fueled by dangerous myths and stereotypes.

This is how many view our society—a view shaped by the toxicity of cultural misconceptions and biases. But the question remains: *What is culture?* Roof and Gendron, like so many others, were guided by stereotypes and myths. These ideologies create violent sleeper cells that continue to leak their putrid venom into our world.

But let's be clear: Stereotype is not culture. While stereotypes can form the skeletal framework of a so-called "culture," they are not the substance of it.

Understanding this distinction is vital as we continue. This chapter serves as a tutorial to guide all readers toward a fair understanding of what culture truly is—and what it is not. Can we look beyond the skin tone and see the deeper humanity within each individual?

A Painful Narrative

I have often borne the pain of narratives shared with me, harsh words that flash before my understanding at unsuspecting moments. Let me be very clear: this kind of social commentary does not only come from those with so-called white skin. I've heard this toxic social caste system perpetuated by Black voices, lighter and darker than my own.

From the foul path leading to the country outhouse to the very benches of the nine-seat institution of justice, the waters of discrimination flow—stinking and deep. The septic flow remains unchanged—stagnant and ever-annoying. We seem unable to move beyond it, trapped in this ongoing struggle with culture. Culture has turned toxic to society, but consider this: society, in turn, has become toxic to culture.

A Culture that Chases its Tail

Okay, let's relieve some tension. What is culture? Culture is one of the countless combinations that define how a group of people live—a set of shared ways of life and standards. It's a pattern that creates a sense of unity among its members, loosely woven together by common beliefs, values, and norms. It's how people in a group try to understand, accept, and treat one another. Culture is the architecture of life within societies, building comfort and cohesion among its members through shared customs and traditions.

Culture might involve a common taste in food, but even this isn't always straightforward. One group may shop at the same markets or attend the same schools, but while one person might be a devout vegan, another might be fully immersed in the art of meat—braised, barbecued, or butchered with love. Culture also encompasses language, clothing styles, music, art, customs, spiritual beliefs, and religion. Culture is like choosing your favorite things that match with what other people like, too. It's about finding a group where you feel you belong, even if you fit into more than one group. It's like finding friends who enjoy many of the same things you do.

Culture shapes the things people in a group have in common, creating a bond that brings comfort among its members. Take the Seventh-day Adventists, for example. Many believe the Bible commands everyone to attend church on Saturday, and some outsiders label them as a cult or assume they all follow a strict vegan diet. But if you look closer, you'll see they are one of the most diverse Christian denominations in North America. Some Adventists eat meat, while others do not. My father, who will soon turn 103 and was a former Adventist minister, does eat meat but chooses to avoid it for his Sabbath meals. I guess you could call him a 'Sabbath-vegetarian.'

Within the Adventist community, there are many differences. Some Black Adventists lean toward the Republican side politically. Many Adventists take pride in academic excellence and can sometimes, intentionally or not, look down on those who don't meet their standards. Racism is a big part of the church within the confines of the North American Division which represents the church organization in the United States. They often idolize titles and positions and continue to debate the role of women in ministry. They can be sharp or subtly critical of those who did not achieve academic success, especially if they didn't attend Adventist institutions. Despite these differences and ongoing debates, they are all still seen as part of the same Seventh-day Adventist culture, even while they often find themselves in conflict with one another.

But culture isn't defined by superficial traits alone. There is no single 'women's culture,' 'white culture,' or 'black culture.' While there may be a Latin-inspired culture that embraces specific foods, music, fashion, dance, and other norms, elements like skin color, regional tastes, or age range are not true measures of a cohesive cultural group.

The term 'Latin culture' doesn't encompass all the people within that group. There are cultures within cultures, creating subcultures. There are gay Latinos, but not all Latinos are gay. In one Latino community, a taco might be rolled a certain way such as in Honduras, while in another area, it's a folded delight. Even when Spanish is spoken, the same words can have different meanings. I remember dizziness I had to maneuver through just trying to grasp the differences between a yellow banana, a green banana, and a plantain—and all the unique ways these foods are prepared and enjoyed as a simple food source.

There is also an older generation, trapped in the dungeons of despair, trying to cling to a past that aligns only with their own nostalgic view of life. This mindset often leads to a clash of cultures—a cultural tension, if you will. These individuals, with their narrow definitions, seek the authority to erase anything unfamiliar, hoping to draw an audience to their limited cultural worldview. Yet, culture is always in motion, and time determines which version survives.

The Dreaded C-Word

Let's dive in headfirst. Culture is vast and complicated, touching every part of human life—our beliefs, values, traditions, and the way we navigate the world. It shapes us, binds us, and gives us identity. But step outside any tightly-knit group of people, and things can get uncomfortable. You may not like how they see the world or connect with others. You listen to their leaders, and suddenly, the group feels like it's moving in lockstep, with their views becoming rigid, extreme, and sometimes hostile to outsiders. You see hints of aggression, subtle digs, or even an undercurrent of violence. This happens when a culture loses its balance and claims ownership of the "one true way." When this happens, individuals stop thinking for themselves, allowing the group's traditions and imagined authority to control their ideas and decisions. Personal thought fades, and they get caught in the trap of groupthink.

That's when a culture becomes a cult.

Now, let's break this down. According to Merriam-Webster, a cult is a group showing intense devotion to a cause, person, or idea. The *Urban Dictionary* puts it even more simply: a cult uses mind control on its followers. It doesn't matter what the group believes in—religion, politics, or anything else. The one common factor? Followers obey blindly, not questioning what they're told. Cults thrive on black-and-white thinking, shun hope, and make their followers think the outside world is wrong. Everyone inside sees the leader as infallible, and those on the outside see a group trapped in narrow thinking.

Here's the kicker: the word cult shares its roots with "culture" and "cultivate." It's all about nurturing something, whether that's ideas, beliefs, or ways of life. But as history shows us, a culture can easily spiral into a dangerous, controlling force when people stop thinking for themselves.

This brings us to the present. We're no longer in the past where these words first appeared. Today, we need to stay alert. The line between culture and cult is thinner than we realize. So, here's a tip: don't let any culture think, guide, or influence - live for you. Embrace who you are, appreciate the diversity around you, and celebrate the many cultures that make this world a rich and colorful place. We may not all agree, but we can meet each other with understanding and create a future where walls fall, and fences become bridges to the entire human neighborhood.

When a Culture Lacks Diversity

One of the greatest challenges faced by societies today is a resistance to diversity, equity, and inclusion (DEI). In the United States, this pushback has evolved over decades, from opposition to Affirmative Action to the current, more veiled attacks on DEI initiatives.

Affirmative Action was introduced as a remedy to address historical injustices, eliminate unlawful discrimination, and foster opportunities for groups that had long been marginalized. However, its detractors coined the term "Reverse Discrimination" to frame such programs as unfair. This term gained traction among those uncomfortable with the implications of societal change—individuals who often did not wish to acknowledge their own biases or the systemic advantages they benefited from.

Interestingly, the term has largely faded from public discourse, quietly placed in the attic of uncomfortable truths. Why? Because it became a symbol of division, even as its implications linger in the undercurrents of political and social debate.

The "Post-Racial" Illusion

The election of President Barack Obama marked a historic moment in American history. Yet, it also exposed the deep-seated racial biases that persist in many cultural bubbles. While some heralded Obama's presidency as evidence that America had transcended its racist roots, others saw it as an opportunity to resurrect old prejudices under the guise of skepticism.

The controversy surrounding Obama's birthplace is a prime example. Despite clear evidence—including the public release of his birth certificate—some continued to question his legitimacy as president. This debate was not just about geography; it was about ideology, identity, and fear of change.

What many failed to notice was the glaring double standard. During the same election, Senator John McCain, Obama's opponent, was born in the Panama Canal Zone. Yet his citizenship was never seriously challenged. The U.S. Constitution is clear: anyone born in the United States or abroad to U.S. citizens is a natural-born citizen. By these standards, Obama's citizenship was indisputable. His mother, Stanley Ann Dunham, was born in Kansas—a fact that rendered her son an American citizen no matter where he was born. Even if President Obama was born on the moon, he was in fact a citizen of the United States of America. Based on current and established law, *you can't trump that.*

The Hidden Roots of Bias

The refusal to recognize Obama's legitimacy was not just about legalities. It revealed the unspoken assumptions that have shaped American culture for generations:

1. The President of the United States must be white.
2. The President must be male.

These implicit biases are remnants of a past built on exclusion, where power was preserved for a narrow segment of society. When these assumptions go unchallenged, they create a breeding ground for intolerance.

When Bubbles Collide

On their own, individual prejudices—contained within personal "bubbles"—might seem harmless. But what happens when these bubbles converge to form a community? The result is often a culture steeped in collective hatred, where biases are amplified, welcomed and reinforced.

Religious institutions are not immune to this phenomenon. In fact, they often become hotbeds for intolerance when they succumb to the gravitational pull of hatred disguised as doctrine. The irony is that diversity—woven into the very fabric of humanity—becomes the target of disdain, rather than a source of strength. Consider this, it is the billions of tiny fibers so woven that keeps the quilt of our humanity intact.

Embracing the Reality of Diversity

The truth is, we are diversely born—not by choice, but by the randomness of nature. To resist this reality is to resist the essence of what it means to be human. The challenge before us is clear: we must move beyond the superficial narratives that divide us and recognize the beauty in our differences. Only then can we create a culture that truly values equity, inclusion, and the richness of diverse identities and perspectives.

Just to Share a Couple of Pennies More *perhaps a nickel*

I wasn't entirely sure where this reasoning belonged. It could nestle nicely here or in the chapter on the Bubble Effect. But why not dig in now? *After all, this is—and isn't—a matter of taste.*

Years ago, back when I still sported a full head of jet-black hair (and a little extra swagger), I was tasked with teaching a Culinary Arts class. One lesson plan required showing a video about taste—seemed straightforward enough. But, in my infinite wisdom, I hadn't previewed the video. I simply gave the prescribed introduction, hit play, and joined my students for the ride. As it turned out, I'm still not sure who learned more that day: the students or me.

The video was a revelation. It explored how taste buds are shaped by where we're raised, the foods we grow up with, and the cultures that cradle us. It showcased the staples and flavors unique to various groups of people.

I should've seen it coming. Years earlier, during a visit to Atlanta, Georgia, I toured the World of Coca-Cola Museum. That experience was a treasure trove of quirky discoveries and even turned me into a Coca-Cola memorabilia collector. Early in the tour, we learned about Coke's history and a fascinating global truth: despite our wildly different palates, one flavor unites us—Coca-Cola.

This fun fact stayed with me as I wandered through the museum, savoring every story. Near the end of the tour, we were invited to sample Coca-Cola and a selection of Fanta flavors from around the world. That's when things got…interesting.

In some countries, sweet flavors reign supreme; in others, bitter tones take center stage. The recipes vary from region to region to cater to local palates. Even in Europe, one Fanta flavor might taste different depending on whether you're sipping it in Spain or Germany.

Then there was Beverly. Oh, Beverly.

One sip, and I was sure I'd just tasted the essence of a soiled baby diaper. To me, it wasn't just bitter—it was *offensive*. Watching others try it was a mix of comedy and solidarity, as their faces twisted into expressions that could launch a thousand memes. Meanwhile, Fanta's Pineapple and Strawberry flavors felt like they'd been engineered to send you straight to the dentist—emergency cavity alert!

The range of flavors, from the syrupy-sweet to Beverly's diaper debacle, was staggering. But the real mystery that stuck with me was this: how can Coca-Cola, with such a universally consistent flavor, get a thumbs-up across wildly diverse palates?

At the time, I didn't fully process the significance of what I'd experienced. It wasn't until I shared that classroom video years later that the answer clicked into place: taste isn't just about food; it's about *where we come from*. Our culture, the bubble we're raised in, profoundly shapes what we crave, tolerate, or reject.

When you think about it, taste is more than a personal preference—it's a reflection of who we are, where we've been, and the cultural spices that season our lives. So, maybe next time you sip something, consider the journey of your palate. And if you're brave enough to try Beverly, well...don't say I didn't warn you.

Taste is the Issue Here

Taste is fundamental, a sense we come by naturally—uncomplicated unless impaired by an external factor like a virus or health challenge. It's an intrinsic part of being human, but how we interpret taste? Now, that's where things get fascinating.

I grew up in Annapolis, Maryland, a place that blends America's early history with a culinary cornerstone: the Chesapeake Bay Blue Crab. This local delicacy, often sold by the bushel, has a flavor and aroma so unique that for many, it embodies the essence of summer. The smell of McCormick's 'Old Bay Seasoning' or 'Phillip's' seafood blends would waft through the air during the warm months, signaling crab feasts and outdoor gatherings.

But life is about movement, and with movement comes new tastes and smells. Traveling introduced me to aromas and flavors far from my familiar Chesapeake roots. A bread bakery has a distinct scent, different from the sweet warmth of a donut shop. The inviting aroma of Rocco's Pizza in Annapolis had its own charm, and even the childhood comfort of McDonald's French fries on West Street carried a nostalgic allure. These smells and tastes weren't just experiences—they were the furnishings of my personal bubble of taste.

I saw this same dynamic play out with my students when they watched the video on global tastes. Their reactions were as varied as the examples shown: from 'Bat Soup' in parts of China to roasted 'Rattlesnake' in the U.S. Southwest. Some students cringed; others were fascinated. The differences weren't about biology but about culture—how we're shaped by the food traditions, norms, and boundaries we grow up within.

But it's not just our palates; our *eyes* are trained for taste too. What looks appetizing—or unappetizing—depends greatly on where we come from and the "taste sheriffs and wardens" that govern our cultural upbringing. These unseen enforcers shape what we view as acceptable, delicious, or even edible.

So how do we break these invisible barriers? One of the most profound ways I've found is by sharing a meal. Sitting down with someone over food says a lot—not just about the act of eating but about the willingness to connect. And when I encourage people to share a meal, I don't just mean passing the breadbasket. I mean trying foods from other cultures, opening yourself to their flavors, aromas, and traditions.

This doesn't mean you'll love everything you try. Take Andrew Zimmern, the famed chef and food critic known for his adventurous palate. He's tasted the bizarre and the sublime—and like all of us, he has preferences. Finding something repulsive isn't about something being "wrong"; it's about being honest. We all live in bubbles, shaped by our unique experiences, and those bubbles cultivate a spectrum of tastes that's as diverse as humanity itself.

But stepping outside your bubble, even for a bite, can teach you something extraordinary about yourself and others. And who knows? That next taste might just become a new furnishing in your bubble of taste.

The Bottom Line on Taste

Taste, at its core, has more to do with culture than the palate itself. While taste buds—gustatory papillae—are biological, our preferences are heavily influenced by the cultures we grow up in. These taste buds, which are sensory organs located on the tongue and other parts of the oral cavity, allow us to experience sweetness, saltiness, sourness, and bitterness. Beyond the biological aspect, much of what we perceive as "taste" comes from the scents processed by the olfactory glands.

But here's the twist: taste is not just about the tongue; it reflects our systems of value and perception. Consider the phrase, "I don't have an easy palate for Westerners." What does that mean? Is it a commentary on Western society as opposed to Eastern nations? An issue between Americans east and west of the Mississippi River? Or is it about food, traditions, or something else entirely—such as taste in music, dress, or dance?

Our taste, in all its facets, extends beyond the biological senses and into the realm of preferences. These preferences are shaped by what we see, hear, and feel. For instance, someone might say, "I have a taste for things that are blue," or, "I prefer smooth textures over rough ones." Even in relationships, taste manifests in statements like, "I'm drawn to people who are smart and accomplished."

The Cultural Blueprint of Taste

Taste, then, is not just a natural instinct but a product of cultural training and influence. From a young age, we're subtly—or overtly—guided by invisible guidelines within our cultural bubbles. These bubbles provide the framework for what is considered acceptable or desirable, often shaping taste in ways we don't even realize.

When one culture observes another that seems to operate by different guidelines—different "taste rules"—there's often a quick attempt to bring the perceived outlier back into alignment. This cultural policing works to reinforce the norm and discourage deviation. This dynamic is why many people are encouraged, either directly or indirectly, to "stay inside the box."

However, such an approach stifles curiosity and exploration. Taste becomes static and dictated by cultural norms rather than personal discovery.

The Transformative Power of Exploration

Sometimes, it takes a human "field trip" to break these confines. Venturing beyond our bubbles—physically, intellectually, or emotionally—can introduce us to flavors, values, and perspectives we'd never considered. It's these moments of exploration that give meaning to diversity and provide value to differences.

Taste, in all its forms, is a reflection of who we are and where we've been. Yet it's also an invitation to explore where we can go. By embracing the variety of tastes—literal and metaphorical—that the world offers, we expand not only our palate but our understanding of others.

Eureka: Taste Relates to culture

The formation of taste—encompassing preferences, appetites, passions, and cravings—is intricately linked to the interplay between individual psychology and collective cultural influence. On an individual level, taste is shaped by sensory experiences and neural pathways that encode preferences as we encounter stimuli. However, these personal inclinations do not exist in isolation; they are deeply informed by the cultural frameworks in which individuals are embedded.

Cultural ties act as scaffolding, shaping and directing the development of taste through norms, traditions, and shared values. For example, a society's collective culinary heritage can establish a baseline for what is considered appetizing or palatable, while its artistic traditions inform aesthetic preferences. These cultural elements are reinforced through repeated exposure, social learning, and the internalization of collective values.

Furthermore, the evolution of taste is dynamic and reciprocal. While culture informs individual preferences, individuals also contribute to cultural shifts through their unique interpretations and expressions of taste. This complex feedback loop underscores the inseparable bond between individual experiences and collective cultural paradigms, illustrating how deeply embedded our preferences are within the social context.

Breakdown from the Armchair Sociologist, me

Think of taste—whether it's about food, art, music, or even people—as a mix of personal choices and cultural habits. On one hand, we each have our own likes and dislikes, based on things we've tried, seen, or heard. But on the other hand, a lot of what we like comes from the culture we grew up in.

For example, if you grew up in a community where seafood was a big deal, you might crave crab or shrimp because it feels familiar and comforting. Someone from another part of the world might feel the same way about noodles or lamb. These cravings don't come out of nowhere—they're tied to our memories, traditions, and the things we see other people enjoying around us.

Culture gives us a starting point for our taste. It's like a guidebook, showing us what's "normal" to like. Over time, we make our own tweaks to that guidebook—maybe by trying new things or traveling to new places. But even when we think we're making totally independent choices, we're still influenced by the cultural rules we've learned along the way.

So, when you think about what people like, it's not just about them as individuals. It's also about where they come from, what they've been exposed to, and how their culture has shaped them. Taste is personal, but it's also social—and the two are always connected.

Here's What I'm Thinking

The world's complexity demands a recognition that monocultural or unilateral thinking is inherently limiting. A mature approach involves cultivating empathy and perspective thinking, acknowledging that no single culture, belief system, or individual viewpoint holds a monopoly on truth or progress. Cultural diversity, much like biodiversity in nature, fosters resilience, innovation, and adaptability. Building metaphorical bridges rather than walls becomes essential to navigating a globally interconnected society. Bridges enable exchange, dialogue, and collaboration, while walls perpetuate division, misunderstanding, and stagnation.

Here's What I am Saying

Think about it like this: if everyone only wanted their way of thinking to dominate, it would be like planting one kind of crop in every field—eventually, the soil would fail, and nothing would grow. But if you plant many different crops, the land stays healthy, and everything thrives. That's what diversity of thought and culture does for humanity.

We don't need more people putting up fences saying, "Stay over there with your ideas." We need architects who can design bridges—ways for us to meet in the middle, share what's valuable, and keep growing together.

It doesn't mean we all have to think alike, but it does mean respecting that others have different experiences that shape their views. By learning from each other, we can make something bigger and better than any one person or culture could on their own.

Cultural Impact

Culture shapes everything—our tastes, values, assumptions, and even what we see as "common sense." When individuals or groups build walls, it often stems from fear: fear of change, fear of losing identity, or fear of the unfamiliar. However, cultures that thrive over the long term are those that evolve through exchange and adaptation. Consider the Renaissance—a period of extraordinary growth driven by the cross-pollination of ideas from different cultures. The bridges built through trade, travel, and intellectual curiosity laid the groundwork for unprecedented creativity and progress.

Similarly, the modern world's most pressing challenges—climate change, global inequality, and health crises—demand cooperation on a scale that transcends cultural boundaries. Wall-builders might protect their immediate interests, but bridge-builders recognize that no nation, culture, or community exists in isolation.

Personal and Collective Growth

On an individual level, the ability to embrace cultural differences enriches life immeasurably. It's in these encounters that we find new ways of thinking, challenge our assumptions, and deepen our understanding of what it means to be human. Collectively, this approach fosters empathy and reduces polarization. When we see others not as adversaries to convert but as co-travelers on the road of life, it becomes easier to focus on what unites us rather than what divides us.

The Perils of Homogeneity and the Value of Diversity

The metaphor of hydrogen and oxygen perfectly illustrates the delicate balance required for stability and progress. Individually, these elements exhibit volatile, dangerous properties. Hydrogen is flammable, while oxygen supports combustion. Yet, when combined as water or when balanced in the air we breathe, they sustain life. This natural interplay reveals a universal principle: diverse components working together in harmony create stability and vitality, while isolating them leads to volatility and destruction.

Psychological Perspective: The Danger of Uniformity

Human psychology demonstrates that a lack of diversity fosters insularity, groupthink, and the amplification of biases. When individuals surround themselves only with those who echo their beliefs, they reinforce their worldview, often leading to rigid thinking. This insularity makes individuals resistant to new ideas and fosters prejudice against those who do not conform to their ideology.

- **Cognitive Dissonance:** Encountering diverse perspectives can create discomfort, as it challenges deeply held beliefs. However, this discomfort is essential for growth and adaptability. Without diversity, people become stuck in a psychological bubble, resistant to change, and prone to seeing the "other" as a threat.

- **Empathy and Understanding:** Diversity forces us to see the world through the eyes of others, fostering empathy. Without it, humans are more likely to dehumanize and even demonize those outside their immediate group, laying the groundwork for discrimination and conflict.

Sociological Perspective: The Fragility of Monocultures

History shows that societies lacking diversity often fall into cycles of oppression and rebellion. When power and resources are concentrated in the hands of one group, those excluded eventually reach a breaking point, leading to instability.

- **Homogeneity Breeds Hierarchy:** In monocultural societies, hierarchies form that place one group above others. This creates systemic inequalities in areas such as race, religion, gender, or class. For instance, autocracies often suppress dissenting voices and favor a narrow elite, leading to widespread dissatisfaction among marginalized populations.

- **Cycles of Oppression and Retaliation:** Marginalized groups, when systematically devalued and excluded, may reach a "tipping point" where they push back, often with great force. Sociologist Charles Tilly's theory of collective action explains how grievances—when coupled with shared identity and resources—lead to uprisings, revolutions, and rebellions.

Historical and Academic Insights: The Pattern of Cataclysm

Throughout history, the absence of diversity has catalyzed destructive conflicts. The examples are numerous:

1. **Colonialism:** The imposition of a single worldview by colonial powers often led to the suppression of local

cultures and traditions. These dynamics bred resentment, resulting in uprisings, independence movements, and enduring global inequalities.

2. **Genocide and Ethnic Cleansing:** In extreme cases, attempts to homogenize societies—whether through cultural assimilation or extermination—have led to catastrophic consequences, such as the displacement of the Native American, the Holocaust, the Rwandan Genocide, or the current and ongoing extermination of Palestinians.

3. **Economic Inequality in Autocracies:** Nations led by autocrats often see wealth concentrated among a small ruling elite, with widespread poverty among the masses. This imbalance inevitably leads to unrest, such as the Arab Spring uprisings.

The Essential Role of Diversity

Diversity is humanity's strongest asset. It introduces resilience, creativity, and adaptability. Consider how biodiversity strengthens ecosystems: a forest with diverse species is more resistant to disease and environmental change than a monoculture. The same principle applies to human societies.

- **Resilience:** Diverse societies are more adaptable to change. Different perspectives offer varied solutions to challenges, ensuring survival in a rapidly changing world.

- **Innovation:** Studies show that diverse teams are more creative and perform better than homogeneous ones. This applies to nations and communities as well, where cultural diversity fosters breakthroughs in the sciences, arts, and governance.

- **Social Cohesion:** While diversity can initially create friction, over time it fosters mutual understanding and unity. When societies embrace inclusivity, they become stronger and more equitable.

The Ignition Point of Inequality

When societies suppress diversity and enforce homogeneity, they risk reaching a "destructive ignition point." This happens when marginalized groups, devalued for too long, rise in rebellion. The pendulum of justice, in these cases, often swings violently, as oppressed individuals seek not just equality but retribution. This overcorrection can lead to further conflict, delaying the establishment of constructive solutions.

The Constructive Path Forward

Avoiding this cycle requires intentional effort. Societies may consider these ideas to ignite a forward motion:

1. **Foster Inclusion:** Create systems that value and incorporate diverse voices, ensuring that all groups feel represented and heard.

2. **Promote Education:** Teach the value of diversity from a young age, helping individuals appreciate differences rather than fear them. Teaching cultural literacy and perspective thinking early can create a foundation for mutual respect and understanding. This includes not only learning about other cultures but also reflecting critically on our own.

3. **Encourage Empathy:** Bridge divides through storytelling, cultural exchange, and open dialogue. Stories shape how we see the world. Diverse and

authentic narratives can act as bridges, helping people see themselves in others and others in themselves.

4. **Address Inequality:** Proactively work to dismantle systemic barriers that marginalize certain groups, ensuring equitable access to opportunities. This take true and not placating leadership.

5. **Leadership**: Leaders in every field must model the courage and humility it takes to build bridges. This means listening, learning, and facilitating connections across divides.

6. **Community Building**: Local efforts to bring different groups together—whether through shared meals, collaborative art projects, or dialogue sessions—can foster understanding on a micro level, with ripple effects that extend outward.

A Vision for the Future

Imagine a world where the default response to difference isn't suspicion but curiosity. Where encountering another culture is seen not as a challenge to our identity but as an invitation to expand it. This is the potential of bridge-building: a world that celebrates its diversity not as a liability but as its greatest strength.

Conclusion: Humanity's Strength in Diversity

Just as hydrogen and oxygen must work together to sustain life, humanity must embrace its diversity to thrive. Homogeneity may seem safe and comfortable, but it is inherently unstable, leading to exclusion, resentment, and conflict. By celebrating diversity, we tap into our collective strength, building a world that is not only resilient but also rich in creativity and compassion.

CULTURAL INCARCERATION AND CULTURAL CONFINEMENT

Cultural Affinity: An Invitation to Understand the Expanding Bubble of Human Experience

Imagine a single bubble—elastic, alive, and ever-expanding. It begins from the earliest stages of life, *sanctum in utero*. Initially shaped by the stimuli and responses of the mother and her environment, the development of the bubble accelerates with the first breath. A new and transforming stimuli then washes over flooding the senses of a newborn. It continues to be shaped by a mother's voice, her world. Each individual's bubble continues to expand under the pressure of a wider and growing world. This bubble is the production center, the main headquarters, of your world, your self—unique, dynamic, and filled with potential. Now imagine this bubble growing, stretching with each new experience, connection, and idea. But what happens when this bubble meets another?

When bubbles collide, they don't simply bounce apart or remain isolated. They blend, overlap, and form something extraordinary—a shared space that transcends individuality. This emergent space becomes community, culture, and identity. It is here, in this evolving realm of mutual influence, where the magic of humanity resides.

Education, at its core, is the great expander of these bubbles. It equips us to embrace the collisions, to see beyond the boundaries of our own realities, and to create a culture that is richer, more inclusive, and infinitely more vibrant. But there's a catch: when bubbles become rigid, resistant to change, or dominated by external pressures, the shared space can transform into a prison—cultural incarceration or confinement—that limits growth, expression, and connection.

So, how do we ensure that our bubbles remain elastic, capable of growth? How do we build a culture that liberates rather than confines? To answer these questions, we must delve into the invisible walls that divide us and the powerful bridges that education, understanding, and shared humanity can create.

In this newly formed space, the furnishings of each bubble—the ideas, values, beliefs, and preferences that individuals carry within them—are not just contained but are also exchanged, tested, and transformed. The environment of the community exerts a powerful force on this process, shaping the tastes, choices, and inner contents of each individual's bubble. Here, we see the beginning of cultural affinity: a fluid yet potent force that multiplies, evolves, and diversifies at varying rates, producing cultures and sub-cultures that are both unique and interconnected.

Like yeast causing bread dough to rise, cultural affinity acts as a catalyst that expands the collective bubble, generating new patterns of thought, behavior, and creativity. It creates a living, breathing culture—a larger, more encompassing bubble that is always in flux, continually shaped by those who can capture attention, convey ideologies, and ignite imaginations.

How do the cultural bubbles we live in shape our choices, beliefs, and the way we see ourselves in the wider world? And more importantly, can we learn to move through this maze of cultural connections to find a truer and more inclusive version of ourselves, both individually and together?

As we grow comfortable in our cultural bubbles, they can start to lose their flexibility and become more rigid. These communal bubbles often develop a strong sense of being "right," which can quickly turn into an "us versus them" mentality. This mindset breeds cultural fears and tensions, dividing us with unseen barriers of prejudice. Over time, these divisions give birth to the many 'isms'—racism, sexism, ageism, and more—that separate us further.

The question then becomes: How do we navigate these divides, remain open-minded, and build connections that bring us closer rather than push us apart?

For many decades, I've witnessed one of the most profound examples of cultural confinement right before my eyes. Only recently have I come to define my experience as something more than just a curiosity—it is a very real and noticeable form of imprisonment. This type of imprisonment starts in a subtle, almost secretive way, gradually incarcerating the bubble of the self. I invite you to consider the abstract reality of this situation.

Some bubbles are arrested against their will; others are persuaded to accept the terms of their own confinement. Often, it begins with a parent or guardian exerting authority over a child's bubble, enforcing control under the guise of responsibility. The child is then led through a process of indoctrination that can range from mildly intrusive to overtly abusive. This pattern is particularly evident in certain religious practices.

As children, we are often encouraged to "follow the leader" without understanding that this seemingly innocent guidance may be the first step into a carefully constructed trap—one that catches us before we have developed the balance and boundaries necessary to stand firm. In my own childhood, I followed the unspoken rules of the house, unequipped to challenge them. Like most children, I was a low-information individual, lacking the knowledge to make sense of my surroundings or to question the fairness of what was happening to me.

My father was a first-generation Seventh-Day Adventist, while my mother came from a third-generation Adventist background. Both were conservative in their beliefs, but my father was often rigid, unapologetically combative, and could easily be seen as easily triggered and sometimes militant in defending his rules—without much regard for a child's capacity to understand or develop reasoning.

The primary tool of my cultural confinement was the relentless emphasis on the word "obedience." We were constantly urged to conform through this overused directive. As children, we were taught to sing songs with lyrics like, "**Trust and obey, for there's no other way to be happy in Jesus, but to trust and obey**." Yet, for a child who had never seen Jesus, these words served as a thinly veiled encouragement to conform to denominational standards and codes of conduct.

From my childhood memories, I recall music being employed as a kind of decoy, subtly coaxing us into the acceptance of our arrest and incarceration within the church's boundaries. Another poignant example was found in the hymn "***I Surrender All.***" We were encouraged to surrender everything to the Lord—an ideal that quickly became a tangled knot of expectations. God, the Lord, and Jesus became synonymous with "The Church," and the church swiftly positioned itself to welcome another new arrestee into its fold. The underlying strategy was clear: get them while they're young.

Leadership would frequently cite the Biblical passage from

Proverbs: *"**Train up a child in the way he should go, and when he is old, he will not depart from it**"* (Proverbs 22:6). This verse was the bedrock of their approach—a method of control presented as divine instruction. These teachings became the foundation of my own developmental incarceration. Whenever I was perceived as deviating from the prescribed path or failing to meet the extra-biblical standards they imposed, I was subjected to brutal humiliation and intense pressure. This felt akin to solitary confinement, a kind of spiritual isolation until I demonstrated a willingness to conform.

The model of my life sets the stage for one method by which cultural confinement begins, but there are countless paths to this end. Not everyone shares my background, and the experience of incarceration for some began in a completely innocent way. I will share some examples. These examples are not exhaustive or absolute, nor do they represent the only observable methods by which the religious aspects of cultural incarceration manifest.

For some, it starts with a seemingly innocent invitation: encouraging a child to bring their friends to Sunday or, for some Sabbatarian sects, Sabbath School. This approach uses children to lure other children, turning the fun and games into a spiritual diversion—a carnival of religious confinement. Once the child is ensnared, the parents and guardians can be more easily drawn in as well. This represents the early-stage level of cultural incarceration.

For others, this process may begin later, during the teenage years—a period often marked by feelings of isolation and the desire to belong. Adolescents find themselves in a vulnerable and confusing stage of transition into early adulthood, naturally questioning their own identities and the realities of the world around them. They begin to examine and re-examine the value of their own "furnishings," seeking new designs that might help them feel welcome within the community of bubbles that surround them.

At this stage, they are particularly vulnerable. They are often honest and open, more willing to explore and challenge their surroundings. They are beginning to sense the contours of a kind of prison, but they may not yet fully understand the prison system itself.

Another common area of challenge, often innocently crafted to draw in the unsuspecting, is the workplace. Those already incarcerated in their cultural or religious frameworks are encouraged to share their experiences and seek out colleagues or friends who are struggling with the pressures of life. These individuals, vulnerable and searching for answers amid life's complexities, become the prey. The often-unaware incarcerated are led to believe that their fundamental beliefs offer solutions to the myriads of bubbles grappling with personal introspections—marriage, family, finances, unmet goals, sexual ideologies, political affiliations—all the ingredients in the mixing bowl of human experience.

Trained to recognize these moments of vulnerability, the incarcerated see an opportunity to draw others into their own cultural or ideological framework. And when these unsuspecting individuals take the bait, they often find themselves in a situation not unlike that of a child who is subtly coerced into conforming.

The examples I've shared from religious or spiritual contexts are just one of many pathways by which a bubble, or community of bubbles, can find themselves incarcerated.

Politics and politicians employ similar tactics to reinforce their chosen brand of confinement. Across the globe, countless models of cultural incarceration exist, each with its unique methods of control. The real challenge arises when those who are incarcerated begin to recognize the constraints of their own prisons.

Who Controls the Prison?

In the first section, I laid out the origins of cultural development and the formation of communities. I showed you how individual bubbles are inevitably shaped by the larger community bubble. If you've been following the theory so far, you've seen how cultural pressure—sometimes subtle, sometimes overt—pushes people to conform. This can turn toxic, corroding the mental, physical, and spiritual vitality of the bubble's host if left unchecked.

I'm not telling you to flee from any religion or political stance. Those choices belong to you, the sole owner of your bubble. If you've reached the age or stage of accountability, you have an inherent right to either conform to or reject any external structure that pulls you away from your personal equilibrium and the best life has to offer.

But now, let's dive deeper. Who holds the keys to this prison of conformity? Who are the prisoners, the wardens, the guards? What about the courts, the parole system, the endless cycle of recidivism that keeps so many returning to their chains? We need to explore these unseen forces—those who control the terms of incarceration and the conditions of release. Let's step into the belly of the beast and see who truly runs the show.

In the vast, open fields of the high plains stands a massive square structure, a monolithic concrete box that, from a distance, reveals neither charm nor menace. The journey here has been long and lonely, the relentless heat of the summer sun beating down, wearing on both body and spirit. But as we draw nearer, this strange edifice seems to swell in size, its presence growing more imposing with each step.

Features begin to emerge from the blur of concrete. What appeared as faint marks in the distance now sharpen into bars and rails. The once plain façade morphs into a complex of rigid, unyielding lines. And then, a sign appears, stark against the bleakness: "Guests are always welcome."

But this is no invitation. It's a declaration, a thin veil over the truth. This is a prison. The road has been long, and night is beginning to fall. As we stand at its threshold, we face a choice: to enter or to turn back, even as the shadows deepen around us.

Life is a relentless force, a ceaseless current that rushes forward with the speed of a fleeting lightning bolt flashing across the sky. It moves so fast that we scarcely notice the exchange of moments — nano second for nano second, an inexorable trade-off that never pauses or hesitates. In this rapid flow, we are often caught in the net of self-analysis, comparing ourselves against the ever-shifting currents of the world around us. At some point, we find ourselves arrested by our own self-perceptions, scrutinizing the contents of our bubble, evaluating the worth of what we hold inside.

Seeking clarity, we turn to others — friends, family, and communities — hoping they will appraise our worth, offer a measure of validation we fear to establish on our own. In our solitude, we sometimes find ourselves tuning into the hushed tones of late-night selling circles, the modern-day snake oil merchants who promise solutions to problems we didn't know we had. They thrive on sleepless audiences, restless souls whose consciences buzz like trapped flies, gnawing at the quiet edges of the night.

We flick through channels, searching for anything to distract from the nagging whispers of doubt, guilt, or longing. These late-night shows replay the memories stored in the bubble, casting shadows and light on the walls of our inner selves — the id, the ego, the superego. We oscillate between hope and fear, those twin spirits birthed from our responses to life's unpredictable acts. Each memory, every mistake, every triumph, hangs like art in the galleries of our psyche — the blessed self, the challenged self, the self-caught in the turbulent spin, often feeling excluded from the spa of human existence.

And so, drawn by the need for answers, we wander toward the community of supposed help. We listen to the voices that promise salvation, solutions, or simply solace. The peddlers of easy fixes and spiritual peace, the guardians of secrets and wisdom, become the characters we unwittingly trust. Before we know it, we step through the doors of the strange, unassuming building — not as guests, but as captives. The prison is not one of stone and steel, but of culture, habit, and expectation. It is built from the familiar and fortified by the comforting echoes of what we've always known — a prison crafted from our own need to belong, to be seen, to be understood.

In that moment, we come to see that the prison has always been there—lurking just outside the fragile walls of our bubble. Yet, it is a prison we enter willingly, drawn in by the allure of ready-made answers and the soothing balm of imagined certainties. We catch a glimpse of ourselves in the mirrors of communal familiarity, only to find reflections that are not quite our own, mimicking us in forms shaped by the expectations of others.

This prison is more than just a structure; it is a finely-tuned community of control. It flourishes on the quiet surrender of individuality, feeding on the suppression of the spirit that dares to question or resist. Its programs, its very machinery, are designed to entice more souls, to keep them ensnared within its invisible walls. This place is not defined by concrete or steel—it is entirely mental, a landscape crafted from beliefs and perceptions, where those who live inside are conditioned to accept the narrative of their own confinement. They consume the limited sustenance provided, barely enough to keep the spirit alive, yet potent enough to convince them to say with conviction, 'I've been convicted.

And so, we dwell in this place, a prison not of walls or iron bars, but of thoughts and conditioned beliefs. It is a prison whose wardens are the very ideas we have allowed to settle within us, the doctrines and dogmas we've inherited or adopted. Every corridor is lined with the whispers of what we should be, what we should believe, and how we should act. The air is thick with the unspoken rules, the 'oughts' and 'shoulds' that shape our behavior, nudging us ever closer to conformity.

Inside this mental prison, the routines are familiar: daily affirmations of beliefs that comfort us, rituals that bind us to our chosen identities, and habits that seem harmless but subtly reinforce our boundaries. The cells are lined not with cold steel, but with the comfortable cushions of tradition and the warm blankets of collective approval. The guards are the voices of authority—religious leaders, political figures, cultural icons—whose words echo through our minds like mantras, keeping us obedient, compliant, and convinced that this is where we belong.

Yet, there are moments—fleeting, almost imperceptible—when we feel a tug, a pull from deep within, a yearning for something more. The walls seem thinner, almost transparent. We glimpse a flicker of light beyond, a world not yet seen, a possibility not yet considered. But just as quickly, the moment passes, and the walls solidify again, thickened by doubt, fear, or the comforting embrace of the familiar. We retreat back to the known, the safe, the defined.

What we seldom realize is that the prison feeds on our fears and thrives on our reluctance to question. It uses our own longing for certainty, for community, for acceptance as its strongest bars. It is built on the paradox that we imprison ourselves by the very act of seeking freedom from uncertainty. The more we crave absolutes, the tighter the prison's grip becomes.

But what if we dared to see the prison for what it truly is? A construct, a fabrication of collective anxieties and inherited assumptions. What if we found the courage to confront the guards, to ask why we must remain confined to these narrow walls of belief? What if we discovered that the key to our release has always been in our possession—a key forged from self-awareness, curiosity, and the willingness to embrace the unknown?

To step out of this prison is not easy. It requires us to dismantle the very structures that have given us comfort, meaning, and identity. It means facing the fear of being alone, misunderstood, or even lost. But it also means finding the vastness beyond the walls, the space where we can grow, evolve, and truly be free. It is here, in this uncharted territory, that we might finally see the full expanse of our own potential—beyond the confines of our cultural incarcerations, beyond the limitations of inherited beliefs. Here, we find the courage to craft a new narrative, one where the bubble expands infinitely, filled with the richness of an authentic and liberated self.

You have it. I have it. We all hold the keys to freedom close to us, whether tucked away in the pockets of our will, hidden in the folds of our intentions, or clutched tightly in the grip of our resolve. Even when life strips us bare of all certainties, those keys remain—perhaps tied around our necks like cherished pendants, wrapped around our wrists like lifelines, or nestled deep within the chambers of our hearts. It may feel distant, but remember, true freedom is only ever a heartbeat away.

The Wardens and Guards of Control

Capitalism isn't a dirty word—but it's not spotless, either. It is the wool from which many of the tapestries that drape the minds of the incarcerated are woven. In its pure form, capitalism offers a remarkable engine for innovation and growth, but it also comes with a cargo of contradictions. It has been both the benevolent wizard promising prosperity and the conjurer unleashing a multitude of evils.

Capitalism has been the relentless force driving those who run and guard the prison, the very architects of the system itself. They are the instructors, the mentors, the creators of commercial advertising—the ones who trained the hucksters of religion and state in the brutal arts of population control. Increasingly, the line between the politician and the evangelist blurs: the politician becomes a preacher, and the preacher speaks like a politician. Both serve to enforce the 'oughts' and 'shoulds' that bind the mind. They are the gatekeepers, whether by self-interest or ignorance, who perpetuate the prison system, often the understudies sometimes without even realizing they are imprisoned themselves.

There is a reality—sometimes a near-fatal one—found within the confines of the prison. This prison has no locks; the bars remain open, even those leading to freedom. Yet, the bubbles—both of the individual self and the collective—retain furnishings crafted by the guardianship of imagination, sustained by fears, and guided by the ever-present question: *What will happen if we reject confinement and seek our own release?*

The wardens and guardians, both real and imagined, are the forces that keep us bound by the traditions and standards of institutions. Though the institutions may differ around the globe, their essence remains static. The designs may vary, but at their core, the cultures that imprison the unassuming are fundamentally the same.

Cultural Incarceration and the Wardens of the Mind

"Often, the leaders of religion and politics function as the wardens and guards of the cultural prison. Every cell and cellblock are under the constant watch of the so-called informed—those who claim to know better and guide others accordingly. This control is voluntary in the sense that every person, beyond a certain age of accountability, has the natural law right to choose their own path. Yet, many remain trapped, either by design or by default.

Some of these captors knowingly keep the culturally incarcerated in check, while others simply follow the directives handed down from above, maintaining an atmosphere of ever-present fear. Each cellblock may look different on the surface, but they all tell the same story—one of a manipulated imagination, trained to accept fantastical truths and romanticized realities. These are the rules, and those who adhere to them are awarded badges of honor, becoming the model prisoners and cultural icons of their communities.

No formal judge issues the sentence for this kind of incarceration. Instead, we bypass the established legal system, accepting the indictments handed down by those who control the cultural narrative. We often surrender willingly, accepting a sentence we impose upon ourselves. It's a mix of curiosity and conformity that leads us into these strange edifices, which, upon closer inspection, reveal themselves as prisons—a phenomenon I call 'Cultural Incarceration.'

Some people testify to being arrested on the road of life, while others tell darker stories of entrapment, finding themselves in a profit-driven house of corrections. In this system, the warden knows exactly what they're doing, but the useful idiot—the middle management guard who seeks status—maintains control over the inmates, keeping them docile and compliant.

Before long, confinement becomes a reality. Some manage to escape, recognizing the open doors and unlocked bars, but others perish within, never acknowledging the truth of their predicament. Let's delve deeper into this issue of 'Cultural Confinement.' This isn't just about imprisonment; it's about sustaining a system that ties into economics—a constant fundraising effort to maintain the power of the wardens, guards, and those convinced to serve as caretakers of the system's wealth. It creates a money-making machine that rewards the top performers.

Prisoners are not always innocent. They often buy into the

prison meals of hopes and dreams, believing they can ascend to the roles of guards or even wardens. They are hypnotically persuaded that the system is waiting for them to rise, through hard work and personal responsibility, while remaining blind to the deliberate controls and limits in place. No legislature sets these rules; they are products of imagination, sold to sustain this peculiar form of civil justice. The system's oppression thrives on the weaknesses of the incarcerated, breaking down personal convictions and demanding conformity to invisible yet unyielding agendas.

Billions of bubbles are contained and branded, each representing a distinct prison house. It's territorial; it's correctional. The public address system continually broadcasts warnings about what happens if we fail to comply with the rules. This house might be a government, a political party, a religious institution, or any societal group that promotes division and segregation into its own gang-controlled cellblocks. The prison culture naturally fosters alliances, driving the 'us versus them' mentality that plagues the world.

So, let's examine this concept more closely. First, you have the bubble representing the individual self. Then, there is the association of bubbles that form a community. Specific communities align with particular cultures, and these cultures make up the populations of various territories. Each culture carries its own handicap, sometimes subtle but often evident when its megaphones reach an annoying pitch. These voices belong to those who have allowed themselves to be imprisoned. They cry out for freedom while simultaneously inviting you to join what they claim is a 'better' cellblock. In reality, they're merely extending an invitation to join their own culturally confined community.

Cultural Confinement

So, we start with the bubble—the individual. Then, this single bubble merges with others to form a community—a collective of individuals. From there, we reach the larger bubble that encompasses a sovereign territory of bubbles—society itself. Society, in essence, is nothing more than a container filled with countless cultures, each built upon a superabundance of subcultures representing every imaginable facet of the human family.

The initial stage of incarceration begins even before birth, as the brain develops within the prison of the womb. The soon-to-be infant has no control over this environment. After birth, the child is introduced to the guardianship of those entrusted with their development—family members and caretakers. These figures help to shape and expand the bubble by supplying furnishings—the beliefs, values, and norms—that define the larger world of bubbles beyond. This represents a transition from one prison to another. At this level, early indoctrination graduates the child into the welcoming arms of chosen communities of comfort. These communities, often composed of familiar faces and trusted authorities, are the larger reaches of the neighborhood, marked by influential figures and celebrated intersections. This stage prepares the child for cultural confinement—a form of captivity imposed without explicit consent.

Cultural confinement is ultimately a matter of choice. It occurs when the individual bubble relinquishes its responsibility for independent thought and surrenders to the rules of the prison house. These rules differ from culture to culture and society to society, but the nature of the confinement remains unchanged until the mentally imprisoned individual decides to break free. Cultural incarceration often starts innocently as a matter of 'following the trusted leader.' However, it frequently evolves into the bubble's willful imprisonment, shutting off access to a more vibrant world beyond the prison walls.

This surrender is marked by an acceptance of the gifts and furnishings offered by the wardens and guards of the cultural penal system—gifts that cause the bubble to expand only within the confines of the prison. Over time, this expansion becomes an isolating surrender to the figures of authority—the wardens, guards, and trusted celebrities. The life that develops within these confines is what I call Cultural Confinement.

To break it down further: Cultural confinement takes place when a warden or a system of wardens imposes their beliefs and limitations on those who have surrendered to their personal and particular worldview. It creates an illusion that no one can rise above the imagined authority of the warden. Even the prison guards are deceived by this construct. But remember—innovations like the airplane, the lightbulb, and the microchip all exist because someone dared to imagine beyond the walls of confinement.

The flaw in the wardens' design is their failure to recognize the vastness of the sky above. They forget that those fortunate enough to have a window view that extends beyond the imaginary bars are naturally inclined to dream of what lies beyond. It is in these moments, when the horizon beckons, that their bubbles expand to hold the limitless potential of freedom. This is where the opportunity for escape arises—a chance to transcend the narrow confines of cultural imprisonment and embrace a more expansive existence.

Recognizing the Signs of Cultural Incarceration and Confinement

To understand how a bubble — whether an individual or a community — becomes incarcerated or begins serving time in confinement, we need to explore the methods for identifying these signs. The period of incarceration often begins with an innocent exploration of our natural curiosities: *What is this? Why is it here? How did it get here? Where is it going?* These are questions not only about the external world but also about the internal landscape of the self.

To delve deeper into this period of incarceration, we must examine the power of group-think and how it shapes our individual preferences and choices — the furniture we select for our bubble. In the group-think zone, irresponsible understanding emerges, driven by the desire to align with the community of bubbles around us. At this stage, we find ourselves reiterating and defending the group's accepted talking points without real research or critical examination. Often, to their applause, the individual, in this context, often dismisses factual history and instead subscribes to an alternate or distorted view of reality.

Here are some indicators that may signal the beginnings of a relationship with the cultural prison system. I call this the Cultural Incarceration Phase:

1. **Loss of Critical Thinking:** Individuals begin to echo the group's beliefs without scrutiny, leading to a decline in independent thought and reinforcing an "us vs. them" mentality that tribalizes communities. Under the wardens' influence, the system discourages unionization and promotes division to suppress collective power. By following these divisive narratives,

we lose critical thinking skills and personal responsibility, leaving ourselves vulnerable and trapped in conformity, effectively putting our minds on autopilot and allowing the group to dictate our thoughts. It is in this phase that the individual automatically conforms to societal, religious, or cultural norms without ever examining their validity or relevance to their own values or beliefs. The absence of critical thinking is a key sign.

2. **Defensive Conformity:** Many within the imprisoned population turn themselves into echo chambers, fiercely defending the group's stance even when faced with contrary evidence. The desire to belong and be accepted by the metaphorical prison community outweighs the pursuit of objective truth. As a result, they become promoters of unchecked falsehoods, viewing any reality-based challenge as a deliberate affront. It is in this incarceration phase that actions and choices are driven primarily by fear—fear of punishment, social ostracism, divine retribution, or failure. The constant anxiety about "stepping out of line" or "offending" is a hallmark of being culturally incarcerated.

3. **Historical Revisionism:** Adoption of revised narratives that align with the group's ideology often involves rejecting established facts or interpretations. This revisionism strengthens the group's identity and sense of righteousness. For example, many still reference the "Burning Bush" incident with Moses, even though the text in Exodus 3:1-4 suggests the bush was not actually burning. Despite the inaccuracy, this

phrase persists across generations because it has been accepted within the community, illustrating how agreed-upon revisions serve to protect the tribe's shared beliefs.

4. **Limited and Limiting Exposure to Different Viewpoints:** A deliberate aversion to engaging with those outside the group, who might challenge its norms, is a critical sign of cultural incarceration. For instance, within certain faith communities, new converts are often advised to distance themselves from family or friends and avoid non-sanctioned literature. The message is clear: "Stay within the fold; outside influences will lead you astray." This kind of guidance fosters isolation from diverse perspectives, reinforcing the group's ideology.

5. **Dependency on Group Affirmation and Approval:** A deepening reliance on group affirming and approval creates a fear of dissent or independent thought. Disagreement is viewed as a serious threat, and there is palpable pressure to conform—deviation is treated as a sin, an unforgivable act of betrayal. New ideas are only entertained if sanctioned by the Warden. This fosters a fear-driven belief and often false security: *If I defend the tribe, the tribe will always protect me.* This phase produces an Overreliance on External Validation (OEV). Here a deep dependence on approval or recognition from authority figures (religious leaders, political figures, celebrities) or social groups develops. This need for validation often trumps personal intuition, desires, or moral reasoning.

6. **The 'Us vs. Them' Mentality:** A tribal or binary

mindset where there is a constant division between "us" (those who conform) and "them" (those who don't). The idea that "we are right, and they are wrong" becomes a tool to reinforce loyalty and obedience.

7. **Language of Submission Emerges:** Phrases, expressions, or teachings that emphasize submission, surrender, or sacrifice to a greater power, leader, or ideology. Language that glorifies suffering, obedience, or martyrdom can be signs that cultural incarceration is at play.

8. **Suppression of Individuality:** This develops as a lack of encouragement or even outright discouragement of individuality, creativity, or unique perspectives. People are expected to fit a mold, to act and think in ways that are predetermined by the group or culture.

9. **Compulsory Rituals or Practices:** Participation in rituals, traditions, or ceremonies becomes less about personal belief and more about maintaining status within the community or avoiding punishment. There is little room for opting out without facing consequences.

10. **Suppression of Curiosity:** Natural inquisitiveness is stifled and replaced by a sense of compliance. Questions challenging the status quo are discouraged—either subtly or through overt threats—in the name of group harmony. Punitive warnings like, "You better keep quiet," or paranoid whispers of, "They are listening to you," enforce a culture where looking deeper, investigating, or seeking answers is forbidden.

By identifying these signs, we can start to understand how cultural incarceration takes root in our lives. Recognizing these indicators is the first step toward breaking free from the invisible bars that limit our potential and stifle our growth. Now, let's explore the difference between Cultural Incarceration and Cultural Confinement. Incarceration occurs when one is either arrested by external forces, convinced to surrender voluntarily, or pressured into submission by the community. Cultural Confinement becomes a long-term state that evolves into the everyday actions of life. These actions, shaped by the accepted norms and "refinements" of the prison environment, often go unquestioned, mistaken for growth or rehabilitation.

Signals and Signs of Cultural Confinement

1. **Feeling Trapped but Comfortable:** An underlying feeling of being stuck in a certain life pattern, belief system, or cultural norm, but with just enough comfort or familiarity to deter one from breaking free. The confined person may feel there's "no better option."

2. **Narrowed Horizons:** An inability or unwillingness to see beyond one's immediate environment or cultural beliefs. New ideas, alternative perspectives, or different ways of living are seen as threats rather than opportunities for growth.

3. **Self-Policing Behavior:** Individuals begin to internalize the norms and rules of the culture so thoroughly that they enforce them on themselves and others, even when no external authority is present. This might include shaming, judgment, or gossiping about those who step out of line.

4. **Resistance to Change:** A strong resistance to change or an inability to adapt to new circumstances. Changes are viewed as dangers that threaten the stability of one's world, rather than opportunities for growth.

5. **Dependency on Familiar Structures:** A deep dependency on cultural, social, or familial structures for identity, security, or decision-making. The thought of stepping outside of these structures often leads to panic or fear.

6. **Echo Chambers and Homogeneity:** Social circles become echo chambers where the same ideas are reinforced repeatedly. Divergent thoughts are rarely expressed, and when they are, they are quickly shut down or dismissed.

7. **The Illusion of Choice:** Individuals believe they are making choices freely, but in reality, all available options are controlled by the same cultural framework. For example, one may feel free to choose their beliefs, yet only within the confines of what the culture deems acceptable.

8. **A Heightened Sense of Unearned Grandiosity:** An inflated sense of authority emerges, where one feels entitled to dictate rules not only within their own culture but to impose them on others. This sense of arrival bestows an illusion of honor and status, fostering the belief that they alone have the right to construct the social order and set the standards for all to follow.

9. **The Need for Unregulated Authority:** The need for unregulated authority often arises, fueled by a vivid

imagination of punitive measures and clandestine retributions against those who defy compliance. This behavior is frequently observed in both religious and political arenas, where dissenters are labeled as 'wicked' or 'sickos.' This extreme stance, a byproduct of prolonged confinement, can even irritate the system's own enforcers. Such individuals may assert, 'I've been here longer than you,' as a trigger for conflict, demanding a return to an earlier state of authority, using their experience and age to assert dominance over others' lives.

10. **The Future is Diminished:** The call for the future turns into nostalgic window shopping of past memories, where unmerited authority is imagined rather than earned. This illusion of power creates a stormfront of vindictiveness toward those who fail to recognize their supposed strength. The quest for growth and development is abandoned, and creativity falters, with innovative ideas incinerated in the crematorium of once-shared hope.

The prison of Cultural Incarceration and Cultural Confinement are real challenges that bubble and communities of bubbles in our society face. However, do not forget. There is an outside where freedom exist. The locked doors and bars are only an imagination played out in the storyline we self-impose – we choose.

Questions to Explore Further

- **What are the dangers of the initial stage of Cultural Incarceration?**
- **What are the psychological and emotional**

consequences of being culturally confined?

- How do these signs manifest differently across various cultures or belief systems?

How can one begin to recognize these signs within themselves and take steps toward freedom?

LET'S RETHINK POVERTY:

Breaking Free from Cultural Confinement

Poverty is often framed as a simple lack of money, but what if we are missing the bigger picture? What if poverty is not just an economic condition, but a form of cultural confinement—one that limits what people can see, dream, and ultimately achieve?

For many, poverty is more than financial hardship; it is an inherited condition, reinforced by systemic barriers, cultural norms, and a lack of exposure to real escape routes. One can work every day and still remain trapped if the only pathways they've been shown lead to the same cycle of struggle. The dishwasher who has never been exposed to opportunities beyond dishwashing may never imagine becoming a nuclear physicist.

Poverty is not just about lacking money—it's about restricted access to information, opportunity, and the belief that something better is possible.

But here's the good news: we can change this.

- **For those who feel trapped in poverty**, this conversation is about opening doors to new possibilities—breaking through inherited limits and rewriting the script for future generations.
- **For politicians and policymakers**, it's about designing solutions that go beyond surface-level aid and work to dismantle the systemic traps that keep poverty alive.
- **For educators**, it's about recognizing that what we

teach (and don't teach) can either confine or liberate minds.

- **For churches and civic groups**, it's about shifting from charity that only sustains survival to empowerment that creates transformation.

Poverty is an issue we all have a stake in because a society that keeps millions trapped in a cycle of struggle is a society that is failing to reach its full potential. If we want real solutions, we have to examine poverty through the microscopic lens of **Cultural Confinement**.

Let's break this down and explore how we can truly help people not just survive—but escape.

Generational poverty often functions like an inherited condition, where cultural norms, systemic barriers, and internalized beliefs reinforce the idea that upward mobility is either unattainable or outside one's rightful place. The **bubble of limited exposure**—whether to education, financial literacy, or networks of advancement—keeps individuals locked in a cycle where the known world defines the possible world.

Poverty is not just economic; it is intellectual, psychological, and social. If poverty is a type of imprisonment, then the key to liberation must involve **expanding the horizon of what is known and believed to be possible**. Remember, there are no locks on the prison doors.

Let's break this down. When we consider the definition for poverty, it seems to be taught like this:

Poverty is when someone doesn't have the resources to meet their basic needs, such as food, clothing, and shelter.

However, poverty can be further explained as:

Poverty is a state or condition in which an individual lacks the financial resources and essentials for a basic standard of living. Poverty can have diverse environmental, legal, social, economic, and political causes and effects.

If we view **poverty through the lens of Cultural Confinement**, we begin to see that it is not merely a lack of financial resources but a **structural and psychological entrapment**—one that is often maintained by systems that claim to alleviate it. This is what I would like to explore. The second definition expands the observation of factors involved in the production of many whose lives seem trapped in poverty.

How Media Reinforces Cultural Confinement in Poverty

Media plays a profound role in shaping societal perceptions of poverty. **Narratives about the poor often fall into two categories: the "deserving" and the "undeserving" poor.** The deserving poor are often shown as hard-working but down on their luck, while the undeserving poor are cast as lazy, irresponsible, or even dangerous. This binary ignores the deeper reality: most poverty is systemic, inherited, and reinforced by limited access to upward mobility.

Consider how news coverage of poverty shifts depending on the **race and location** of the people affected. When economic hardship strikes a **middle-class** or suburban community, it is often framed as a **temporary setback**. But when it exists in historically poor neighborhoods, it is presented as **chronic and inescapable**, reinforcing stereotypes that those living in poverty belong there. This confinement is both **psychological** (convincing the poor that this is their reality) and **cultural** (limiting societal empathy and action).

Politics and the Maintenance of Cultural Confinement

Policies aimed at helping the poor often carry an underlying **ideological bias**. Some political forces promote **"bootstrap narratives,"** implying that poverty is an individual failure rather than a systemic issue. Others promote policies that create **dependence rather than empowerment**, ensuring that people have just enough to survive but not enough to **escape confinement**.

For example:

- **Welfare policies** sometimes include work requirements or restrictions that keep recipients in low-wage jobs with no opportunity to advance.
- **Educational policies** in poor communities often receive less funding, leading to **poor schooling**, which then limits job prospects, continuing the cycle of confinement.
- **Redlining and housing policies** have historically prevented economic mobility for entire communities, creating generational poverty.

All of these political mechanisms reinforce a **barrier of limitation**, making poverty not just a lack of money but a lack of **alternative pathways to success**.

How Charity Can Sometimes Reinforce Cultural Confinement

Charity, when done without an **empowerment focus**, can inadvertently **cement cultural confinement** rather than alleviate it. Programs that only provide **temporary relief**—like food distribution without financial literacy, or housing without career training—can unintentionally **sustain poverty rather than solve it**.

The problem isn't charity itself but the **framework** in which it operates. If charity is given in a **hierarchical way** (the powerful give to the powerless), it reinforces **dependency** rather than transformation. True poverty alleviation must focus on **expanding opportunities, skills, and networks**, not just addressing immediate needs.

Escaping the Cultural Confinement of Poverty

The key to breaking free from **poverty as cultural confinement** is **access to knowledge, alternative narratives, and exposure to possibilities beyond the bubble**. Solutions must include:

- **Education beyond the basics**, including financial literacy, critical thinking, and career planning.

- **Policy reform** that focuses on true upward mobility rather than maintaining a dependent underclass.

- **Narrative change**, where stories about poverty emphasize **systemic barriers and real solutions**, rather than blame or pity.

- **Community-driven empowerment programs** that help people take ownership of their future rather than waiting for outside help.

I believe most forms of poverty can be addressed in a way that brings together those on both sides of the economic divide. The key is expanding opportunity and breaking free from the confinements of the past. Throughout history, creativity, innovation, and invention have been the launching pads that have propelled individuals—though too few—beyond poverty's grasp. The truth is, the prison doors are not locked. **Cultural Confinement affects many, and too often, those who share the same constraints unknowingly reinforce the generational cycle of no escape.** It's time to rethink the way forward—together.

PERSPECTIVE THINKING

The Power of Perception

Take a trip with me back to my early childhood. I want you to see as much as you can. Imagine a small, drafty house on an almost quiet street. Check out my boyhood home where the walls could barely hold the noise, the laughter, and sometimes, the tears of eight souls living under one roof. The salt-box structure groaned under the weight of life's daily pressures, like it had more stories to tell than the concrete block on its mortar foundation and the wood covered walls could handle.

My wife really wasn't fond of the house I'd bought later in life on Primrose Road. It was my best attempt at home ownership. That house was a huge upgrade from that four-room salt-box home I grew up in. By 1968, that tiny house was bulging with eight of us. Take a trip with me back to my early childhood. I want to share and expose you to a good portion of my development. I invite you to see as much as you can.

My father worked tirelessly, a federal employee at the U.S. Naval Academy by day and a taxi driver by night. He had side hustles too—painting, bus driving, whatever he could find. And during the warmer months, he tended a garden that to a child seemed to stretch forever. Of course, I was his 'apprentice,' though I felt more like a full-time farmhand, working not only our garden but also my granddad's garden as well. They weren't small plots either—no, these were vast enough to keep our family supplied with fresh produce well past the harvest season.

Now, my mother, she was a force in her own right. A homemaker, but so much more—crossing guard, store clerk, and part-time housekeeper for what seemed to be wealthy families nearby. The times weren't easy, but they were familiar. Many Black women in my neighborhood did the same, keeping homes spotless while quietly navigating the divide between employer and servant. Momma did it all without complaint, just like countless mothers who made sure families were fed, clothed, and cared for, even if the pay didn't reflect the work.

Sure, they paid her, but the dynamic always left a bitter taste, especially when I noticed the subtle divide between servant and employer. Sometimes it was like a living echo of what many Black people had survived. Some of these families formed genuine bonds with us, weaving into the fabric of our lives, even if it was through that unequal lens. Some of the people she worked for seemed to have clung to the remnants of a social order that felt like something straight out of *Roots*—not exactly the world I wanted to grow up in, but it was the one I knew.

We were a two-parent household—six kids, two parents, all cramped into that tiny salt-box home. Each of us kids developing different bubbles, each forming our own perception of life. My sisters saw one world, governed by strict rules, institutionalized righteousness, and the ever-watchful eye of the church. Meanwhile, my brothers and I were coming to terms with what it meant to grow up in a world that didn't always offer kindness to young Black boys. We felt the constant pressure of becoming men in a world that could be cold and often indifferent. Like my brothers, I felt the pressure of becoming a man in a world that often-withheld kindness. The world was different through each of our eyes, though we shared the same family, family name, and surroundings. As a kid my eyes were open, even though I did not understand my vision but, I was watching—observing life, maneuvering through what I now call the labyrinth.

There was also the world outside our walls, a world where history wasn't just something we read about—it was happening in real-time. The Vietnam War. The Civil Rights Movement. More Assassinations. I was just a kid, barely old enough to understand what was going on, but I felt the tremors. I guess you can say I was just a toddler when President Kennedy was shot, the somber conversations that followed. I was old enough to remember my mother's tears when Martin Luther King was assassinated, and again, just two months later, when Bobby Kennedy met the same fate. These weren't just names on the evening news—they were real people, real losses, real matters thrusting themselves into my little world. These guys had great value in my community that was measurably on the verge of societal change.

The world around me was like a kaleidoscope—always shifting, always changing. In those years, the country seemed to be coming apart at the seams, but for me, life was still about the little things. My father's taxi sat in the driveway, and my mother's hands seemed permanently soaked in dishwater or furniture polish. The grown-ups whispered about assassinations and riots, but for me, the real excitement was watching the snowplow clear the roads after a storm, or catching glimpses of those psychedelic Volkswagen vans rolling through town, painted with peace signs, flowers, and groovy slogans.

But even in the midst of all that chaos, there were quieter, personal moments that shaped me. I remember the cold drafts that crept in through the windows of our house, even after we covered them in plastic. And yet, somehow, those drafts felt insignificant compared to the real kind of draft that took people I knew including family members away.

My cousin Louis C. Byrd—he was more like the closest thing I had to a big brother. He lived right across the street with my grandparents, and he used to dress me up, put on my socks and shoes, and carry me out of the house. We'd walk to the Parole Shopping Center, where he'd buy me donuts and my own little bag of Utz potato chips at the bakery. I can't forget that bakery smell.

Cousin Louis and I would take hikes running errands to the A&P on West Street. Sometimes it was a stroll to get some meat from the butcher at Richmond's little dark grocery store with those unforgettable wooden floors that would bend and creek seemingly with every step. I often felt like I was king of the world as I would pony up and take my ride on his back.

As a young child I wasn't given a clear definition of the draft. The house I grew up in was definitely drafty during the winter months—plastic covered the windows, but it didn't stop the cold. I remember the whistling in the house when the harsh winter storms would defeat the plastic covered windows. That 'Duotherm' kerosene stove, our source of heat, worked overtime, the same way my family did to keep things together. Sure, our home was drafty during the winter but like my granddad's home, we put plastic over the windows to avoid the draft.

A lot of guys left because they could not control that draft. Community members and church friends like Pat could not deal with this draft thing. They all got caught up and taken away in the Army. That draft didn't just steal loved ones; it stole our sense of normalcy. I was learning fast. My innocence was thinning out, and I learned to coat the cracks with humor. What else could I do? Humor was my shield, my security blanket, against the loss and the stupidity of it all—war, race, struggle, hunger, and cold. I was just a kid, watching men go off to fight, come back broken—or not at all—and wondering if this was what being a man meant. Is this my future?

The adults dealt with each delivery of loss in their own ways, but as a child, I found myself absorbing their emotions, layering them with my own confusion and fear. Yet, nothing could warm the chill when news came of another life lost overseas.

Then one day, Louis was gone. The whistling winds of the annoying draft they kept talking about came like a thief in the night, stealing away my cousin and others from the church and community. And just like that, a whole chapter, one of my many chapters of my childhood closed. I didn't understand what was happening then, but I remember the pit in my stomach, the way my mother's eyes clouded over with worry, how she pressed her lips together when she talked about 'the boys going off to fight.' War wasn't just something on that small black-and-white TV anymore. The draft and the war had reached into our home and pulled Louis right out of the picture.

The news was always on in our house, with Walter Cronkite, Chet Huntley, and David Brinkley becoming permanent fixtures in our living room. I remember the grainy footage of marches and protests, the voices of people demanding justice—fighting, demonstrating, screaming for a better world. History wasn't something distant—it was hot and cold blasted into our living rooms, onto our streets, into our schools. History was making impacts drilling deep into the invisibilities of our souls. But as children, we took it in through a lens we barely understood.

I can't forget this. Some Black guys and some white guys started growing big hair. They started passing around that word brotherhood and very interesting cigarettes. Music was changing on the local WANN Hoppy Adams Show. It was changing on WSID, WYRE, and WUST out of Washington radio. The spiritual music was developing a new beat with a little more bass. Jazz and blues were introducing what we call today 'Old School'. We were starting to sneak around Daddy's church driven rules for music.

And then there were the Hippies, with their long hair. They too, like many of the black guys, wore colorful dashikis. They accessorized themselves with dark and oversized sunglasses. They also began dancing to a different and developing tune. It was a strange cocktail of love and war, anger and hope.

Yes, both black guys and white guys were growing supersized hair. More and more, both wore colorful dashiki shirts and dark sunglasses. Everybody was fighting for something while the Hippies were loving. The Peace sign was appearing more and more as I caught glimpses of those psychedelic Volkswagen vans rolling through town, painted with peace signs, flowers, and groovy slogans. In the hot summer, people were getting 'cool'. Some guys would talk a lot about 'getting high'. A few guys were so energized that they got fired up. A few guys got so high on new ideas and energy that they were literally out of this world or as the groovy people with the many colors was saying, "Far out." These guys got so high that they literally left this world. They left the planet. Neil Armstrong actually stepped on the moon. He, like the many he temporarily left behind, made the sizable impact on me.

The world was exposing itself to me and I didn't close my eyes. Just as the exposure brought tears and worry, I was exposed to the lightening of comedy. I was exposed to the Rowan and Martin Laugh-In show. Actor Arte Johnson was saying over and over, "very interesting." Like the characters on that show, the Smothers Brothers were causing me to laugh as well. Black and white society, just like the black and white televisions were becoming technicolor. 'Chico and the Man' became a new match up. 'All in the Family' became the mirror of absurdity. The color in TVs was transforming us more than just a technologically defined colorful way.

Meanwhile while all this was happening, I was still figuring out my place in all of it. The world outside my window was exploding with change, but I was just trying to keep up with my brothers, running through the house with plastic on the windows to keep out the cold. The adults had bigger things on their minds—like how to survive in a world that didn't always make sense—but for us kids, the biggest challenge was staying out of trouble and making sense of the labyrinths we were born into. I was just a kid trying to make sense of it all, and yet, I was surrounded by these grand themes of life: war, race, power. The labyrinth of my early years was filled with these moments—some small, some earth-shattering. The assassinations, the riots, the men going off to fight in Vietnam, the hippie movements—everything was shaping me, even if I didn't see it or understand it fully.

It was as though I was being dragged through history by the scruff of my neck before I even knew what history was. Sometimes, it felt like I was in the middle of a movie I didn't buy a ticket to see. From the Vietnam War to watching men walk on the moon, history was the backdrop to my childhood. I watched it unfold, piece by piece, in the faces of my parents, in the tears of my mother, and the grunts of my father as he worked another double shift.

But there was also the bubble of innocence—a weird balance of not understanding the weight of what I was witnessing. Kids still played kickball and hopscotch in the streets, and the Good Humor ice cream truck bells still rang through the neighborhood. We could hear the melodies of the Mr. Softee truck, the yell of the fish man selling fish from his truck, the snowball man, there were a lot of trucks selling things. Adding these trucking merchants to the so many other happenings, we could often find pockets of joy, even in the dirty cracks of life.

Even as a young child, I was building perspectives. I didn't know it then, but every event, every tear from my mother, every switch, belt, strap, yardstick, shoe, slipper, spatula and other crazy objects that connected with my bare buttocks was significant. We would get blamed for things we didn't do – especially if it was an adult telling the lie. The stories about the boys going off to war, every cold draft of change blowing through the many windows of my life were indeed furnishing the bubble of my life. This wild ride of real-time videography was causing me to follow that floating feather caught up in the breeze of time. Giving my attention to that seemingly innocent and random feather would eventually shape my world.

You see, as I look back, I realize that I was standing in the eye of a historical hurricane, too young to understand the winds swirling around me but old enough to feel their force. There was the tension of the Vietnam War, the energy of the civil rights movements, and the sadness of assassination, after assassination, after assassination. It felt like the world outside my little bubble was constantly shifting, but in our home, we were trying to hold it together with whatever we had—faith, family, music, imagination, and hard work.

And that's where the humor kicked in. You see, when you're a kid living in the middle of all this, you don't realize the gravity of it all. My cousin Louis was off in Vietnam, but in my mind, he was on some big adventure, maybe even riding one of those cool helicopters like the ones I saw on TV. The black-and-white news broadcasts showed all the chaos, but as a child, I learned to laugh in the face of it. Dank humor, sarcasm—that was how we covered up the pain. It wasn't ignorance; it was survival. When the world around you seems to be falling apart, you find ways to protect your bubble from popping.

And yet, there was a strange, unintentional ignorance, too. I didn't fully grasp the cost of what was happening. Vietnam was far away. The marches were in other cities. The civil rights leaders were people on TV, not people I could touch. But I could feel the ripple effects, and so could my family. The cracks in our community's bubble were everywhere, even if we didn't always talk about them. The reality of our lives—poverty, racism, the struggle to survive—was wrapped up in the larger story of my America.

That's why, as a kid, I thought everything was just the way it was supposed to be. But now I know better. Now I see how all those moments—the laughter, the tears, the cold drafts, the historical explosions—shaped my view of the world. It was all part of the labyrinth of life, the journey that each of us walks through day by day and in our own way.

I was just arranging the early furnishings of my bubble back then. I was being forced by time, age, and adult supervision. I was being guided by one side, or limited sides of the story, but little did I know, I was also laying the foundation, receiving the building blocks, blueprints, and drafted measures for what would be constructed as my perspective.

Think about it, the curtain raised on my life a little before the assassination of President Kennedy. My earliest days coincided with the passing of the Civil Rights bill, the Voting Rights Act, the famous, great, powerful and moving 'I Have a Dream' speech which was delivered less than an hour from my home.

Think about it, I was a year old when Medgar Evers was assassinated. A little after my third birthday a minister and Civil Rights leader Malcolm X was assassinated. I remember walking into the house and seeing my mother pressing clothes. Her face was wet with tears as she told me someone had killed Dr. King. I can't forget the humid heaviness encased in the sadness.

Think about it, almost two months later, I saw my mother's tears again. When she told me somebody killed Bobby Kennedy. With all the tear producing drama of the 60's, I recall moments of hope, too.

Think about it, In the late 60's Loving v. Virginia case had overturned laws against interracial marriage, shaking up the very fabric of society. Two months later, I watched through a kid's eyes as Thurgood Marshall, whom I was told, was black like me. They let this black guy finally have a seat. Somebody gave him a chair of power on the United States Supreme Court.

Think about it, during this early period of my life, I watched a lot of TV. Walter Cronkite, Chet Huntley, and David Brinkley, were developing as household names. There was the CBS Evening news, ABC News, NBC Nightly News rapidly developing as old white men telling us about protests, marches, and the war like it was a movie we weren't allowed to be in.

Think about it, I saw more and more elephants in the room and donkeys too—oh, they were everywhere on the news too. People were changing. People were waking up through the magic of that old black and white TV. Pictures and videos of people were marching and demonstrating in the streets in big cities across the U.S. Our nation was having a time and *it was alive.*

This was a rapid run through the opening scenes of my life. Without question, I was a child of the 60s. Life was both slow and fast—an era of extremes, where the cold and the heat of societal tension collided. It was a time of darkness and yet, light was breaking through. Atlantic City saw its share of battles, and public faces—on the streets, in the media—were getting darker, taking on shades of my own reflection. Televised faces were shifting, slowly starting to look like mine, like ours. Hope was nipping at the horizon, casting a faint but growing glow.

I was receiving the early furnishings of my bubble, that personal world we all carry, one shaped by the forces around us. No longer was I wandering aimlessly through the labyrinth of life; I began to walk it with intent, with purpose. This intent was the firstborn of my perspectives, a creation molded by the friction of my experiences and my surroundings. All around me, polarities were shifting. The atomic structures in the many rubber bands of society were vibrating, excited by the tension, causing movement, friction, and change. I was learning the art of paying attention.

The opening scenes of my life were like everyone else's: I was starting to figure things out, starting to see how I fit into the world. Right in the middle of it all, my brother Emory was born. But not long after that, another baby brother arrived, so Emory lost his spot yielding to Clarence as the youngest in the family. It felt like there was a whole construction project going on in my life—changes I didn't ask for, but they were happening anyway. And all of this before I even turned ten.

My baptism, by full immersion, had a deeper meaning than anyone could really grasp. Around the same time, some guys were heading off to Woodstock and coming back with a new attitude—charged up and ready to challenge the system. They had a new look and, stereotypically stated, a very interesting smell. A cloud, a beautiful cloud, seemed to follow. They were rebelling, and the establishment wasn't ready for it. Honestly, it still isn't. That's my story of the 60s, and I'm sticking to it.

It took me a long time to understand myself as undergoing a natural and spiritual renovation. I now realized that I am and will continue to be under construction. I am a living work in progress. What I became aware of, I am presenting to you. This story is told so many different ways by observers of the same period of time. We were witnesses of time that intersected with events. Our stories may differ but, unless embellished, each one is true. Such realities and the retellings of the 60's experience are the reports of perspective.

Can we take a quick leap from the 60s to the 21st century? I want to bring you to a moment that really shaped my understanding of what I call 'Perspective Thinking.'

Earlier, I walked you through my resume as a kid in the 60s, under ten years old, trying to make sense of the world. Those events didn't just mold my personality; they built my perspectives. Now, let's fast forward to a different scene — one that was just as pivotal in shaping how I see things today.

It's January 17, 2000. That's the day my twin sons, Jack and

Brandon, were born. They were so tiny, but even then, I knew I was looking at two distinct perspectives waiting to bloom.

Fast forward a few years. The boys are just about three years old. As I mentioned earlier, my wife wasn't too thrilled with the house I had bought for us. To me, that house was a huge upgrade. It had more space on one floor than the entire interior of the house I grew up in. But from her perspective, it was different. She grew up in a much larger home with more bedrooms, bathrooms, a basement you could really use, and a fireplace — complete with central air. My childhood home? We had a kitchen table, no dining room, no dishwasher. We *were* the dishwasher, eight mouths and sixteen hands. They had cups and glasses, we had old mayonnaise and jelly jars.

The house I bought was an up for me; for her, it was a down.

See, the house isn't just a physical place — it becomes this perfect example of how perspectives shape our reality. I was proud of the house. It was a step up from the crowded home I shared with seven other people. For her, it was a step down from the spacious home she had known, one rooted in her family's German Catholic heritage. Meanwhile, my roots went deep into a Black American history marked by stories passed down from a grandfather born at the turn of the 20th century and a father born in 1922 who had witnessed a lot by the time we were growing up in the 50s and 60s.

The point is, perspective changes everything. And back then, those differences in perspective were on full display in that house.

She wasn't happy with it, though. She wanted new windows, a new washer and dryer, and a bathroom remodel upstairs.

Here I was, trying to serve the community, host a local TV show, give weekly radio commentaries, work the night shift, raise twin boys, and now—on top of all that—become a bathroom remodeler.

As I was remodeling the upstairs bathroom, I was also juggling the responsibilities of taking care of our boys. Most of my day was spent with them, but somehow, I found time between cooking, cleaning, laundry, reading, writing, and even working on the car, to squeeze in some renovation work. It wasn't easy, and I had to get creative to make everything fit into a very tight schedule and budget.

One day, while I was tearing down the old drywall around the bathtub, an idea hit me. I had these large pieces of drywall that were just going to be thrown out. But instead of tossing them, I thought, why not make use of them for something fun? I could turn this into a project with the boys.

So, I remember pulling out a huge slab of drywall and propping it up against the hammock, near the round picnic table in the backyard. I figured we could have some fun with it — maybe draw on it, turn it into something creative. It wasn't just about the drywall; it was about finding ways to bond with the boys while squeezing creativity out of every moment.

The two little guys were playing in the yard when I called them over. I had some markers with me, thinking they'd enjoy drawing on the wallboard I had set up. They looked to me, waiting for direction, so I started drawing numbers as they called them out. One, two, three, and so on. We were having a great time until I got to thirteen. Brandon, with excitement in his voice, shouted, 'Thirteen!' But Jack? Jack gave me a strange, confused look, and then with a confident smirk, said, 'No, daddy. B.'

I paused, surprised. 'No, Jack, what is this?' I was determined to make sure he saw the number thirteen the way I saw it. But Jack wasn't budging. 'No, B, daddy,' he insisted. And then, in a move that completely stunned me, he put his little finger to my lips and said, 'No, daddy! B!' His tone was almost angry, as if to say, 'How could you not see this?'

I was at a loss. I knew they both understood their numbers, so why was Jack acting this way? Maybe it was too much excitement for one day, I thought. So, I stopped the activity and sent them back to play in the yard. Jack hesitated, lingering for a moment, and quietly said again, 'B, daddy.' There was such disappointment in his voice.

As I started cleaning up and carrying the large slab of wallboard back to the deck, it hit me. I took a second look at the number I had written. My penmanship had made the one and three run a little too close together. What I saw as thirteen, Jack saw as the letter B. And Jack was right. It wasn't willful defiance. It was his honest perspective.

This experience was one of my first clear lessons in Perspective Thinking. I had set up the game for them to tell me what they saw, and Jack had done exactly that. While I insisted on what I *meant* to show, Jack saw what was *there*. And that's where perspective comes in—seeing things from a different angle, sometimes even more clearly than the one who presents it.

Years later, my marriage to their mom ended, and I moved to Georgia. There, I met someone new, Kathleen. In this new relationship, I realized how much of what I took for granted about culture—things like where we eat, what we eat, or what church we attend—were things she had never been exposed to. Kathleen is white, raised in a white community, attending a white church. I often found myself hypervigilant, trying to shield her from awkward or rude behavior that I knew might come our way.

In our relationship, I began to notice how cultural divides quietly shaped perspectives, even in subtle ways. Kathleen, with her kind heart, would often apologize for other people's poor behavior, or brush off offensive remarks with, 'Oops. I didn't mean that.' It reminded me of all the excuses I'd made over the years—little concessions to avoid tension or discomfort. But there were moments when I had to step up and say something, not just for her sake but for my own. I was noticing more and more microaggressions—those quiet, almost invisible acts of exclusion that make their mark. And when people would follow up with, 'I didn't mean it,' I realized that intention didn't always erase impact.

We had moved to Eastern Oregon, to a place with its own fraught history—Pendleton, once a Sundown town. If you're unfamiliar with the term, a Sundown town was a place where non-whites were deliberately excluded, often through threats or violence, ensuring the town remained 'all-white.' Pendleton was one such place. Today, it's a tourist spot, and I encourage anyone to visit. But before you go, take a moment to read up on the Pendleton Underground and Oregon's constitutional history. You might find yourself amazed by how deeply racism was embedded in the laws of this state—a reality far different from the multi-cultural Mid-Atlantic world where I was raised.

Living in Pendleton was a stark contrast to my experiences back East. And this history, as uncomfortable as it is, needs to be faced. Some may argue that we shouldn't dredge up the past, that it's better left forgotten. But I believe this: If you don't want to deal with bad history, then don't make bad history.

The term 'WOKE' has become a cultural buzzword in recent years, often ridiculed or vilified by those who see it as a threat. But at its core, being 'woke' is about awareness—about seeing things as they really are. Back then, we didn't call it 'woke.' In Christian circles, we spoke of 'The Great Awakening'—periods in American history when religious fervor swept across the land, prompting people to examine their lives and the world around them with fresh eyes. There were four, maybe five, great awakenings in the U.S., the last of which stretched into the period just before the Civil War, including the Millerite Movement of the 1840s. These awakenings stirred religious piety and often came with a promise: America could be made great if its people returned to righteousness. Sound familiar?

Today, certain groups, especially among the alt-right and Christian Nationalists, argue that being 'woke' is somehow sinful or evil. But every Christian movement I've known has been about turning on the lights, waking the sleeping masses, and bringing them to some form of truth or salvation—whether spiritual or social. In other words, being 'woke' should mean waking up to injustice, to inequity, to the need for change.

Each of these examples, whether historical or personal, is rooted in perspective. Perspective is not a lie. It's the lens through which we view and make sense of our experiences. There is no such thing as an 'alternative truth.' A lie is simply a lie. But as we position ourselves to view the same event or situation from different angles, we begin to see the layers and complexities of what is true for each of us. Jack saw the letter B. I saw the number 13. Both perspectives were real, shaped by how we were looking at the same thing.

Perspective Thinking, at its core, is about acknowledging differences without dismissing them—or the people behind them—when our understanding of reality diverges. It's about recognizing that while facts remain constant, our interpretation of them can vary based on the unique experiences that shape our inner worlds. We see what we see through the lens of our personal bubbles. What I am postulating is that our perception of reality is what's truly in question. We're not imagining a rushing river on a dirt road when no water is present; we can both observe the dirt road together. While we may define it differently, we cannot see a rushing river that isn't there.

Perspective Thinking Defined

Perspective Thinking is *the intentionally cultivated ability to consider the various viewpoints through which individuals may observe, define, and interpret the same experiences, shaped by honest reasoning within their personal bubbles. We see the same; we interpret differently.*

While living in Augusta, Georgia, I found myself in a tight spot, navigating a social clash that had become an undeniable part of daily life. I noticed how some people carried a sense of entitlement, creating a clear discomfort in their interactions. This unspoken supremacy often pushed others—including myself—into that familiar 'go along to get along' position, where you concede to maintain peace, even when it goes against your better judgment.

In dealing with these growing frustrations, I found myself sitting at the desk next to the bed, closing my eyes to think. The annoyances were piling up. Why was she automatically right about everything? Who made her the authority? Why did I always have to cater to her preferences—whether it was food, music, art, or anything else? These questions kept circling in my mind, and they began to guide me back to memories of my two sons in our backyard. One more question I wrestled with in Augusta: What unwritten rule says you can't serve barbequed ribs at the White House?

That last question—about the barbequed ribs—was both interesting and very real. I remember being on a worksite one day, just before Barack Obama's election, when an argument broke out between Burt and Nate. Burt was openly racist, his worldview shaped by the rogue descendants of the Confederacy. He despised the growing belief that the United States might actually elect a Black president.

Before I go any further, please read this excerpt from the United States Constitution:

CONSTITUTION OF THE UNITED STATES OF AMERICA—1787

ARTICLE II.

SECTION 1.

Paragraph 5

"No Person except a natural born Citizen, or a Citizen of the United States, at the time of the Adoption of this Constitution, shall be eligible to the Office of President; neither shall any Person be eligible to that Office who shall not have attained to the Age of thirty-five Years, and been fourteen Years a Resident within the United States."

Let it be clear—assumptions and imagined entitlements should not be mistaken for the actual document we hail as the 'Law of the Land'. Notice I did not say the law of the world. I'm specifically referring to the Constitution of the United States. Often affectionately called a 'living, breathing document,' it has no soul except the one we, as citizens, breathe into it from the depths of our collective spirit. The Constitution does not govern the sovereignty of any other nation on earth. It was granted to us, the citizens of the United States, for as long as we respect it, nurture it, and allow it to evolve. We, the people, are its life support. It's our shared energy that keeps its heartbeat alive. Yes, it skips a beat now and then as times change, and it is not infallible. That's why it leaves room to grow with us. For this reason, the Constitution allows for Amendments.

The highest rule of law, the CONSTITUTION OF THE UNITED STATES OF AMERICA, clearly outlines the qualifications for serving as President of the United States and the executive power vested in that office. These are the constitutional qualifications for holding the presidency:

- Be a natural-born citizen of the United States

- Be at least 35 years old

- Have been a resident of the United States for at least 14 years

We've attached additional qualifications to the presidency—ones that are not found in the Constitution. Until 12:00 pm on January 20, 2009, many believed, and some still do, that to serve as president, one must be white and male. Barack Obama, a true African American, shattered that notion when he was sworn in as President of the United States.

The Constitution never stated that the president must be male, and I believe, if we are alive, we will see a woman elected to that same office. The document also doesn't require the president to be heterosexual, conservative, liberal, Republican, or Democrat. It doesn't mandate that the president must be a Christian or a believer in God at all. If an atheist were to win the support of the majority, they too could be sworn into the Office of the President, according to the Constitution.

The CONSTITUTION OF THE UNITED STATES OF AMERICA is not subject to personal interpretation; it is the foundation of our nation's laws. It serves as the seat, holder, and protector of our civil rights. Until recently, it was a sanctuary where every U.S. citizen, nationalized citizen, immigrant, and migrant could recognize the sacrifices made through protests, wars, bloodshed, and even death. It embodies the nation's honor and values, reminding us of the trust we, as citizens, uphold.

No, indeed, the Constitution is not a matter of perspective, nor should it ever be. It must serve as the impartial and vigilant guardian of the state, protecting all who meet the qualifications bestowed by birth and naturalization.

Both Burt, an easily angered white man, and Nate, a young Black American, viewed the presidency through the tinted lenses of their inner visions. Nate looked through a lens of hope, thrilled at the prospect of living in a nation led by someone he could relate to, at least in terms of skin color. In stark contrast, Burt viewed the same picture—the election of 2008—through the lens of a hate-driven past. To emphasize his point, Burt hung a Confederate flag at work, a gesture I felt crossed the line. He remained shackled to the traditional viewpoints he had always known, yearning for America to stay the same. This clash highlighted the stark differences in their perspectives.

Nate often teased Burt to provoke a reaction, sometimes inviting an audience for added effect. I always found it entertaining to watch Nate get Burt riled up. On this particular day, however, things felt a bit different. 'Come here, Brother

Harris,' he called to me, a glint of mischief in his eye. 'I want you to see this.' He led me around the corner to a spot where he knew Burt would be working. As we arrived, others joined us, eager for the spectacle. The old, ruggedly aged white man looked up, clearly caught off guard in that moment.

'Hey, Brother Burt!' The energy was palpable, and though the Tea Party had yet to begin, it felt like the air was charged. I wasn't sure what group, if any, this cantankerous man belonged to, but his agitation was evident. I could almost see the tension straining against the thick lenses of his dark, bone-framed glasses. My brows furrowed as I found myself drawn into the unfolding drama.

'Brother Burt! Are you ready? I can smell the barbecue—the ribs sizzling on the grill at the White House. Are you coming, Brother Burt?'

I could tell these guys had been exchanging energy. Burt went from a casual 15-mile-per-hour zone to a dangerous supersonic speed, breaking the sound barrier in no time flat. "I told you; you can't have barbecue, ribs, fried chicken, or collard greens at the White House!"

I promise you, the prohibitions against ethnic foods are found nowhere in the Constitution or the founding documents of our nation. This was a perspective Burt held, shaped by the limited furniture in his bubble. For some reason, the guys often considered me the intelligent one in the workspace. I was known for negotiating peace to keep things running smoothly and on schedule.

I think I had built up a bit too much confidence in Burt when he turned to me and asked, "Explain to the guys; only sophisticated food is served in the White House." I think he was telling me, only foods that he imagined would be found on rich white people's tables would be found in the White House. So, I braced myself for what would struggle to come through his lips. Burt shot me a death stare, as if betting all his confidence on my answer. I felt I was about to fail his expectation. My empathy extended even to this racist mole of a human (at least, that was my perspective). Burt checked nearly every box of the so-called forgotten white underclass. He wasn't particularly smart, yet he had the confidence to believe he was smarter than any Black person who had ever lived, dating back to when God supposedly painted the skin of a cursed people black.

In my mind, I had already called it. It was like those fast, garbled words you try to say with a dentist's tools still in your mouth, all slowed down in awkward motion: "Ain't that right?"

No Burt, that's not right," I responded, as the room erupted into laughter. The assembled audience, arranged for fun, unintentionally humiliated a human being. Nate immediately seized control. "They ain't gonna be cooking in the kitchen. They gonna be on that smoke pit in the back yard," he added, continuing his ribbing of the racist ball of energy Burt had become. The guys laughed at Nate's relentless teasing. Even some of the white guys joined in, understanding Burt from their own perspectives. But Burt had his own perspective too. Each person there carried their own story, a face of hidden agendas cracked open from the egg of perception.

Perception is a powerful force—capable of both destruction and sparking creative genius. It becomes constructive when we make a genuine effort to see the world from another person's point of view. While we may never fully reach 100 percent understanding, we can come closer to seeing what they see rather than what we assume. This approach is essential for finding those few fragments of common ground that exist, waiting to be discovered.

This is the story of how I grew up. This is the story of who I am. This is the journey of my perspective. As a child, my journey began on the perspectives of well-meaning people who, often, were simply ignorant. Yes, ignorant—driven by beliefs rooted in darkness, holding onto candles that had long since lost their flame. They were the racists and those who responded to racism. They were the illiterate preachers who built our fear-based traditions. They were the shadows of superstition, crowned as our saviors.

The pendulum of society swings swiftly from left to right, carrying with it the weight of guilt we all share. This guilt is the negative charge in the stations of our perspectives—the force behind the rose-colored lenses through which we see ourselves, and the dark, villainous visions we project onto those we don't understand or care to know. Perception is seeded in our personal bubbles, but the seeds come from somewhere. We are the growth of past seasons, the spring of old perspectives, and the inevitable fall of futures yet to unfold. Our blossoms become our furnishings.

Let me explain:

First may I repeat my definition of **Perspective Thinking (PT)? PT is -** *the intentionally cultivated ability to consider the various viewpoints through which individuals may observe, define, and interpret the same experiences, shaped by honest reasoning within their personal bubbles. We see the same; we interpret differently.*

I saw a Christmas tree ornament. Another person saw a simple ball. One saw paganism. Someone else saw a decoration. One person noticed color. Another saw art. Some saw money well spent, while others saw money wasted. One labeled it evil; another saw the effects of capitalism. One noticed the inscription of a Bible text, and someone else saw the exploitation of Christian funds. Some saw the exploitation of the poor, while others saw a money-making opportunity.

Yet, they all gazed at the same object. Each could defend their perspective, and each was accurate according to the furnishings crammed into their bubbles. But then came the guy who walked up and saw the round, colorful goose egg—destined for his breakfast table. Let's just say, his perspective changed.

Burt saw a nation that had his back. No matter what happened, Burt believed the government was his safety net, a blanket of protection for his hopes and dreams. To him, that government would always be controlled by people who looked like him, thought like him, and carried out policies that aligned with his civic beliefs. His views weren't born with him—they weren't blood-bound or genetic. They were instilled in him by older generations, old musty furnished bubbles, who wanted the world to follow their civic and cultural understandings.

In Burt's world, it was the duty of police officers to stop and punish anyone who didn't fit into their idea of a natural order—an order where people were supposed to be white and Christian. Anyone who didn't fit that imagined design of superiority wasn't deserving of help from the government. Those with more melanin in their skin were seen as poor, lazy, tricksters living off government resources that, in Burt's mind, were meant only for people like him—people fortunate enough to be seen as white.

Non-whites weren't supposed to get jobs, not because of

their abilities, but because of their skin color. They weren't supposed to hold positions of power, especially ones that put them in charge of people like Burt. In his mind, no non-white person should be President of the United States, because, although it wasn't written in law, he believed that the Founding Fathers intended it that way. Even though there was no document to back these beliefs, many U.S. citizens, like Burt, had been led to believe the same.

This is why so many clung to the idea that minorities, especially Black Americans, only got hired because of Affirmative Action. Today, the words "Affirmative Action" have been replaced by "Diversity, Equity, and Inclusion," the trendy acronym DEI. But the argument remains the same—an old, worn-out narrative that fuels the bubble Burt lived in, staining and distorting his vision of what America was supposed to be.

Nate's idea of America carried its own set of unwritten expectations. He was energized by the prospect of living in a nation where the president would give voice to his dreams, dreams planted deep by the cultural seeds of generations long passed; generations of hope. His worldview was shaped by ideologies passed down through his community, carrying the weight of a historical narrative that was both a burden and a source of resilience. Nate's sense of identity was steeped in stories of survival, resistance, and hope—echoed in the lines of James Weldon Johnson's poem, *Lift Every Voice and Sing*.

That song was an anthem of hope, casting rays of sunshine onto a dismal background of often perishing dreams. It inspired those able to see beyond what was, into what could be. The words spoke directly to the heart of Nate's experience, painting a vivid picture: "Stony the road we trod, bitter the chastening rod, felt in the days when hope unborn had died."

For Nate and many in his community, these words held a weight that transcended the page. They captured a feeling so severe, so historically entrenched, that it painted a cultural background where unborn hope often felt aborted—strangled by the bitter hands of injustice. Yet, that same narrative also carried the spark of resilience. The anthem declared a future not yet seen but desperately yearned for. Nate held onto that hope, believing that the rise of someone who looked like him to the highest office could represent the beginning of a new chapter—one where his community's hopes could finally take root and flourish.

Nate, while standing on the edge of this grand possibility, couldn't help but see Burt as a relic of a time long overdue for change. Yet, despite Burt's blatant racism, Nate continued to call him 'Brother.' There was something in Nate's cultural upbringing that didn't allow him to completely dismiss Burt, perhaps because, in Nate's world, every step forward had to be accompanied by a fight for inclusion—even for those who might oppose it. Nate's bubble wasn't tethered to the founding documents of the country, but rather to the lived experience of generations past, who had marched, bled, and cried out for freedom that was still, even in 2008, far from fully realized. In his heart, he was living the unfulfilled dreams of his ancestors, dreams that echoed in every line of Johnson's song. But as he faced Burt, Nate wasn't just confronting a man—he was confronting a mindset, one that had tried to keep his people down for centuries. And in his mind, that confrontation was part of his duty, part of the legacy he carried forward. Like Fannie Lou Hamer, Nate was "Sick and tired of being sick and tired."

Burt and Nate, though sharing the same blistered hands and aching backs, were bound by more than just the labor they toiled under. What united them was their frustration—an internal fire fueled by the sense that they were not being seen, heard, or understood. Yet, instead of seeing each other's struggles as interconnected, they allowed the chasm of their imagined realities to divide them. Burt's frustration stemmed from a fading belief in an America that would always protect his place at the top, while Nate's hope was rooted in the desire for an America that had never truly existed for him or his ancestors.

Neither man had a nuanced understanding of the political system they placed so much weight on. Burt thought the government was there to guarantee his dominance, while Nate believed it could finally lift him out of centuries-old subjugation. But what they didn't grasp—what so many fail to see—is that the President, no matter how much power the office seems to hold, is bound by the system. A system of checks and balances, of compromise and constraint. Neither Burt nor Nate saw that their frustrations couldn't be solved by one person in one office. Their civic education was built on myths passed down, not facts they had engaged with. And that's a dangerous place to be—because it's easy to project all hopes or all fears onto a single figure, without ever confronting the deeper mechanics at play.

Can you see the power of perspectives at play? Perspective Thinking is an intentionally practiced art born of the cultivated ability to stop and consider the other person or persons varying viewpoint. I am not saying that you must agree or legitimize their codes or beliefs. Each is free to observe and absorb those things that are comfortable within the confines of their bubble.

The problem comes when one determines the furniture contained in other bubbles and seek to manage its arrangement. All definitions personally held are based on a combination of personal affinities and alliances within the acculturated score. It is in this segment of understanding that two or more people may interpret the same experiences but, define such experiences amazingly differently. It is an observed fact; we see the same; we interpret differently.

Nate ribbed Burt by teasing him that the Obama White House would have barbecue—smoked ribs, dripping wet and sticky with one of America's most delicious regional flavors. The conversation was so intense I could almost smell the smoke, see the ash-covered wood embers glowing, and feel the familiar, mouth-watering scent of fat dripping onto smoldering flames; oh baby – I could hear the sizzle.

But in Burt's mind, the smoke rising wasn't from the pit of cultural celebration Nate imagined. No, Burt's furnishings of a past era, of superiority, likely revolved around an entirely different image: kitchen maids in aprons, black tux butlers (all in natural blackface, of course) silently serving White House guests. His mind likely summoned scenes straight out of a Norman Rockwell fantasy from the *Saturday Evening Post*, where order, control, and hierarchy were evident in every gloved hand and nodding 'Yes ma'am.'

Those 1950s-era images never moved from Burt's main floor, never changed with the times. His imagination was busy, painting an overseer in a spotless white apron—likely a white woman, eyes keenly fixed on the culinary staff, awaiting any slip in their 'place' with silent obedience.

Of course, to be fair, this is 'just my imagination running away with me' on my wild and happy to be the writer playground. I can picture the whole scene: the dressed turkey or standing rib roast, the steamship round being masterfully carved, the gentle tinkling of champagne flutes, and water goblets filled to just the right level. I see the plates and sterling cutlery placed with precision, the kind of perfection you'd expect at a White House dinner.

But then, I can't help but imagine the splashes and inevitable stains on white lace tablecloths, the red-streaked napkins as guests wipe their lips between bites of ribs. And why not? The Memphis-born, Kansas-raised, Texas-bred pitmaster might've served up some dry-rubbed and sticky-wet glazed ribs that had everyone toasting and cheering between bites, while a live jazz ensemble hit every right note, keeping the party going all night long.

Big question?

What happens when imagination fills in the blanks, choking off the mind from the endless possibilities alive in the vastness of reality? What is the outcome when the true image—the one that's right in front of us—is overlaid with imagined myths and fanciful legends, staining the inner walls of our thoughts? I don't know for certain, but perhaps we can ask the police officer suspended from duty or placed on desk duty, now wondering how they lost sight of the bigger picture. Maybe we can ask the waiter who deliberately overlooks a certain table, choosing service based on biases they've absorbed over the years.

Could we ask the bank or insurance company that continues to red-line communities, turning away from the reality of those people's hopes and dreams? Maybe we turn to the teacher who subconsciously devalues a particular class of students, or to the parents and students who don't even see the systemic disrespect and underpayment of their own educators.

It's worth asking: **What happens when Burt and Nate can't find a way to refocus their frustration on the bigger picture instead of their own misunderstandings of each other?** What's the cost of their failure to look beyond the limitations of their bubbles, selfishly seeing only the furniture handed down from generations past?

A Real Talk About Perspective and Imagination

Maybe it's time for a real conversation—a deep dive into the way we see and understand the world.

Some things operate by the power of perception and the authority of an image, rather than by the facts themselves. In a society driven by appearances, choices often overshadow chances. Yet, real change never arrives without challenge. We've mastered critique, but have we truly learned to observe? Have we trained ourselves to look beyond the surface, to notice the simmering frustrations that erode trust? Are we truly listening, or is our collective comfort with hitting the snooze button drowning out the alarm calling us to wake up?

As humans, we carry an innate artform: imagination. It's what allows us to dream, create, and interpret the world around us. But imagination is not without its flaws. Too often, we invoke it to fill in the blanks of a story, especially when discomfort arises. There's a culturally conditioned reflex to create answers where none exist, to impose meaning where there is ambiguity. And filling in the blanks is not the same as perspective.

Imagine this: a story is told with gaps—unanswered questions. Our immediate discomfort with those gaps pushes us to bridge them, not with truth, but with assumptions. Those assumptions often reflect our frustrations, stereotypes, or prejudices, rather than objective reality.

Consider the late commentator Paul Harvey. He masterfully filled in the blanks with researched, compelling narratives, always ending his segments with, "Now you know the rest of the story." But in everyday life, filling in the blanks is rarely this thoughtful. Instead, it becomes an untrained reflex—a habit of imposing our biases onto others.

Take this scenario: A man drives an expensive vehicle. Someone assumes, "He has no business driving that car. He must have stolen it." This isn't perspective; it's cultural conditioning. It's the imagination running unchecked, filling in a story that doesn't exist.

This behavior has real-world consequences. Look no further than the controversial and often harmful "stop-and-frisk" procedures. Despite laws meant to curtail it, the practice persists, justified by claims like, "The person fit the description." But did they? Or was it the officer's imagination, shaped by cultural predispositions, that filled in the blanks?

This happened to me in "the Real West" - Pendleton, Oregon. My wife and I had just moved to this small town, where Black residents make up less than a fraction of a percentage of the population. One day, an officer watched me uncomfortably and disrespectfully close. His eyes invaded my personal space. Eventually, his constant glaring scarred my wife. The next day I saw him and stopped him. I asked him to come to my home. I explained to him, from the inside of my living room window, my perception of what he had done the previous day. I told him how it made my wife feel and how it embarrassed and made me feel. He admitted that my facts were indeed accurate concerning his behavior. His reasoning? He said he'd received a report of stolen bags from a local shopping center. When I asked, "Did they find the person?" he replied, "Yes." He then admitted, "The person we were looking for was white."

I paused, and then I asked him to take a good look at me. "Not only am I not white," I said, "I'm a dark-skinned Black man. I don't even resemble white." To his credit, he admitted his mistake. He later became a friend and even a protector when the Klan threatened me with an unscheduled visit.

But here's the question: Was his initial suspicion of me a matter of perspective or the product of an overactive imagination? Did his imagination, fueled by cultural biases, cast me as a criminal before seeing me as a new member of his community?

When imagination replaces perspective, the results can be devastating. It destroys trust, especially when the very people tasked with serving and protecting allow assumptions to dictate their actions. The imagination we employ when crafting stories about those we find uncomfortable isn't perspective—it's prejudice, and it's wrong.

The Intentionality of Perspective Thinking

I sat at the desk next to my bed in Augusta, Georgia. On that desk, I placed a white sheet of printer paper. I remembered a lesson my son Jack had taught me—it was there all along, waiting for me to realize it. It was a secured intellectual deposit he made to his dad that continues to pay dividends in helping me to understand many of the complexities shared with me in counseling challenges squeezed from a never dry washrag of differences. It was the number thirteen, a code that unlocked a simple thought that could help undermine our differences and bring light to a better understanding of our collective human family. I started drawing.

I was known as something of a sketch artist once. At sixteen, I wanted to make a little cash to boost my personal fortunes. I didn't have the artistic abilities that my oldest brother Carl discovered in his later life, but thanks to my uncle Ches, I was able to sell a good number of prints I had drawn of the Maryland Statehouse. I could place on paper what I had floating in my head. And what I discovered back then, as I'm rediscovering now, is that the simplest images often carry the most powerful messages.

The number 13 was my focus and the key to a theory I developed. From the center of the page, I drew a six-by-five, three-dimensional version of the number thirteen. I sat there, looking at the page, asking myself, 'What am I missing?' It was there all along. I saw a 13. Jack saw a B. The two of us saw our same realities in the exact same moment. The little man Jack wanted his big man daddy to stop and consider what he was seeing. Jack saw the letter B. I failed, at that time, to notice how observant he was.

I was, in fact, mastering my superiority as father and teacher. I had spent years learning how to critique and correct. This was a production of my community, my culture, and the guidance that taught me to be right and never wrong. I grew up in a church that condemned anyone who did not follow our teachings. Only recently, I have come to admonish church leaders, telling them that we have a long history of chastising more than we baptize. That little closed-minded church was in the process of incarcerating a calculating kid. I almost believed what they were teaching whether directly or indirectly. They wanted me to believe that we knew why they, those beyond our heaven bound doors, wouldn't follow us. It was simple: They were controlled by the Devil and the Catholic church. Everyone seen as not being a part of our practice was to be seen only in a negative light.

What an idiotic and unverifiable way to exact condemnation on all those who reject, don't understand, or are simply oblivious to our teachings.

From the start, I was raised identifying my young friends and community members as 'Heathens' and 'Infidels.' We boasted the only intellect on the planet; that was until we needed one of the specialties that only the world could provide. The Emergency Room Doctor may have been a 'Heathen,' but he was trusted to handle our aches, pains, breaks, and sprains. That toothache that hurried moms and dads off to the Dentist who may have been seen by an 'Infidel,' but he was certainly spot on in delivering Novocain and laughing gas to calm us for that filling or extraction to be completed. Hell, nearly 100% of the items we used in everyday life were products produced by people and faces we never knew or would ever know existed.

We did not care about affiliations when the comparison was with necessity. We didn't care about the sexual orientation of the person who made my parents and grandparents eyeglasses. We didn't care about the person's mental challenges who delivered milk and eggs from the farm. Our local church teachings were off the chain, stupid in our critiques and failures to understand others. That was our training. We were taught to produce 'Blanket Statements' that defined everyone under the banner we selectively placed above their heads.

But after years of driving in a wrong and inappropriate direction, Jack's daddy made a turn on 13th Street. That turn wasn't just a lane change or a change in route—it was a change in perspective, in understanding, in the very way he began to see the world. Maybe it wasn't obvious at first. Like most journeys, the shift was gradual, but once made, it was impossible to go back.

It wasn't just Jack's dad making this turn; it was the realization that my whole upbringing—our culture, our teachings, our critiques—had been narrow, skewed, unfair, and very incomplete. We had been living with blinders on, seeing only what was selfishly convenient and ignoring the rest.

As I took that turn, it became clearer. There was a world beyond our bubble. People weren't heathens or infidels, just humans navigating life like the rest of us. And slowly, I realized that 13th Street wasn't just a place on a map, but a metaphor for perspective—a shift from rigid thinking to a broader, more inclusive understanding.

For the first time, that number thirteen helped me to see people for who they were, not for the labels we had lazily slapped on them. Doctors weren't 'Heathens' when we needed them, and teachers weren't 'Infidels' when they shaped our minds. We were not the complete story of the 'sheep' and the 'goats.' The world was not neatly divided into categories of 'us' versus 'them.'

But change, even one as necessary as this, wasn't easy. Many in our so-called Christian community resisted. They clung to the comfort of their labels, their criticisms, their certainties. It's hard to let go of the idea that you're always right, that your worldview is the only true one. Sort of like the phrase, "God's true church." Some turned a blind eye, others lashed out, claiming that the world outside had corrupted me and I was trying to corrupt their 'purity.'

Yet, the more I journeyed down that proverbial 13th Street, the more I realized how much richness, how much complexity, and how much beauty existed outside of the confines I had been taught. It was humbling to acknowledge that I didn't have all the answers, but it was also liberating. It freed me from the suffocating need to be right and opened up the possibility of learning from others.

The turn on 13th Street wasn't about abandoning my values, but about expanding them, about understanding that we are all part of something much bigger than our little bubbles. It was about embracing the intentionality of Perspective Thinking—choosing to see beyond our limited viewpoints and accepting that the world is full of different realities, each as valid as our own.

It was the Jack perspective of an image I could only define from my perspective the incarceration of my careless confinement to that image of thirteen that helped me understand something profound: two or more people can be correct in their assessments of reality, and yet, they may see things very differently. No, I'm not promoting that 'alternative truth' nonsense. Let's be clear—there's no such thing as an alternative truth. A lie is a lie, and the truth is not in it. But within the bounds of truth, there exists the undeniable fact that our perspectives—our mental furnishings—can shape how we experience and interpret the world around us.

We can observe the same real thing, like a work of masterpiece in an art museum. The art itself is real, the brushstrokes, the canvas, the pigments, all tangible. But the conclusions we draw, the emotions it stirs in us, the meaning we assign—those vary, depending on who we are, what we've lived, and how we've been taught to see. These are not falsehoods, but the honest reflections of our individual perspectives.

As I sat, gazing at that seemingly magical three-dimensional number thirteen, it became clear how easy it is for honest people to reach different conclusions. From the top, one might simply see two parallel dashes. From the left, obscuring part of the one, someone might report seeing a three, an eight, or even as 3-year-old Jack did - a B. From another angle, you might notice an eleven. And at the right distance, where the numbers seem to touch, yes—someone might indeed see a B.

This didn't mean any one of us was wrong. We were all seeing what we were seeing. It was real to us, shaped by where we stood and how we looked at it. The truth of the thirteen remained unshaken, but our observations, our mental furnishings, defined the way we interpreted it. We understand from the inside of the bubble. We are trained from the outside trainers who are also teaching from limited bubbles. Often, we may find ourselves confined by the very community of bubbles that are no better off. They are those whose furnishings not only look but, feel and smell similar to our own. Perspective matters, not because it alters truth, but because it informs how we engage with reality. Sometimes a little movement may not hurt. We can call such a movement 'consideration'.

THE DIFFERENCE BETWEEN A LIE AND PERSPECTIVE

Let's make this clearer

A **lie** is intentional deception. It is when someone knowingly distorts or denies reality with the purpose of misleading others. A lie has no basis in truth and seeks to create a false narrative or hide the actual facts. For example, if the sky is blue and someone says it's green, that's a lie. The person is consciously ignoring the truth in favor of spreading misinformation. Lies deny what is real, replacing facts with fabrications, and they hold no weight when confronted with the truth.

Perspective, on the other hand, is how we interpret reality based on our personal experiences, upbringing, culture, and environment. Perspective is not a distortion of truth—it's a viewpoint, a lens through which we see and understand the world. Unlike a lie, perspective is built on the actual truth, but it acknowledges that people may see the same event or situation in different ways. Two people looking at the same painting might describe it differently—not because one is lying, but because their personal backgrounds influence their interpretations.

Let me explain again what my son Jack saw. We really have a developing need to understand and not underestimate the power of personal perspective. Perspectives can change when multiple angles are shared. Let's reexamine the 10 ft. tall three-dimensional number "13" now standing in an open field. From one angle, a person may see the number clearly as a "13." From another angle, it could look like a "B" or even an "11." None of these observations are lies—they are all honest perspectives based on where the observer is positioned. The object remains a "13," but the way it's perceived varies based on location of observance and the interpretation of perspective.

My conclusion: Jack did not lie. Jack shared with me his personal and defendable perception. That was his intelligent perspective.

A **lie** ignores the truth, trying to replace it with something that isn't real. **Perspective** interprets the truth, shaped by a person's unique view of the personalized observances of the world around. Understanding this distinction helps us navigate conversations where different viewpoints arise, reminding us that not every differing opinion is a denial of truth—it could simply be a different perspective on the same reality. In short, perspective is not about denying reality but interpreting it.

Making It Work:

The intentional art of Perspective Thinking finds its strength in the field of consideration. It begins with the act of stepping away from our fixed position on a matter and consciously moving to the vantage point of another. From this position, we begin to realize that what the other person sees is shaped by their unique experiences and worldview. While we will never perfectly see through their eyes, we can gain a deeper understanding—a momentary glimpse—into the mental and emotional 'furnishings' that shape their perspective. This can only happen when we intentionally commit to understanding the perspectives and positions of others.

Perspective Thinking is not about agreement; it's about comprehension. The power lies in this: by recognizing the difference between how we interpret an experience and how others do, we open the door to clearer communication and more meaningful dialogue. In practice, this might look like taking the time to ask questions, listen deeply, and resist the urge to immediately counter. Instead, we reflect on what might be driving the other person's view. This is not to justify, but to understand—and therein lies the potential for real growth.

When we demonstrate our willingness to visit another's perspective, we make it easier for them to consider ours. In fact, we may find that our own perspectives were not as clear—or even as real—as we once thought. Perspective Thinking gives us flexibility in a world that increasingly feels inflexible. It unlocks the power of diplomacy, answering simple but imposing questions like 'Why do they eat bread?' and 'Why do they eat rice?' And even more introspectively, it asks, 'Why is it my business?' or 'Why do I need to know?'

Perspective Thinking teaches us what *is* our business and what *isn't*. It moves closer to difficult realities—unthreatening, yet fully engaged.

Consider the young girl who hasn't yet seen her thirteenth birthday, a child who has become the object of her older brother's violent affection and force. Do we truly understand the term *statutory rape* when we fail to step into her perspective? Using Perspective Thinking, we can see through her eyes: the sting of embarrassment, the weight of shame, and the haunting fears she now lives with. Sadly, by giving her space to share her experience, we may also confront the tragic reality that she has been driven to believe this is how life is, and that she should be proud to be a mother before thirteen.

Perspective Thinking frees the mind from Cultural Incarcerations and Confinements. Perspective thinking expands the bubble by welcoming new and updated furnishings that help to beautify communities and up-value the cultures. Perspective Thinking welcomes back the true well-trained thinkers to civic education and civic duty. Perspective Thinking reduces the impacts of racism, xenophobia, homophobia, transphobia, and many other phobias that are really resulting from fears of those demeaned. Fears of the indigent and oppressed will open creative doors providing much needed assistance beyond the usual dismissal and scorn.

The intentionality of Perspective Thinking has far reaching impacts. Creatively, we can produce new ways and avenues to defeat challenges that seem impossible to overcome.

The Applied Art of Perspective Thinking

Perspective Thinking is more than a concept; it's the applied art of consideration. It's about stepping out of our bubble, however comfortable or familiar, and moving toward understanding—recognizing that differences in viewpoints don't always need agreement, but they do deserve respect. This simple, yet transformative act can open doors we never imagined.

In the evolving workplace, Perspective Thinking is a winner. In human resources, it fosters an environment where diversity isn't just a goal but a thriving reality. It's the tool that can dismantle biases, reduce conflicts, and create inclusive spaces where everyone feels valued. In leadership, it becomes the foundation of empathetic decision-making, allowing leaders to make choices informed by multiple viewpoints, resulting in more effective and impactful outcomes.

Conflict resolution? Perspective Thinking is the key that unlocks new approaches. When we understand the root of a conflict through the lens of someone else's experiences, the solutions become clearer, fairer, and more sustainable. Imagine the power of this in communities, organizations, or even on a global scale—bridging divides once thought impossible.

This simple concept, when practiced intentionally, becomes a tool to defeat challenges that once seemed insurmountable. Perspective Thinking is an evolving, adaptable solution for modern life's complexities. It doesn't just help us understand others—it transforms us into better listeners, leaders, and human beings, paving the way for a future where barriers fall, and connections flourish.

Let's ignite some Discussion

Questions for Understanding Others:

1. What assumptions am I making about this person's perspective that might not be true?
2. How would I feel if I were in their position, facing the same challenges?
3. What experiences or values might be shaping their beliefs and reactions?
4. Have I taken the time to listen without judgment or the intent to correct?
5. What biases or stereotypes could be clouding my ability to see their perspective clearly?
6. How would this conversation change if I approached it with curiosity instead of certainty?
7. What cultural or societal influences might have shaped this person's worldview differently from my own?
8. What common ground can I find, even if we disagree on important points?

9. How can I show empathy without necessarily agreeing with their perspective?

10. In what ways could their perspective offer me new insights or ways of thinking?

Introspective Questions:

1. How often do I challenge my own perspectives and invite alternative viewpoints?

2. Am I more focused on being right than on understanding the other person?

3. What personal biases might be preventing me from seeing the situation clearly?

4. Why does this person's perspective make me uncomfortable or defensive?

5. What do I stand to learn from considering another person's viewpoint, even if I don't agree?

6. When was the last time I changed my opinion after genuinely considering someone else's perspective?

7. How willing am I to acknowledge when my perspective might be limited or flawed?

8. What have I learned about myself in situations where I disagreed with someone's perspective?

9. Am I creating space in my life for perspectives that challenge my own, or am I surrounding myself with people who only reinforce my views?

10. What is one belief or viewpoint I hold that could benefit from the insight of another perspective?

MAN IN POPULATION

(In other words, spiritual manipulation – Another type of Cultural Incarceration and Confinement)

I wasn't always a man. Like everyone else, I started life outside my mother's womb, and from that moment, I was left mostly to the guidance of my family and those they trusted to shape my world. From the start, I was part of a controlled society. If you're honest, you'd likely agree that you were raised in a similar, closed environment—protected, in a sense, from the dangers or influences outside of your personal bubble.

Our early years are typically shaped by those around us—parents, guardians, or other authority figures. These people control who we associate with, the conditions of our upbringing, and what we're exposed to. As children, we don't have much choice in these matters, whether we're rich or poor, regardless of our race or gender. Our choices are metered and limited.

My father, now 102 years old, was a member of the United Methodist Church. Growing up in a Methodist family, I spent time in the places where he once lived and got to know the people and social order that once swirled around him. I built close ties with many members of the United Methodist community, and they taught me a lot. I learned their creeds, their rituals, and also their superstitions and beliefs—ideas passed down through generations.

These communities were sheltered. A few key families within these circles held control, safeguarding their traditions and secrets. But even then, much of what we learned, whether true or not, shaped how we saw the world.

Now, as I reflect on this, I can see the lines between intentional manipulation for gain and unintentional manipulation wrapped in tradition. Sometimes, people knowingly influence others to maintain power or control. Other times, traditions simply continue, without questioning, and the manipulation happens unintentionally—wrapped in a belief that "this is just how things are. I saw many of those communities as very sheltered.

I began to notice that many of the beliefs they seemed to live by weren't truly grounded in any form of reason tied to the Bible itself. Instead, the pastor's role in several of these congregations appeared to be measured by their showmanship and ability to entertain. It wasn't about the message; it was about controlling the emotional experience to such a degree that goosebumps and cheers became the measure of success. Young people, seeing this, thought to themselves, 'I can do that too,' and for many, this was considered their call to ministry. In that tradition, preaching often started with a biblical text or story, but quickly veered off into personal or political commentary. These preachers became the mouthpieces of God in the eyes of their congregations, shaping thoughts and beliefs in ways that were often disconnected from scripture and grounded more in spectacle.

In the mid 1950's my dad had been taking so-called Bible studies from some well-meaning members of the Seventh Day Adventist church. His wife, my mom, was a third generation Adventist. She was rather laid back in her enforcement of her beliefs. I was never really certain of what she believed because we did not discuss it much. I think she believed that the Bible told everyone to go to church on Saturday.

In reflecting on my upbringing, especially with the Seventh

Day Adventist influence through my parents, I noticed that many of the beliefs and practices, though sincerely followed, were not always based on reason or even rooted deeply in the Bible. They were often traditions that were passed down, almost unquestioned, and sometimes absurd, from generation to generation.

One such practice was the belief that financial giving equated to pleasing God, and for many, this went beyond mere tithing—it became a form of sacrifice, even to the point of going into debt. My mother taught us that we were to earn money and give it to God. In that order I learned that God was synonymous with the church. Whenever God needed money, we were to go into our pockets and sacrifice. So as a child, I saw no distinction between the church and God. If the church called for money, it was as though God Himself had a hand in my pocket. Over time, I realized that this wasn't just an expression of faith—it was an unintentional manipulation born from tradition.

People, in their genuine desire to be blessed or to earn divine favor, often put themselves in difficult financial situations because the church, synonymous with God in their eyes, demanded it. There was little space to question why God would want them to suffer materially for the sake of financial sacrifice. These beliefs were seldom debated or reasoned through; they were just followed.

This kind of manipulation is subtle. It doesn't come from a place of malice—it comes from deeply entrenched tradition. But it still binds people to actions that, if examined, might not align with their well-being or even the core teachings they believe in. The conflation of church, tradition, and God is powerful, and unless one steps back to think critically, they may find themselves caught in a cycle of blind adherence. This, to me, is the real danger: when manipulation becomes so ingrained in tradition that we don't even recognize it for what it is.

Daddy wasn't much different. He became the first Seventh Day Adventist in his family. He became the enforcer. I believe that is why my mother did not share much when it came to dogma or the regional or local teachings of the church. They both lived honestly in the belief that they held membership in God's true church.

The teachings of the church were at the core of the family's fundamental structure and code of beliefs. Often, we would hear what the Bible said. People who could not read were often telling us what the Bible said. In our home culture, I would read. We were encouraged to listen to Bible stories and Sabbath School lessons. On Saturday's were had to go to church. We were trained to regurgitate what we had learned from our daily Bible lessons that were really statements of obedience to the denominational indoctrination and control. The system guided what we were to believe, think, and understand. If we repeated what we were told to repeat, then we were safe in the Ark of Safety; or the Ark of Jesus. If we didn't care or got it wrong, we could be compared to the Heathens and Infidels that would not join our church family.

Believe it or not, there were members in that little church that ate food. They ate real chicken (you know – the "cluck cluck" kind). I mean we had some of the best fried chicken that one can imagine. My mother would make a mean, I mean, that lady pushed the boundaries of taste upward when she made meatloaf. We had hamburgers, hotdogs, turkey, bologna and many other meats. I enjoyed venison or deer-meat when it was available. But one of my favorites that we would fight over as kids was getting that additional piece of beef sausage. The smell, the taste is still moving tastebuds in my memory today.

Some members of our church were vegetarians. They pushed a vegetarian diet that included meat substitutes that were sold by the denomination. Yes, there were brands like Cedar Lakes, Loma Linda, and Worthington Foods. We often were pushed to live in both worlds. Sometimes the pressure silenced our mouths but not our taste. We had to decide who we would surround ourselves with and who we would not. We were told what to eat, how to dress, what we could drink, where we could and couldn't go, and who would be our friends and who we would hate. There I said it – "Hate."

The other thing we learned as children is that Jesus is here. We also learned that Jesus went away. Even more, we learned Jesus is coming back. He'll be back within the next couple of weeks was pushed on us on a weekly basis, and that he's only coming back to get Seventh Day Adventists that don't eat meat. Some would teach us, as some continue to do it today, that meat eating makes God angry.

By now you've got me figured out. I catch a good laugh now and then. I'm often humored by the contradictions of faith. As a child I was led to believe God had guardian angles and recording angels that followed you everywhere you went. They were taking notes on everything you do and speak. They monitored your relationship to God's true church (you may guess by now who that is). Jesus was going to burn up and destroy all those who had an opportunity to accept the Seventh Day Adventist message.

Jesus was going to throw non-Adventist, and people like us children that did something naughty, into the lake of fire and brimstone and that was going to be their end, and if we did not do everything, they ordered us to do that end would be ours as well. When Jesus, that we were talking to this morning, who is with us always gets back, we will go with him and from that point, we will live 'Happily ever-after.' All my friends, and all those who refused to do what daddy or the church said to do was going to be executed along with Satan, his angels, the Pope, Catholic people, those with physical disabilities, those with mental disabilities, rich people, and those who speak with an accent. To be more brutal in my description, God is going to destroy people who, by our account, talk funny. I learned all of that before my first day of school.

What a scary life that must have been you may say. No, it wasn't scary at all. Understand this please, that picture I hope to have painted is of a mentally controlling segment; a small swath of my earlier days. We were free to be children, to grow to meet other children. We were encouraged to meet older children and adults. Others were always under the microscope of suspicion. There were test they had to past to reach the inner-circle. They were judged by the fact that they ate meat – especially that meat coming from the pig. I learned that many Black people in my community ate everything, I'm told from the 'rooter' to the 'tooter.'

White people ate ham and bacon and pork hotdogs. As Adventist, we were supposed to be like the like the imagined life and existence of 'white people.' What is that supposed to mean? Picture that, we were to assimilate ourselves into a cultural mimic of those we often spoke about in negative terms and tones.

We were almost fully stricken Pentecostals in my early days. Our choir and church services were exciting and energetic especially when those conference people came. Those people were the creme de la crème, the cream or the crop (I never figured that one out), they were the 'Best of the best.' People used to jump up and spin around and go into fits that sometimes had them to pass out or be taken out – sometimes to the hospital. Some would get so caught up in the spirit that they would froth or foam at the mouth.

Then some white guys in black face came. Things changed. The music changed. The preaching changed. We were getting refined. We were getting ready for Jesus to come and the one distinct thing that would not be accepted was living black while black. We had to distance ourselves from the culture. We had to become more critical of the culture – the community in which we lived. We were suspicious about everyone and every intention. We were God's true Israelites of the last days. Yes, we were the spiritual Israel – God's chosen people. We were the remnant, of the remnant, of the remnant. We were cut out and set aside. We would be protected during the coming last days events.

They were going to shut down our Sabbath keeping churches, and by order of the Pope, forced into Sunday worship. It was all about the beast. Those who worship the beast. Those who were worldly, the ring wearers, those who wore jewelry of any kind, those who have ever thought about anything in which the word sex could be even imagined were to be destroyed. The only things we had to do was be good, eat good, wear used clothes, be humble, don't smoke, don't drink beer, don't drink any tea that was not supplied by the church (Kafree Tea), don't speak to people we have not vetted, hate the people whom the adults hate, and follow one source, one stream of information. This is the truth, as long as it is supplied by Your Friends the Seventh Day Adventist. Wow! I've said a whole lot and haven't even begun to cover the name Ellen G. White.

Momma meant well. Daddy meant well. The old people who had no children who gave advice on raising children meant well. Those who taught the Bible but did not read because they were illiterate meant well. All of these people were very protective at times. They often fought for an imagined and self-serving reality that was utopic and fairytale-ish. Often the reality was the 'man in population was taken advantage of by manipulations that fed the instigated imaginations of what they learned could be. Another way to say this, heaven is everything you don't have but want. It is the streets or pure gold, the gates of pearl, the heavenly foundations produced by every precious stone that we assign value. It is the dream of those who served as tenant workers that never owned land of their own. In heaven they are promised their very own gardens and vineyards. Remember this, 'All dogs go to heaven.'

We had what we called 'socials' from time to time. It was a time when we would come together in Sister Parker's house or the small room in the back of our little church; our base of all knowledge. At the social, we could play, eat cake, drink punch, eat potato chips, enjoy artificial hotdogs and not listen to music or dance. We could play games like 'Hide and Seek.' We could watch one of the new sinners that they ran away from the church because he did a magic show during the social event. Everyone in the circle meant well. We were the original MAGA's (Make All Great Adventist). Whatever they told us, or demanded of us, we believed.

They showed us pictures of bad people. They looked like me and us. The Devil was a dark angel. They showed us people who were going to heaven on picture scrolls. Seemed to me heaven was only made for white people – you know white adults with Caucasian colored children who pet lions. It was our task to become like the people they despised. All along, not knowing the population of earth in the present and the 6,000 to 8,000 years of human existence that preceded the current living population, only 144,000 would be saved and they will not be meat eaters. It was the culture of that little church that life centered around. In short it was a cult.

Many, who don't understand this point, are going to be infuriated by my commentary. We like many Christian cultures and other religious viewpoints around the world that produce a one road, one avenue, one way of understanding reality, break down into the same and fundamental category. We were a cult. All of this scaffolding of a human life was possible because from the start, there was control.

When the baby, the toddler, the young child has no reference point of the outside world that exists beyond their reality. They can be told anything. Be careful of those who dominate you and push you and your community for control. Be careful of those who teach that knowledge is bad. Be careful of those who present you with dilemmas and are the only ones capable of supplying the antidotes and answers. Such answers to the envisioned dilemmas are usually an intentionally guided scenario of the ancient 'us' vs. 'them' setup. They often teach their listeners the, 'They are your problem' gimmicks, ploys, and smoke screens.

Since the beginning, history has repeated the same story of human control. It happens in religion, politics, even in media control. We learn early that we are first sheltered and guided by those who love us, those who claim to care about our futures. This raises the question, are we steering our own intellectual journeys or following pre-programmed routes? Are we losing or being steered away from the art and privilege of critical thinking? Are we all caught up in the social order that robs us of our individual rights to consider and understand the realities of human existence around us? Are we the 'Man in Population' or are we the careless product of sometimes intentional, sometimes unintentional 'Manipulation?'

Manipulation can be both intentional and unintentional. Those well-meaning people who taught us the Bible I believe were unintentionally assisting in driving our viewpoints and the mass production of cultural created fears. They told us the rights and wrongs and packaged them in an 'If you don't do it our believed way' a sadistic God is going to set fire to you and slowly kill you to his joyful sorrow.

Everybody who made me uncomfortable is going to hell. Everybody who does not believe as I do is going to hell. Everybody that does not share my faith is going to hell. Every lifestyle I am uncomfortable with is going to hell. Everyone who humiliated me is going to hell. Everybody who saw me as stupid because I had dyslexia and did not know it is going to hell. Our nation is going to hell because they refuse to vote for one guy or gal.

We are becoming who we are and who we were. We are repeating the same playbook that has been around since BC or BCE times. We have gone from the verbal instructions to get to other places. Later, after the tangible development of mapping and maps, we were able to follow mapped instructions. We could get from point A to point B and beyond guided by maps. The map evolved. Today most of us are guided by the technology of Global Positioning Systems

(GPS). Many of us can find our way very efficiently. Many vehicles are guided by this same technology. However, many struggle behind the stress of rather than being a thoughtful member of the neighborhood, we are guided to suspicion and outright hate. We are told what our enemies are up to.

In our little cult, the child was taught that the enemy was the devil. Then they went on to demonize every human being and situation, real or unreal, that made the teachers of our so-called faith and cultural equivalents uncomfortable or scared. I am believing more and more that just as GPS provides convenience, it has the unwelcomed capacity to dull our map-reading skills.

Consider this, external influences may offer comfort but can also weaken our critical thinking. We can reclaim this "manual control" by fostering awareness, encouraging reflection, and promoting intellectual freedom. In other words, is it possible to influence thought responsibly without crossing into manipulation? Influence, when ethical, should guide people toward deeper understanding rather than direct their conclusions. The human family needs, more than ever before, a more intentional approach to shaping our worldview rather than being passively molded by external forces that narrow our scope and responsible reasoning. Jesus taught his followers to love their neighbors. Many of the current American, so-called and self-titled, followers of Jesus driven influences teach us to despise our neighbors.

How did all of this happen? Our parents taught us to look both ways before crossing the street. We got excited over the blindfold. Somebody said, "Close your eyes and follow me." We forgot how to read; missing the detours, 'ONE WAY' warnings and 'DO NOT ENTER' signs. We forgot we were safer holding hands.

I remember when the UPC codes first started appearing on products in stores. The power-brains of fear started to bring to our attention this was the mark of the beast. Everything the snake oil hucksters don't like are a mark of the beast. Education is a mark of the beast. Science is a mark of the beast. The Covid vaccine they use to insert micro-chips and other technologically advanced items are pumped into the population as tracking devises so that the 'One World Order' can track our every move. How deranged, the man in population who has no reference point that exposes manipulation. At what point does a mentally responsible patron of faith, politics, and current cultural leanings ask the very vital question, acting out of genuine belief or out of a sense of duty to a tradition that hasn't been honestly questioned? Consider this, you just may be the proper goose but, much of what is directed in your direction may be a manipulative use of propaganda.

THE POWERS OF IMAGINATION

The role of imagination in shaping reality, possibilities, and potential futures.

If you're reading this, you're likely already aware that some pretty wild thoughts circulate in the world around you. People imagine all sorts of odd and far-fetched interpretations of reality. The challenge is that many of these imaginings remain confined to the mind, rarely venturing beyond that space. Comedian and radio personality D.L. Hughley nailed this idea when he said:

"The most dangerous place for Black people to live is in white people's imaginations."

That line struck a chord with me because I immediately grasped the layers of meaning behind it. In my own experiences, I've witnessed how people grab onto a fragment of information and run with it, creating entire narratives based on little more than a sliver of truth. Once this fragment slips into their mental bubble, it doesn't remain isolated. Their imagination—what I like to think of as the 'interior designer' of the mind—kicks into high gear, rearranging the furnishings of thought to accommodate this new and/or strange piece of data.

This process happens instantly. Before you know it, people's minds are warping and reshaping that information to fit comfortably into their pre-existing worldview. It's a mental reflex, an almost unconscious act of ordering and molding ideas into something familiar—something that aligns with their expectations, beliefs, or even fears.

Imagination, then, becomes a mirror of the quirky,

sometimes distorted interior of our minds. It reflects not just what we know but also our insecurities, desires, and misunderstandings. It can transform the mundane into the extraordinary, swing wildly between sanity and absurdity, and reveal hidden truths or amplify falsehoods. It sets the stage for the stories we tell ourselves, stories where we are often the unaware actors following a script we don't fully understand.

For instance, take Grandpa Joe—G Joe for short. G Joe is your classic grumpy old man with deeply traditional views, the kind who sent his wife to church while he stayed home, bemoaning the day the neighborhood got "invaded" by people of different races. He spends his days glued to his favorite news channel, soaking in the steady drip of confirmation bias, clinging to an America he believes once existed.

Now fast forward to Thanksgiving. The family is all gathered, but there's an added element of tension: Bob and Jim are bringing a friend from Liberia. Each family member is imagining how this will play out, mentally rearranging their own "furniture" to accommodate the new dynamic. In their minds, they've already scripted parts of the conversation, projected G Joe's inevitable outbursts, and prepared their responses. Every person in that room is living a slightly different version of the same event in their imagination.

This is the power of imagination: it shapes how we perceive the world and how we expect reality to unfold. It is the driving force behind human creativity, innovation, and problem-solving. Every invention, every piece of art, every social movement began as a seed of thought in someone's imagination. From the first tools our ancestors created to the latest technological breakthroughs, imagination has pushed us forward.

But just as imagination can inspire the lime-light of greatness, it can also lead to darkness. Left unchecked, it can become a prison for some. There's a thin line between imagination as a force for hope and possibility, and imagination as a spiral into despair. For some, when their inner world becomes clouded by negative thoughts, the imagination starts to spin dark stories, crafting an existence where there seems to be no escape.

Imagine a person replaying their past mistakes and regrets, furnishing their mental space with pain, self-doubt, and loneliness. The imagination, which once built dreams, begins to build walls. It warps their sense of reality, convincing them that they are trapped, unworthy, or hopeless. The vibrant world of possibility slowly darkens into a humid dense fog and suffocating maze.

When imagination turns this way, it can push someone toward the deepest despair—where suicide feels like the only option. In these moments, the person's mental bubble becomes a house of horrors, filled with stories that convince them there's no light at the end of the tunnel. The imagination, meant to be a liberator, becomes their captor.

But that's not the end of the story.

The imagination that brings people to such dark places can also be the key to their liberation. Just as it can build a prison, it can also tear those walls down. The same powerful force that creates narratives of despair can be redirected to write new stories—stories of hope, resilience, and endless possibilities. The truth is, the imagination is yours to control.

Yes, there are times when it may feel like your imagination has taken the wheel, driving you into places you never intended to go. But the real power lies in recognizing that you are the author of your story. Your imagination is not something that controls you; it's a tool that you can wield to shape your reality. And when you understand that, the possibilities are limitless.

Every great invention, every revolution in human history, began with someone who dared to take control of their imagination. They envisioned a world not as it is, but as it could be. That same power lives within each of us. We can choose to imagine a brighter future, not only for ourselves but for the world around us. When we learn to harness our imagination, we become the architects of possibility, the creators of change.

The key is learning to recognize when your imagination is working against you. When those dark thoughts begin to creep in, you must confront them and ask, *"Is this the story I want to tell? Is this the reality I want to create?"* In doing so, you reclaim the narrative. You decide whether to dwell in fear or move toward possibility.

So, the next time you catch your imagination wandering into the shadows, stop. Take a breath. Remind yourself that your mind is a powerful force, and it is yours. You can choose to direct it, to rewrite the stories that no longer serve you, and to create the future you desire.

Imagination is the spark that ignites the flame of human progress. And you, my friend, are the keeper of that spark. Now, go light the world.

Positive Aspects of Imagination:

1. **Creative Force Behind Innovation**: Imagination is the engine of human progress. Every invention, every piece of technology, and every artistic creation started as an idea, imagined in the mind. From the wheel to

space exploration, it's our ability to picture what doesn't yet exist that leads us to innovation.

2. **Vision of Potential**: Imagination allows us to envision not only what *is*, but what *could be*. It helps us think outside the box, solve problems, and push boundaries beyond the constraints of our current reality. Whether it's through art, science, or social progress, imagination shows us the paths we can take toward a better future.

3. **Empathy and Understanding**: Imagination isn't just for creativity; it also fuels empathy. It allows us to place ourselves imaginatively in someone else's shoes, to understand perspectives and experiences beyond our own. This mental flexibility can break down barriers between people, leading to stronger connections and more inclusive societies.

4. **Personal Empowerment**: Imagination gives individuals the ability to rewrite their own narratives, to break free from limiting beliefs, and to envision a different version of themselves. Whether it's imagining a life of success, overcoming personal challenges, or picturing a more fulfilled version of oneself, imagination is the foundation of personal transformation.

Negative Aspects of Imagination:

1. **Distorting Reality**: When unchecked, imagination can lead to distorted views of reality. As comedian D.L. Hughley said, *"The most dangerous place for black people to live, is in white people's imaginations."* This observation underscores how harmful stereotypes, born from biased imagination, can lead to prejudice, fear, and

systemic injustice.

2. **Filling in the Blanks with Bias**: People often take incomplete information and use imagination to "fill in the gaps." This is where imagination becomes dangerous. Rather than seeking truth, the mind crafts false realities based on fears, biases, or misinformation. These imagined narratives can lead to unfair judgments, actions, or policies that negatively affect entire communities.

3. **Imagination as a Tool for Manipulation**: When wielded with malicious intent, imagination becomes a tool for manipulation. History is filled with examples of powerful groups using imaginary threats, false narratives, or conspiracies to control populations. In modern times, we see this in politics, where misinformation is used to incite fear, manipulate votes, or reinforce harmful ideologies.

4. **Isolation and Insanity**: When individuals become too trapped in their own imagination, they can lose touch with reality altogether. This detachment can lead to isolation, paranoia, and in extreme cases, mental instability. People who live more in their imagined world than in reality may struggle to engage with others or face the truth about their surroundings.

Bridging the Gap Between Imagination and Reality:

Imagination, when guided by reason and empathy, is a creative force for good. But when imagination is distorted by bias, fear, or self-interest, it can become a tool for destruction. Our challenge is to harness the positive aspects of imagination while guarding against its potential to deceive or harm.

We must remain vigilant and question what we imagine. Are we creating something positive, or are we filling the unknown with harmful assumptions? By being honest with ourselves and expanding our awareness of reality, we can better control the power of imagination and use it as a tool for progress rather than a gravity driven vortex for regression.

Before I Leave This Section

It had been a grueling day. I'd worked through lunch, skipped breakfast, and was running on fumes. On my way home, I stopped at one of my favorite grocery stores. It had the most incredible deli. This place wasn't just about food—it was an experience. The warm, yeasty aroma of freshly baked bread, the smoky scent of wood-fired pizza, and the crisp tang of fresh produce created a symphony of smells that would make anyone hungry. You could pick up various soups and fresh vegetables along with any other items you may need from the local market.

All I wanted was one of their fresh made to order legendary subs. I was hoping to eat it on my way home during rush-hour travel. I wasn't going to pick up much speed but, I could sure put down one of their fine deli sandwiches. It would be just enough to get me through that rush-hour traffic. Besides, I was not really up to during my drive home.

In the store, it was my turn. They called my number at the deli. The staff behind the counter laughed as I piled on the toppings. I was ordering things that my wife would often protest when she was with me. I was getting it all: a buttered and toasted sub-roll, a thick slathering of mayo, an overloading swipe of hot pepper hoagie spread, a heaping pile of smoked turkey, a mixture of muenster and provolone cheese, crisp romaine, perfectly sliced tomatoes, red onions, and their famous homemade pickles. Some banana peppers, black olives, a drizzle of oil and vinegar. It was dusted with freshly cracked mixed peppercorns and fragranced with some nice blessings of oregano—it was a masterpiece.

They wrapped it all up; squeezing my culinary expectations into what would be to me white gift-wrapping and sent me off to get into another line to pay as they called the next number in line. As I stood in line waiting to pay, someone in line ahead of me turned and smiled. She had a very welcoming look. I thought maybe she was going to tell me I could go ahead of her being I only had one item; well two if you counted my coke. Yeah, I had a coke and a smile, as she continued to fix her eyes on me.

"I know you," she said.

I froze, trying to place her face. It was vaguely familiar, but not in a way that made sense. She looked different from anyone I thought I knew: dressed casually in jeans and a very nice shirt. She was holding milk, a carton of eggs, and a loaf of bread. Her smile was warm, kind.

"You do?" I asked, tentatively.

She chuckled. "Yeah, I'm the one you're always chasing down the driveway with that big dog of yours on trash day. You tend to run a little late most weeks. You know," as her kind and pleasant laugh continued. I didn't get it. She told me what street I lived on and described my house. She told me how beautiful my home and community were. And just like that, it clicked. Of course. I saw her—him, I mean, *her*—every week, but never like this. Without the orange safety vest, the heavy work gloves, or the truck, she was almost unrecognizable. Clean, relaxed, and just... human.

"Oh! Right. Wow, sorry, I didn't even recognize you out of uniform," I stammered.

"No problem," she said with a shrug. "It's nice to meet you when I'm not hauling your trash."

We laughed, and she asked me my name. I told her both my first name and last, with pride as we shook hands. Of, course she had set her items on the counter by then. I knew she was telling me the truth when I noticed the tattoo on the back of her hand.

I asked her what made her choose to be a garbageman; she was so beautiful. She shared a little about her family: her kids and her husband. Her husband worked two jobs while she was in school. So, she told me how she took the job on the garbage truck to help support her household while her husband went back to school so that he did not have to work two jobs. They wanted to stay in their community; especially with the kids in school.

"Wow," I said, still processing. She had been this figure in my mind—a "garbageman," part of the scenery of my life. And here she was, a whole person with a name, a story, a family, and dreams. I realized she was a regular person. I thought she was one of those hard women that had a voice like some dude. I really didn't care. She was a service worker. I was a professional.

I nodded along as she continued talking, but if I'm honest, I barely absorbed her words. My mind was spinning with the realization of how much I had filled in the blanks of her life with my own assumptions.

"Well, it was great talking to you," she said eventually, lifting her small bag of groceries. "Have a good one. I'll see you soon.

Don't be late," she said laughing as headed for the doors. "Take care."

"You too," I said. And then she was gone.

On the drive home, I thought about the encounter. For months, my wife and I had joked about "the garbageman," never once stopping to consider *her* life. We'd speculated about who "he" was, imagined "his" rough-and-tumble personality, and even decided "he" probably didn't have kids but might enjoy a beer or two or three after work.

We didn't even acknowledge that the garbageman could be a woman. She wasn't a person in our eyes—just a role. And now? She knew my family name. She knew that my office was in the same town that she lived in. She shared a piece of her family story with me. She had shattered the caricature I painted in my head.

When I got home, I pulled into the garage. I grabbed my folders to go over as I prepared for tomorrow's meetings. She got me. She snuck-up on me as I leaned across the seat to grab the white bag that had converted into a trash bag. She said, "Surprise!" I said the 'D' word. I was busted. My wife greeted me with her usual suspicion.

"What did you eat?" she asked, wrinkling her nose. "Your breath smells like onions."

"Oh, just a sub," I said, waving her off. I needed an immediate and emergency level distraction. I remembered the garbageman. Here's how that went:

"But guess who I ran into at the store?"

She raised an eyebrow. "An old friend?"

"Nope. The garbageman."

Her eyes widened. "Wait, really? What was he doing there?"

"*She*," I corrected, a little sharper than I meant to. "She was buying groceries. And we talked. She's married, has kids, and her husband is in school. She's really nice."

"Wait, she's a woman?" my wife asked, genuinely surprised. "Huh. I guess I never thought about it." Her eyes widened. Her eyebrows raised. "I can't believe it," my wife said, shaking her head. "I always thought…" She trailed off, and I knew exactly what she meant.

We had both filled in the blanks about this woman's life with assumptions based on her job and appearance. But standing in that grocery store, she wasn't "the garbageman" anymore—she was a hardworking mother, a supportive wife, and someone who showed kindness to strangers even after a long day.

"Neither did I," I admitted. "We've been calling her 'the garbageman' for months without even considering her as a person."

My wife nodded slowly. "It's weird, isn't it? How easy it is to just… not see someone for who they really are."

"Yeah," I said, thinking back to her smile at the store. "We owe her better than that."

"She asked and I told her our names."

"That's great. Did you get her name?"

"Oh! I never thought about asking."

"How could you?"

"Well, I guess at the end of the day; she's still the garbageman."

My wife just shook her head. "You gave her our name. You could have politely asked her name." She just shook her head. She just shook her head. She shook her head. Later that night, as I thought about the encounter, I realized how often we define people by a single aspect of their identity. It's easy to forget that everyone has a story, a family, accomplishments and struggles of their own. I made a note to myself: never again would I let assumptions define someone I hadn't taken the time to understand.

THE REACTIVE MIND

How reactions, often rooted in emotion and impulse, shape actions and decisions.

I entered Oakwood College in 1980. One of my many favorite classes was An Introduction to Psychology. I did not know at the time my curiosity would carry me further to study Clinical Psychology, Geriatric Psychology, and other areas in this field. I was so curious that I wanted to study the Psychology of Religion.

Religion, not just the areas of so-called Christian religion often fascinated me. How is it that something so abstract can guide many people into doing some of the most outrageous things, believing some of the most outrageous things, and paying out of their resources that often clash with their material resources outrageous sums of money. Here's how it works in many areas of European and Western guided Christendom. God loves you – NOW PAY UP! The believer is guided to purchase faith on the installment plan. In giving intervals, the faithful is guided to give of their resources to enrich the institution of so-called believers. They are told, "This is God's money." However, God's money must be taken to the bank to cover the expenses of the institutions and their outreach programs.

When I observe the statuary, the thematic architecture and literal artistry in music and the many other ways to put on display the advertising highlights of one's institutionalized faith practices, I find myself astonished.

I am reminded of the story that had passed my way. A pastor entered his church one Sunday morning. It was cold. He wanted to prepare the church for the soon to arrive parishioners. He decided to turn on the heat. However, the furnace did not respond. He immediately called an HVAC specialist. The serviceman examined the system and concluded that the system was quite old and needed to be replaced. The pastor asked, "Well how much would that cost?' He was told more than $15,000. The pastor thought that was excessive, but he also realized the heating system was indeed old. He rapidly developed a plan.

The Pastor presented his plan to the congregation. "I know it is cold in God's house this morning. As you know, our heating and cooling system has treated us with amazing comfort for many years. It has been with us for funerals, weddings, baby services, counseling for those with an array of issues and troubles. It has been with us for decades and served us well. This morning when I came in, I turned up the temperature so that you would be comfortable in God's special house. This morning our beloved heating system said as Jesus said on the cross, 'IT IS FINISHED!' We need a new system. I don't want to send this lovely caring church into debt. We can pay for this in one morning service. It is going to cost us $20,000. We have enough people to do just that if we would just dig a little deeper in the storehouse of God's everlasting love."

He went on to encourage the people of faith. "I am going to put in the first $1,000. God has been good to me. Some of you can give cash and some can write checks for more. We just need some amazing people of faith to put their money where their heart is. Let's play some giving music as we guide the baskets and buckets through the congregation of the assembled. We can do this."

What he failed to tell the congregation is, that when the

service had ended, he took his money back. He explained it as a needed ploy to encourage the believers.

There was a little old lady in the church. She had recently lost her husband. He had been sick for some time. She lived off their combined income. They were together in their giving; making many sacrifices. But now, with her husband gone, she was struggling. It was a continued expense to make choices between needed medicines and food on her table. She was falling more and more behind in her housing and utility expenses. Impacted by the loss of a nearly lifelong friend, a husband, the father of her children, she was now falling into the despair of what to do. She was losing control. This dear lady gathered herself. She made her way to the local bus-stop. She decided to ask the pastor for help. She arrived at the church. She was invited into his office. She sat down. With tears, she poured her heart out. She explained her struggles as she asked for help. "Please. Can you help me?" The pastor responded, "I certainly will." He then invited her to pray. He will continue to pray that God will help her. End of that story. Hmm!

The things that we do. The things that we are led to believe. The many contradictions that we have woven into the fabric of our lives.

The reactive mind is a concept that refers to the unconscious dimension of the human psyche, which operates primarily through a stimulus-response mechanism. During my freshman year of college, I embarked on the study of psychology. Although my academic performance may not have reflected it, I was deeply fascinated by the subject. However, my experience in the classroom was marred by a professor who not only dismissed me as a student but also seemed to disregard my worth as a person. My imagination suggests that I didn't fit the mold of what was expected. This college, affiliated with a prominent Christian denomination, held certain cultural and social expectations that I did not meet.

I lacked the background of those who had previously attended prestigious black institutions associated with the denomination. I was not a 'blue-blood' black Christian, and I often perceived myself as 'less than,' receiving little respect from some. I was not connected to the elites of the church, and my father and my prior scholastic accomplishments were, in the eyes of some, relegated to the mental 'trash heaps.' The challenges I faced were formidable. Yet, amidst this environment, there were individuals who recognized my intellectual potential and encouraged me to persevere. The mountain I faced was steep, but it was not insurmountable. With their support, I was motivated to continue my ascent toward the summit.

The insights I gained from my freshman psychology course proved invaluable in helping me to understand both myself and the broader world. They provided me with a deeper perspective on the purposes and complexities within the world around me. As I mentioned earlier, I had a strong interest in exploring the psychology of religion, but I found no such course available. Consequently, I had to make do with the resources and courses that were offered.

One of my favorite magazines was *Psychology Today*. I enjoyed reading it as much as I did *Reader's Digest* and *National Geographic*. These extracurricular readings greatly expanded my intellectual horizons. *Psychology Today* frequently featured ads about metaphysics, which piqued my curiosity. Perhaps this would help me gain a deeper understanding? Eventually, I decided to explore it. What I discovered led me down the proverbial rabbit hole, leaving me with more questions than answers. I learned more about myself in the process. However, certain principles and foundational insights had a strong pull, drawing me back to the core teachings and well-established principles of psychology.

In Psychology 101, I was introduced to the concepts of 'Stimulus' and 'Response.' Two particularly impactful studies were the Pavlovian experiments by Ivan Pavlov and the behavioral experiments conducted by B.F. Skinner. The key takeaway was the relationship between cause and effect, suggesting that behavior in living beings can often be predicted. The stimulus-response theory, a well-researched concept, posits that learning and behavior can be understood through the interactions between stimuli and the responses they provoke.

This theoretical framework, which has evolved into a proven ideology, originated from early concepts of conditioning—a behavioral process where a response becomes more frequent or predictable in a given environment due to reinforcement. Variations of the stimulus-response theory have long served as the dominant explanation for conditioning. One notable version of this theory proposed that the mere occurrence of a new response to a given stimulus, such as in Ivan Pavlov's experiments, where dogs were conditioned to salivate in response to the ringing of a bell, exemplifies how behavior can be shaped through conditioned associations.

In other words, the 'Stimulus-Response Theory' remains a foundational framework in psychology, offering an explanation for how individuals react to external stimuli. This theory posits that learning and behavior can be understood through the interactions between stimuli and the responses they elicit. Now, let's delve deeper into this concept, exploring the logic that underpins it. The key focus here is on *reaction*. The environment—both atmospheric and human—plays a crucial role in shaping behavior, reinforcing the idea that behavior can often be predicted and controlled by understanding and manipulating stimuli.

As humans, we possess learned behaviors that often operate beneath our conscious awareness. These behaviors can either draw from a wellspring of goodness or tap into darker impulses rooted in malevolent influences. Here, I introduce you to the concept of the 'Reactive Mind.'

Our lives, filled with vivid memories, often harbor hidden stimuli that, when unnoticed, can trigger automatic reactions in our behavior. Consider the widespread issue of posttraumatic stress disorder (PTSD), where past traumatic experiences serve as triggers for reactive behaviors. While I may not be an expert on PTSD, I understand how unresolved issues from our past can provoke immediate emotional responses to situations that feel familiar and often seem beyond our control. Reactive behavior typically manifests as an instant emotional reaction to such stimuli, whether these triggers stem from past events, a friend's comment, or a partner's mood. In psychology, this reactive behavior can be observed when individuals alter their behavior or performance because they are aware of being watched. This change can be either positive or negative, depending on the context.

Being reactive often manifests as blaming others for one's choices, indicating that a person is driven more by emotions than by rational thought. Negatively, this suggests a low emotional intelligence, where the reactive individual may come across as blaming, resentful, insecure, or angry. In recent years, many Americans have become increasingly reactive, leading to visible divisions within our communities, marked by anger and rage. The social fabric of our nation is frayed by individuals with low emotional control, sometimes resulting in violence and even death.

Long-held resentments, stoked by careless rhetoric, have been unleashed, tearing away the veil that once concealed our true feelings toward others. There was a time when we valued community, where we cared about our neighbors and they seemed to care about us. However, due to our myriad differences—cultural identities, religion, race, income, sexuality, political polarization, and environmental concerns—negative energies have been amplified, leading to hypersensitivity. The result is a once-loose thread of human connection that has unraveled into an ever-widening tear. Reactive behavior creates the moth-eaten holes in our social fabric, leading some pessimists to fear that we may never be able to repair or reunite the human family.

The question I pose is, when did all of this begin? Allow me to introduce the 'Bubble Effect,' a personal theory I've observed over time. It examines how and why we understand our actions and words, how we determine what is right or wrong, and who assumes the authority to govern the lives of those who do not share our beliefs and principles. We have crossed countless cultural boundaries without pausing to ask ourselves: who gave us the authority to dictate the lives and choices of others? In other words, who appointed us as the cultural GPS?

MYTH CONCEPTIONS

Examining cultural and societal myths and how we can evolve beyond outdated beliefs.

A myth is often defined as a person, idea, or thing whose existence—whether historical, present, or future—remains unverifiable. But can a myth be futuristic? As the writer, I say yes. Myths are not just relics of the past or distortions of present realities; they are also projections of what we believe we cannot achieve.

It is a myth to claim that human creativity has limits. The dream, the determination, the will to search and innovate are evidence that we can make possible what was once unimaginable. To say that we will never record the sense of smell, for example, is a myth rooted in today's limited understanding. There is no conclusive evidence—no absolute measurement—that can truthfully define what human will and spirit cannot achieve. Yet far too often, we succumb to "myth-informed" beliefs, surrendering to defeat because we've been told that certain horizons are beyond our reach.

In truth, a myth is often the product of misinformation—an artwork that convinces the well-meaning that our future is predetermined, that the days of innovation are over, and that we are nearing the end of possibility. But time, in its essence, has no end. Even if everything ceases to exist, the story of time continues.

From the planting of the first seed, the hunting of the first meal, to the moment you read these words, we stand on the shoulders of giants, gazing forward from the peaks of progress. We've come so far—not just in distance, but in depth, understanding, and the unleashed power of human potential.

The long road behind us is a testament to our resilience; the path ahead is a promise of what's possible. We've come a long way—and this is only the beginning.

In this section, I invite you to embark on a thoughtful and patient journey with me. Together, we will unravel some of the deeply embedded myths that have traditionally shaped our intellectual lives. My hope is that, as we navigate this terrain, I can offer you a unique lens through which to examine these cultural and historical constructs, a perspective that has profoundly shaped my own thinking.

Across civilizations, we often find ourselves entangled in webs of belief—myths that, over time, become ingrained in our worldview. Many of these myths are fear-driven, and we unknowingly accept them as foundational truths. As they take root in our minds, they shape not only how we think but also how we engage with others, making it challenging to reexamine or discard what might actually be detrimental. The harm these misconceptions cause can be deeply personal, yet their impact extends far beyond the individual, sometimes rippling out into entire societies.

In this exploration, I invite you to pause and reflect with me. Let us examine these myths critically and with curiosity, pushing past their deceptive allure. What truths lie beneath the surface, and how might this journey shift our understanding of ourselves and the world around us? I am excited to share this with you, and I encourage you to remain open as we uncover new insights, together.

I've spent much of my life walking on eggshells, carefully taught to tread lightly around others because of how easily people can react when their beliefs are questioned. But as time has passed, I've learned something crucial—sometimes, you have to crack those eggshells if you truly want to move forward. I was reminded of this during a conversation with a friend over coffee, where we talked about how difficult it is to challenge ingrained ideas. People often cling to the familiar, holding on to accepted beliefs, sometimes losing sight of the reality right in front of them.

It's never easy to take an honest look at ourselves, to admit when we're wrong, and to seek out new ways of thinking. But this is exactly what we must do—forge new partnerships, embrace innovative ideas, and work together to build lasting relationships that push the ongoing development and evolution of humanity forward. The future of our global society depends on our courage to confront uncomfortable truths and grow beyond them. Only by doing so can we unlock our collective potential and create the world we hope to see.

Here are 20 'Myth Conceptions' that stand out to me; *there are so many more.*

1. "Myth: Absolutely."

Let's begin with a word we all know: "Absolute." How often have you heard it, used it, or perhaps even believed in its promise? In truth, all things and ideas that lie ahead of us are not absolute; they exist only in a predictive state, shaped by what we think might happen. To be absolute implies that we can foretell the future with complete certainty. But consider the phrase, "I have absolute faith in their ability to get the job done." What I am really expressing is my strong trust in their capability—yet it's not guaranteed. The future remains an unknown.

Think about how we use this word: "Are you absolutely

sure he will agree?" or "Is she absolutely sure that she can?" Such questions are no more reliable than an oath sworn by an unrelenting liar who promises absolute secrecy. The only thing keeping them from breaking that promise is their personal choice to be trustworthy—not some unshakable certainty.

Now, imagine December 16, 1903. My grandfather was just a four-year-old boy. For those who were listening, there were rumors about two brothers who believed they could invent a flying machine. At the time, a confident genius remarked, "I am absolutely sure if God wanted man to fly, He would have given us wings." My grandfather, like most, didn't see what was coming next. Within 24 hours of that statement, the world witnessed man's first flight.

More than a century later, here I am, the grandson of Emory Harris—a man born before humanity took to the skies. Someone, so certain about the future, was wrong. It reminds us: dream big, and never limit yourself by the absolutes of today. Reach for the stars, because the future may defy all current certainties.

2. Myth: "Time Will Be No More."

Let's start by examining some familiar phrases: "Time is about to end," "We are in the last days," or "Time is winding up." These expressions often come from those who simultaneously profess a belief in eternity, and yet, they speak with certainty about the imminent end of time. This paradox is worth exploring. Personally, I grew up in what one could call an "End Time" home. Religion had a firm grip on our understanding of the world. From an early age, my siblings and

I were immersed in a worldview that said we were living in the last days—a notion fed to us almost constantly.

This idea, it turns out, is not unique to my upbringing but is part of a much broader cultural legacy. It stretches back to the Millerite movement of the mid-19th century, where the idea of an "end time" reached a fever pitch. William Miller, a Baptist minister and farmer, declared that he had uncovered a mathematical formula based on Biblical prophecy, which predicted the imminent return of Jesus Christ. His followers trusted this interpretation without question. The date was first set for October 1843. The failure of that event is now part of religious history. But Miller persisted, claiming he had miscalculated, pushing the date forward by a year to October 22, 1844.

Needless to say, the second prophecy also failed. That day became known as "The Great Disappointment." Miller's followers were left devastated—not just spiritually, but in many cases, materially, as they had given up their homes, possessions, and livelihoods in anticipation of the apocalypse. Miller had also sold many of his Millerite Apostles or Gullible Adherents white ascension robes. So, some had even donned themselves with white ascension robes in expectation of being carried off into the heavens.

What followed was not just a crisis of faith but also a sociological phenomenon that we can recognize today as *cognitive dissonance*. Faced with undeniable evidence of their error, some of Miller's followers doubled down on their belief, clinging to increasingly far-fetched explanations to reconcile their shattered expectations. From this movement, various Adventist groups emerged, including the largest of them, the Seventh-Day Adventists. These movements, united by the idea of Christ's imminent return, share an "Adventist" theology. In reality, any religious group that teaches the return of Jesus is Adventist in theory, regardless of denomination.

It's interesting that Miller might have saved himself considerable trouble had he more closely examined the same Bible he was using to make these prophetic claims. In Matthew 13:31-32 (KJV), we find a clear statement: "Heaven and earth shall pass away, but my words shall not pass away: but of that day and that hour knows no man, no, not the angels which are in heaven, neither the Son, but the Father." Further reading in Matthew 24:36 reiterates the point: "But of that day and hour knoweth no man, no, not the angels of heaven, but my Father only."

Despite these warnings, the idea of the "End Time" has had an enduring appeal, transcending the Millerite movement. And here lies the heart of the matter—*time* as we know it is not about to end. In fact, "time ending" is a myth, a futuristic concept that is, by nature, unverifiable.

Now, let's delve deeper into what time actually is. Time, in its most essential definition, is a nonspatial continuum. It allows us to measure the progression of events from the past to the present and into the future. But here's the key: even if the world, as we know it, ceases to exist, time itself does not end. It continues because time is not tied to the existence of human life, Earth, or even the cosmos. Time is an infinite concept; unbound by the physical limitations we often impose on it.

Let's break it down even further. Think back to the number line you learned in elementary arithmetic. The line begins at zero, but it stretches infinitely in both directions—negative and positive. Similarly, time stretches infinitely forward and backward. The future is not an endpoint; it is a continuation; existing on an inescapable continuum. So, when someone says "time is winding up," they are misunderstanding the very nature of time itself. It doesn't wind up, it doesn't end—it simply moves forward.

In the context of eternity, time is merely a tool—a way of organizing our experiences, our histories, and our expectations of the future. But time is not something that ends. Even if all human life were to disappear, the continuum of time would persist, just as it has before us, and will after us.

The future is not a fixed point waiting to be reached; it is an open, ever-expanding space of potential, shaped by human imagination, creativity, and will. Our task is not to fear the future but to engage with it, to fill it with meaning, and to leave our mark on the continuum of time itself.

3. Myth: "People who love the Lord are full of hate."

This myth arises from a widespread misconception that those who profess a deep love for the Lord are also judgmental, hostile, or even hateful toward others, particularly those who don't share their beliefs, personal self-images, or lifestyles. While this stereotype has been reinforced by many unfortunate examples, it doesn't reflect the core teachings of Christianity or the true journey of spiritual development.

In reality, those who genuinely love the Lord are striving to develop and extend love—*not condemnation*. This distinction is essential and must be understood both by those within the faith and those observing from outside. To love the Lord, in its truest sense, is to embrace the essence of love itself, as embodied in Christ's teachings. Jesus made this clear when he said, "Love one another as I have loved you" (John 13:34).

However, here's where the myth gains traction. As so-called Christian people, we tend to *chastise* more than we *baptize*. In other words, many who identify as Christians have mistakenly equated their role with being judges, quick to condemn others for perceived sins or failings. In short, many so-called religious practitioners, especially many within the Abrahamic lined faiths, have positioned themselves as social observers and gatekeepers. This is profoundly a out of control behavior noticed in the Westernized tendencies of the outgrowth of European designed and churches of the United States. This inclination toward chastisement can overshadow the more central Christian calling—to baptize, to welcome, and to guide others into a loving relationship with God. The focus becomes more about enforcing rules and less about fostering relationships, which is at the heart of Christian love.

This has led to the perception that Christians, particularly those who claim to love God the most, are often the most harsh, critical, hate-driven, and unkind. It's a distortion of what the faith intends. While it is true that some individuals and groups have allowed personal biases and cultural values to color their religious expression, the essence of loving the Lord is about grace, love, humility, and forgiveness.

Christianity teaches that love is patient and kind, that it does not boast, and that it is not easily angered (1 Corinthians 13:4-7). Yet, the myth persists because there is a gap between *aspirational faith*—what Christianity teaches—and *lived faith*—how some Christians behave in the world. This gap is where misconceptions, like the one we are discussing, take root.

The challenge, then, is for Christians to close this gap. They must model love in its purest form, rather than condemnation, as they navigate their faith journey. True Christian love involves recognizing our shared humanity, offering compassion, and fostering understanding—even in the face of differences. In doing so, they can counteract the myth that their faith is rooted in hate and show that it is, in fact, built on the supreme foundation of love.

4. Myth: "All politicians are crooked. All politicians are for sale."

It's an easy, often tempting narrative to buy into—especially in an era where trust in leadership is at a low point and corruption scandals seem ever-present in the news. However, this blanket statement simply isn't true. It oversimplifies a complex landscape and ignores the individuals who enter public service with a genuine desire to make a positive impact.

To assume that *all* politicians are driven solely by greed or power is to overlook the many who stand firm in their integrity, serving their constituents with a sense of duty. Public office, at its best, is an arena where leaders balance competing interests, navigate bureaucracy, and make hard decisions that affect the lives of millions. The reality is that politics attracts a wide spectrum of people—some corrupt, but many dedicated to public service and positive change.

Moreover, painting all politicians with a broad brush of distrust can lead to apathy, disengagement, and a toxic political climate. It's important to hold our leaders accountable and to call out corruption when it occurs, but it's equally vital to support and encourage those who are working honestly for the common good. Public cynicism should be directed at the systems and structures that perpetuate inequality and corruption, not at every individual within the political realm.

This myth fuels disengagement, yet it is only by staying informed, participating in the democratic process, and supporting leaders who stand for accountability that we can help nurture the kind of political culture we want to see.

5. Myth: "I know what happens when we die."

This statement is one of the most pervasive and deeply ingrained beliefs in human culture. But the truth is, no one really knows what happens when we die. It's a mystery as old as humanity itself, and while many claim certainty, that certainty is often rooted in belief, not in verifiable knowledge.

Belief systems around the world provide a wide array of answers to this question. Some speak of an afterlife, others of reincarnation, and still others suggest that death is simply the end. Each of these perspectives is valid within the cultural and spiritual context from which it arises, but they remain beliefs, not facts.

Saying, "I know what happens when we die," is akin to claiming, "I'll get muscles when I eat spinach like Popeye." It's a nice thought, rooted in stories and traditions, but it's not based on evidence that can be proven. It's comforting to have beliefs that help us make sense of our mortality, but it's important to acknowledge that they are just that—beliefs, not certainties.

The beauty of this mystery is that it invites contemplation, reflection, and humility. It forces us to confront the limits of our knowledge and to recognize that death, like life, is something we're all trying to understand. And in that search for understanding, different people, cultures, and religions have come up with many answers, but none that can be definitively proven.

In this case, the myth isn't just about death itself; it's about our human desire for certainty in the face of the unknown. Instead of holding onto a rigid belief, perhaps the more powerful approach is to embrace the uncertainty with curiosity and respect for the many ways people try to understand the end of life.

6. Myth: "They left our church. That means they left the Lord."

Leaving a religious institution or a church does not automatically signify a loss of faith or abandonment of the divine. It's a myth to equate departure from a structured belief system with leaving the Lord. Faith is inherently personal, not confined by church walls or membership rosters. People walk away from churches for many reasons—personal growth, shifting beliefs, or simply the need for a new spiritual journey—but this decision doesn't strip them of their connection to a higher power, nor does it mean they've forsaken their spiritual path.

One of the fundamental teachings of the Christian Bible is the freedom of choice given by God from the beginning. The choice to believe, the choice to follow, the choice to love—all are integral parts of human free will. The United States Constitution enshrines a similar principle: the freedom to choose, which extends to religious affiliation. Globally, humans are endowed with the natural right to make choices that reflect their personal values and evolving beliefs.

What many religious communities fail to acknowledge is that leaving a church doesn't always reflect a rejection of the Lord, God, or even the values that religious teachings represent. Faith is personal—it arises from individual experiences, reflections, and inner dialogues. It is not a pre-packaged system handed down through tradition or culture. Each person's faith is formed by their own mental and spiritual journey, shaped by their unique perspective and lived experiences.

When we reduce someone's departure from a religious order or organization to *"leaving the Lord,"* we ignore the complexities of human belief, growth, and freedom. Exercising one's choice to step away from a church should not be interpreted as stepping away from spirituality. True faith can exist outside institutional boundaries, and it is deeply personal, evolving as people explore the broader realms of their inner understanding and convictions.

7. Myth: "I'm praying that they will accept God."

On the surface, this phrase sounds like a compassionate, spiritually driven sentiment. Yet, when examined closely through psychological and sociological lenses, we see a more complex dynamic. The prayer, while likely well-intentioned, can often carry an underlying assumption: *my* belief system is the only correct one, and therefore, others need to align with it.

Psychologically, this can be described as a form of *confirmation bias*. The person praying may already be so deeply invested in their particular worldview that they see anyone who doesn't share it as incomplete or misguided. The prayer becomes an act of reaffirming their own beliefs, rather than a genuine expression of concern for the other person's spiritual journey. It's as if they're asking for divine validation of their own religious stance, expecting God to convince others to join their fold.

This also introduces an element of *cognitive dissonance*. The person praying might feel uncomfortable that someone they care about does not share their faith, and the act of praying becomes a way to soothe this discomfort. It's easier to hope for God to "fix" the other person than to confront the diversity of beliefs and choices that make up human experience.

Sociologically, this prayer reflects the social pressures within many religious communities. In these environments, shared faith is often equated with moral alignment and community belonging. The pressure to have loved ones conform can come from a desire to preserve group cohesion. For the person praying, the wish for someone to "accept God" may be less about spiritual salvation and more about ensuring that person remains within the cultural or social boundaries that define their personal religious community.

This kind of prayer often ignores the principle of *personal agency*. Every individual has the right to make their own choices, including how they relate to spirituality, God, or any higher power. The act of praying for someone to adopt a specific faith can unintentionally bypass that individual's autonomy, pressing them to fit into a mold that is not of their own making.

As the saying goes, "That person you're praying for may be praying too," and in their prayers, they might be seeking their own unique relationship with spirituality or asking for others to respect their freedom to choose their own path. That other person may be praying for you.

8. Myth: "His perception is wrong."

Nope! His perception isn't *wrong*—it's just *his*. What he sees, he sees! From his unique point of view, he's not sharing your perception, but that doesn't automatically mean he's wrong. Maybe what he sees is like looking through a foggy windshield—he might need to clean things up a bit. Sure, his perception could clash with logic or scientific facts (like thinking the Earth is flat... sorry, Flat Earthers!), but that doesn't make it *wrong* on a purely perceptional level. It's like wearing glasses with the wrong prescription—you're still seeing something, just not clearly.

9. Myth: "He doesn't know what he's talking about."

You've probably heard this before, right? Maybe you've even thought it yourself when someone shared an idea that seemed out there or just plain crazy. But here's the thing: just because someone's idea is different or you've never heard of it before doesn't mean they don't know what they're talking about.

Take the story of Fred Smith, the founder of FedEx. Believe it or not, his idea started as a college project—an idea about getting packages from point A to point B overnight. His professor thought it was nonsense, too impractical, and not worth pursuing. But Fred didn't give up. He knew something others didn't. He had a vision, a spark of innovation, and the guts to follow through. Today, millions of people use FedEx worldwide, proving that what some people dismiss as "crazy" can actually change the world.

This kind of thinking has been around forever. Think about Thomas Edison, the guy who gave us the electric light bulb. Back then, people thought lighting up a room was only possible with oil or kerosene lamps. Edison came along and flipped the switch—literally! Now, we have everything from incandescent lights to LEDs, and it's all because someone like Edison refused to listen when they told him, "You don't know what you're talking about."

The point is, just because an idea sounds wild doesn't mean it's wrong. It's about listening, paying attention, and being open to possibilities. It's easy to dismiss someone because what they're saying doesn't fit with what you know—but maybe they see something you don't. Maybe they're onto the next big thing, and instead of brushing them off, we should take a closer look.

Inspiration is where ideas are born. Innovation is where they take off. And the truth is, sometimes those so-called "crazy ideas" can change the world.

10. Myth: "She comes from a

bad family."

Such an observation is an example of how society's labels and judgments can limit the potential of individuals based on the actions or reputations of their relatives. It's a myth that not only promotes narrow-minded thinking but perpetuates cycles of discrimination, unjust criticism, and missed opportunities for those caught in its web.

The idea that someone comes from a "bad family" is rooted in comparative and biased perspectives. I believe such a statement often stems from values that are affirmed within particular cultural bubbles—what we deem "bad" in one context may simply reflect a different set of experiences or circumstances. This myth has been used to prop up harmful systems such as racism, classism, and xenophobia. It's a judgment that carries generational weight, affecting not only the individual but often entire families, all due to a lack of understanding and empathy.

When we place individuals into categories based on their familial backgrounds, we ignore their potential, drive, and resilience. We fail to recognize that no person is defined solely by the actions of others in their family. The myth implies that a person's environment has irreversibly condemned them, shutting the door on their potential before they've even had a chance to walk through it.

A powerful counter to this myth is the story of that one sister, whose dedication to her community and belief in the power of education not only shattered the narrative of "bad family" but also set the stage for remarkable achievements—like her son's graduation from the United States Naval Academy. This is a testament to how a single person's positive influence can break through stigmas and inspire others to rise above unjust societal expectations.

Programs like Big Brothers Big Sisters operate on this very principle. They recognize that every child, regardless of where they come from, has incredible potential waiting to be unlocked. By pairing mentors with young people, they challenge this harmful myth by offering new perspectives and opportunities for growth. These programs prove that no child, regardless of their family's reputation, should be reduced to their background or circumstances. Instead, they should be nurtured based on their individual capabilities and dreams.

Ultimately, the idea of a "bad family" comes down to the limitations we place on others and ourselves.

Consider this, if she, the one that comes from a so-called bad family, is in your view, I invite you to find a mirror. Look into the mirror. Most mirrors are a glass opaqued on the opposite side of view. As you look into the mirror, you can see the present. That present moment slips away in a fraction of a nanosecond. Other than that moment, the person looking into the mirror can only see an image of the past. All known personal history is part of that person viewed in the mirror. We cannot see beyond the reflection. I think this is what Paul was asserting in 1 Corinthians 13:12 where it is written, *"For now we see through a glass, darkly; but then face to face: now I know in part; but then shall I know even as also I am known."* It is only the eternal mystery of time, the greatest reader of potentials and possibilities. Time unravels the mysteries of the present transporting us to the moment.

It is time that forever flows beyond the reality of the seen to measure the depths of the unseen things inherent in each of us. She came from a bad family? Perhaps, what we saw as bad was good for her. We don't wear heavens eyeglasses. Standing in front of a mirror only shows us the past; we see what's been, not what's possible.

We often judge based on superficial or incomplete information, forgetting that the person in front of us has the power to rewrite and reproduce their narrative.

To move beyond this myth, we must realize that personal growth, potential, and success are not determined by family history. They are shaped by choices, opportunities, and, most importantly, by those who have the courage to see beyond what society has written for them.

The next time someone says, "She comes from a bad family," we should challenge them to look deeper. What potential is being overlooked? What good might come from a situation we deem undesirable? The possibilities are endless if we learn to stop focusing on where someone comes from and start paying attention to where they're going. As observers, we all have the potentiality to be a boost.

11. Myth: "Nothing good can happen here."

I'm all in when it comes to believing in possibilities. I understand the difference between probability and possibility. Probability measures how likely something is to happen, while possibility? Well, that's the immeasurable potential that anything can happen, regardless of the odds.

One Sunday morning, I visited a small Methodist church in Salem, Oregon. After the service, I had a conversation with the pastor. He shared something with me that stuck: the church we were standing in had been fire-bombed—multiple times. Why? Because some members of the local community didn't welcome or appreciate the presence of an African Methodist Episcopal Zion (AME-Zion) congregation. That's right—this church had been attacked with Molotov cocktails because of the color of its congregation.

As shocking as it was, the pastor didn't flinch while telling me this. Instead, he talked about how the church kept rebuilding. They even installed a bulletproof shield behind the pulpit. And here's where it gets interesting. As the attacks continued, something unexpected happened: white members of the community started attending the church. They figured that if white people were seen worshipping there, it might deter further attacks.

My response? "This church is special." The pastor asked, "Why?" I said, "Because I know one thing—there's definitely been fire on the corner of Sunnyview Road and Fisher! And where there's fire, there's potential." That unexpected response lit him up.

This church, born from a fiery past, became a glaring example of potential, not just for its members but for the entire community. The attacks that were meant to divide and destroy instead brought people together across racial lines. It's an incredible story, and it reminds me that just because the odds are low doesn't mean the possibility isn't high.

You see, I come from a very racially divided church. They've got ministries aimed at growth, but those invisible walls of division are strong. The probability that they'll break those walls down? Pretty low. But the possibility? That's high. It all depends on the will of the people. Many will say things like, "Young people aren't engaged because of the devil, sin, or the 'end times', but look around. Young people aren't leaving faith; they're finding community in places that build bridges, not walls.

If you've ever been to the food court at the mall in my city, you'll see what I mean. There's more unity in that food court than in many traditional churches. Young people are pulling together with ropes of common community, while the old ropes of division—those used to lynch and divide—are becoming relics of the past.

When people say, "Nothing good can happen here," I say the potential for something good is always present. It's just waiting for the right moment and the right people to ignite it.

12. Myth: "She lacks the ability to reason."

No. She reasons according to her understanding. Her decisions are mindful, shaped by the experiences, knowledge, and perspectives she holds within her personal "bubble." It's not that she can't reason—it's that her reasoning comes from a unique set of experiences, just like anyone else.

Every one of us operates from our own bubble, filled with the things we've learned, the beliefs we've absorbed, and the environments we've lived in. To say that someone "lacks the ability to reason" is to assume that there's only one way to think or process information. But in reality, reasoning is deeply personal—it's informed by upbringing, culture, and countless life experiences.

Imagine someone who has lived their entire life in a room furnished with just a few pieces of knowledge, limited in scope but solid in foundation. You wouldn't expect them to think exactly like someone who's been exposed to a much broader world, with a variety of experiences and diverse perspectives. That doesn't mean their reasoning is invalid—it just means it's built from what's inside their room, inside their bubble.

We often judge others based on the belief that they lack something we have, but the truth is, every person's reasoning reflects their reality. What may seem irrational or limited to one person might be the most logical decision for another, given the walls and windows of their world.

Instead of dismissing her reasoning, we can try to understand where it comes from. If we step outside our own bubble for a moment, we might find that her perspective makes sense when viewed through the lens of her experiences. And if we engage with her, if we share our own reasoning and listen to hers, that's where growth happens.

True intelligence isn't about judging someone else's way of thinking—it's about recognizing that reasoning is always shaped by the world each person knows. We all reason from the bubbles we live in, and when we come together, we can start furnishing each other's bubbles with new ideas, deeper understanding, and greater empathy.

13. Myth: "He has very little potential."

This statement, though often made with conviction, reflects a fundamental misunderstanding of human potential and the complexity of its development. The idea that one can definitively assess another person's potential is inherently flawed because potential is not static, nor is it easily measurable. In reality, it is the unlocked code of chance within the universe—combined with environmental influences, personal resilience, and learned abilities—that ultimately determines the boundaries (or lack thereof) of an individual's potential.

Human potential is not merely a product of observable traits or current capabilities; it is deeply intertwined with opportunity, access to resources, mentorship, and the capacity to adapt to life's challenges. To suggest that someone has "very little potential" is to overlook the dynamic interplay between these factors and the innate, often unpredictable, ability of individuals to transcend limitations imposed by circumstances.

The Limits of Predicting Potential

Forecasting human potential typically relies on measurable probabilities—grades, standardized test scores, social background, and other quantitative indicators. However, while these metrics can be useful in predicting short-term outcomes or identifying specific strengths, they fall short of capturing the holistic and often latent capacities of an individual. For instance, a person may face a series of roadblocks—socioeconomic hardship, educational inequality, or systemic discrimination—that skew the perception of their potential. These obstacles may inhibit immediate success but do not reflect the person's true capabilities or the future potential that might be realized in different conditions.

What we often fail to acknowledge is that potential is far more fluid and context-dependent than we assume. People evolve in response to life's experiences, challenges, and opportunities. Their capacity to adapt, innovate, and persist in the face of adversity often surpasses initial predictions. What's more, many individuals' potential remains latent, awaiting the right combination of circumstances—such as mentorship, education, or access to resources—to be fully realized.

Chance and the Universe's Role

Chance plays a critical role in the development of potential. The randomness of life, from the opportunities we encounter to the obstacles we face, creates an unpredictable environment where potentials are either nurtured or stifled. Sociologist Pierre Bourdieu introduced the concept of *habitus*—the deeply ingrained habits, skills, and dispositions that individuals possess due to their life experiences. The environment in which a person is raised, their cultural capital, and the challenges they face all contribute to shaping their habitus, and by extension, their perceived potential.

But while environment plays a significant role, it does not account for the myriads of factors, both internal and external, that unlock or hinder potential. One's personal resilience, creativity, and ability to adapt to changing circumstances are intangible qualities that can dramatically shift what a person is capable of achieving. These qualities cannot be accurately measured at a glance, nor can they be easily predicted.

A Better Approach: Offering a Running Start

Instead of presuming the limits of one's potential, it is more constructive to focus on creating environments that offer opportunities for growth, rather than placing roadblocks in their path. By removing artificial barriers—whether social, economic, or educational—we provide individuals with the tools and resources necessary to unlock their potential. The process of self-actualization often requires a running start: access to knowledge, supportive networks, and spaces that encourage experimentation, learning, and failure as part of the growth process.

As educators, mentors, and fellow human beings, it is not our role to judge another's highest potential but to support their journey towards discovering it. We must recognize that potential is a spectrum, influenced by the intersections of environment, experience, and chance. By equipping people to better adjust to and maneuver the experiences of life, we enable them to transcend immediate limitations and expand their horizons of possibility.

Conclusion

In sum, no one can definitively determine another person's truest or highest potential. It is shaped by countless factors—many of which are beyond our immediate perception or control. Rather than asserting judgments about someone's capacity based on limited or biased criteria, we must acknowledge the profound uncertainty and boundless possibilities inherent in human potential. True potential is not a fixed quantity to be measured or assessed; it is a dynamic, evolving force that can only be fully understood in the context of one's entire life journey.

14. Myth: "I can't believe he said that."

Well, if you can't believe he said that, then... why are you telling me? I mean, if it's so unbelievable, wouldn't that be a sign to just let it go? But no, here we are, you pulling out this third-hand piece of gossip like it's some kind of priceless relic, when really, it's just a game of telephone with a few missing brain cells.

You *heard* he said something, but you don't believe it? Alright, so we're at a crossroads of logic here. On one hand, you don't think it's true. On the other hand, you're eager to share it with me like its breaking news. It's like trying to convince someone you didn't steal a cookie while chewing with crumbs around your lips and on your shirt. If you didn't believe it, wouldn't you just *not* say it?

Look, the whole "I can't believe he said that" routine is really a way to slip in a little gossip under the guise of disbelief. It's like saying, "I'm shocked… but also kinda thrilled." It's like serving up scandal on a silver platter but trying to pass it off as concern. The real truth is, sometimes, people love a good "I can't believe it" moment—just as long as it's about someone else!

So, next time you hear, "I can't believe he or she said that," take it with a grain of salt… and maybe a whole lot of buttered popcorn.

15. Myth: "You need money to succeed."

No, money is not the root of success—it's a byproduct. What you truly need is a thought, an idea, and a burning desire to bring that idea to life. Before there's ever a dollar to spend, there's a spark in the mind that sets things into motion. Look at people like Tyler Perry, who didn't start with wealth but with determination, grit, and a vision. He began by sleeping in his car and writing plays, pouring his passion into his work until the world couldn't help but notice. The truth is, you don't start with money—you start with a solution to a problem, an idea so powerful that it can't be ignored. That's the atomic energy of reality, the force that drives success.

When you focus on creating value, the practical points and buyable options will naturally fall into place. The world is full of seekers—people looking for a service, a product, or a story that fills a need they didn't even know they had. If your idea addresses that need and you're willing to put in the work, the money will follow. Success is built from imagination, dedication, and the willingness to act. Money? That's just one of the tools you pick up along the way.

16. Myth: "Those who don't share my Christian views are pagan."

No, those who don't share your Christian views are not pagans—they're people. People with their own minds, thoughts, and, most importantly, a natural right to explore and embrace their own understandings of reality. Just because someone doesn't walk the path you do doesn't make them lost. Maybe, they're just walking a different road, but headed in the same direction: seeking truth, connection, and meaning in life.

The truth is, people don't have to subscribe to Parson Millbrook's interpretation of the universe to be good, moral, or spiritually aware. They have the right to ask questions, to doubt, to explore their own beliefs, or to reject them entirely. Demonizing those who differ from your views doesn't make your faith stronger—it makes it more brittle, incapable of bending to the complexities of a diverse world. It's not about labeling someone "pagan" or "other." It's about recognizing that we all come from different walks of life, shaped by various experiences and teachings.

And let's face it: the world isn't just black and white, good or evil, "us" vs. "them." It's more nuanced than that. Maybe the so-called "pagans" aren't worshipping idols; maybe they're just finding a different language to express their spirituality. It's time to let go of this myth and start seeing people as they are—complex, thinking beings—rather than reducing them to labels from an outdated playbook.

17. Myth: "If I do the things my church teaches to honor God, I will be protected from every evil and harm."

Let me tell you, life happens. It doesn't care how often you go to church, how many verses you memorize, or how earnestly you pray. No ritual, no set of rules, no matter how sacred, can shield you from the unpredictable ups and downs of existence. There is no magical armor, no spiritual vaccine that immunizes you against all of life's hurts, struggles, and challenges—not even the ones labeled as "evil."

Think about it: You can do everything "right," and still, life will find a way to throw curveballs at you. It's not about a lack of faith or some failure on your part. It's simply the reality of the world we live in. Health issues arise, loved ones pass away, relationships falter, and yes, sometimes, the worst things happen to the best people. That's life moving moment by moment, and it doesn't follow our expectations.

Even the best of us—the most faithful, the most devout—

experience hardships. But here's the truth that often gets lost in the myth: honoring what you believe in isn't about avoiding pain, it's about building the resilience to face it. Your faith isn't there to act as a force field against life's tough times; it's there to give you strength, perspective, and community to help you get through them.

Life, at its core, is unpredictable. But in those moments, when you feel tested, that's when what you believe matters most. Not because it keeps the bad things away, but because it helps you navigate the storm when it comes.

18. Myth: "Things are only going to get worse."

I've heard this sentiment echoed so often, usually by those whose minds are anchored in fear of what's to come, clinging to the belief that our best days are behind us. But let's take a step back and really look at the trajectory of human progress. Whether you count history in BC (Before Christ), BCE (Before the Common Era), AD (Anno Domini), or CE (Common Era), one thing is crystal clear: We've come a long way, baby.

Just think about where we started: in caves, scratching at the earth for survival, barely able to communicate, and constantly at the mercy of nature's unpredictable fury. Today, we've mapped genomes, walked on the moon, and developed technologies that allow us to connect across the globe in seconds. We're creating solutions to problems that previous generations couldn't even dream of solving.

But fear—fear has a way of narrowing our vision, doesn't it? It can make us think that every step forward is somehow a step toward disaster, that every change is a sign of impending doom. It's the 'last days' mentality, rooted in a fatalistic view of the future. It's like having blinders on, unable to see the incredible advances that have been made in medicine, communication, human rights, and technology.

I get it—change can be unsettling, and not every shift in society feels like progress. But history tells us that with every step forward, we've overcome massive challenges and learned to adapt. The future isn't a guaranteed descent into chaos. In fact, it's filled with the potential for new innovations, better solutions, and deeper understanding.

Here's the truth: fear won't save us, but action, curiosity, and hope can. The same spirit that allowed us to move from crude tools to AI technology is alive today. Yes, there will be tough times ahead, but we're equipped to handle them better than ever before. The best days aren't behind us—they are right in front of us, waiting for us to take hold of them.

So, let's keep our eyes open. Let's break free from the chains of pessimism, and look to the future with the same spirit that has brought humanity this far. We've been through worse, and we've always found a way to make things better.

19. Myth: "You cannot cure diabetes."

It's astonishing how many people who profess belief in miraculous powers—whether through faith or magic—are quick to declare what cannot be done by the hands of medical science. Just because something hasn't happened *yet* doesn't mean it never will. They said flight was impossible, but then the Wright brothers soared through the sky. They said landing on the moon was a dream, but Neil Armstrong took that first historic step. The distance we've traveled—from the invention of the wheel to self-driving electric vehicles, from sun dials to atomic clocks—proves that human ingenuity is relentless.

There may not be a cure for diabetes, cancer, blindness, or hearing impairments today, but research is constantly in motion, much like the wheel itself. With each step forward, we edge closer to answers. From primitive cave drawings to touchscreens that connect us across the globe, human curiosity, determination, and resilience never wane. We strive, we innovate, and we solve the riddles that once seemed impossible. As long as we continue to push boundaries, the human race will keep moving forward—driven by hope, invention, and the will to ease the pain and loss that confront us all.

The future is never as limited as it seems—it's only as limited as we choose to believe.

20. Myth: "They have an Alternative Truth."

No. Truth has no alternatives. Truth is based on facts. Many of the things we hold dear aren't exactly rooted in fact—they're more about clinging to our cultural confines and traditions. Let's take a historical example: In the early 1600s, the scientific observer Galileo Galilei dared to challenge the prevailing belief of the time, the geocentric model, which held that the sun and planets revolved around the Earth. Galileo's *heliocentric* view, which correctly placed the sun at the center of our solar system, earned him punishment from the Catholic Church, which had the "truth," or so they believed. They were convinced the Earth was the center of the universe, and anything suggesting otherwise was heresy. Oh, really?

In my own life, I was similarly presented with "absolute truths." I grew up in a strict Christian sect that insisted we had the complete and unquestionable truth. Our mission was to convert others to our way of thinking because, we were told, we held the truth. But here's the thing: I grew up. I realized we didn't. In fact, we had limited truths even about the very religious sect we followed.

The more I studied, the more I understood that many of the so-called "truths" we clung to weren't grounded in reality—they were products of tradition, superstition, fear, and a refusal to question. Just like Galileo, who challenged the understanding of his day, we need to be willing to challenge the "truths" we've been handed, especially when they conflict with fact and reason.

In my early years of school, for example, I was taught that the sun was the center of the universe. But by the time I reached middle school, my imagination took me beyond that. I believed that the sun, being one of billions of stars, was just one example of many stars with planets revolving around them. This wasn't in the textbooks, but I was curious. I had a curiosity born imagination. My teacher called me a few unkind things for daring to question the traditional view.

Looking back, I realize: very few *stupid* people write books. The pursuit of truth is not about holding onto outdated or comfortable ideas—it's about continuous learning, questioning, and evolving with new information. "Alternative truths" are just opinions, biases, or misunderstandings dressed up as facts. Truth is singular; it's the foundation that withstands scrutiny and stands the test of time.

The difference between truth and belief is important. While beliefs can vary and even conflict, the truth does not bend to fit individual or cultural preferences. The truth is rooted in evidence and reality, even when it challenges our deepest assumptions. If anything, the history of Galileo and my own journey remind us that truth is not always what we've been taught. Sometimes, it requires us to dismantle what we've always known in order to see the world as it truly is.

Consider this: Rigid belief systems often masquerade as "truth." If you don't understand anything else that I share, please take this and move it around a few times in your privately owned thought process – you know clear the air of your personal bubble. Like old bread, if may have been inviting when fresh but, ignorance often becomes moldy and stale. Just because Joe the plumber tells you he knows how to perform heart surgery because he saw it online and can save you money; RUN. He may lead you to believe he would be better than any surgeon representing the Mayo Clinic or even Johns Hopkins but RUN when he tells you for $150, he can perform such a surgery in a hotel room; again RUN. When he tells you that you cannot trust your doctor because today's doctors are DEI hirers and products of Affirmative Action – RUN. He is not telling you the truth. Real truth is independent of cultural or personal biases.

ENERGIES IN MOTION

The balance between potential and kinetic energy in human actions—understanding our control over potential.

The potential of human abilities is astounding. As I reflect on my life, I often find myself returning to the lessons I learned from observing my father. We had a complicated relationship, especially during my early teens when we frequently butted heads. Despite the friction, I loved him dearly. He was a strong-willed man, particularly when it came to his religious beliefs, which, in my view, he took a bit too seriously. If I ever suggested this to him, I doubt it would even occur to him to ask, 'What do you mean by saying that?'

My father's religious convictions left me with gaps and questions, ones that were difficult to reconcile even at a young age. What puzzled me more was that these questions often went unchallenged in the larger community—points of view were static, unyielding to any form of critical scrutiny. I learned a great deal from him, however. Chief among those lessons was the deep respect for the church. To him, the church was the embodiment of God on earth, and we were members of God's true church. Our family, in his eyes, was chosen to set an example, to be a moral compass for others in the community.

Saturday church service was central to our identity and our testimony to the world. Yet, 'the world,' as my father saw it, was surprisingly small. It was mostly confined to the people on our street, those he worked with, or relatives from his side of the family. Anyone beyond that small circle was categorized as being under the influence of demons. We were to shun them if they didn't share our beliefs. For my father, his responsibility was not only to guide our family but also to argue and correct anyone who saw things differently.

Violence played a crucial role in maintaining control in my father's world. He was a staunch believer in corporal punishment, and growing up under his roof, I learned just how easily he could be triggered by anything that clashed with his rigid ideologies. His strict demand for us to follow his rules and beliefs often led to awkward situations when we interacted with others. What he didn't realize was that, when he wasn't around, we were left to fend for ourselves. Our peers ridiculed and mocked the oddities of the strict conformity he imposed on us—conformity that didn't mesh with the world outside our home.

But my father wasn't so different from many other dads of that time. He wanted others to see our family as 'good,' as a shining example of God's grace. We were to represent the best of what the church and faith could offer. In his eyes, those who didn't follow our beliefs were condemned to hell. Of course, he never used that word, as he considered it a curse word—something we were strictly forbidden from uttering. Any use of profanity in our house could lead to swift punishment, often meted out with violence.

Now, it's important to note that my father wasn't a violent man by nature, but he did have a serious and easily triggered temper. When things didn't go according to his plan, he resorted to corrective measures that often-included beatings. To a child, this was simply the way things were done. This was the genesis of my understanding of discipline. It wasn't until much later that I began to question it.

Interestingly, this approach wasn't unique to my household. When I visited friends in the neighborhood, I often saw similar threats of violence. It wasn't uncommon to hear mothers—many tired, some with a beer in hand—threatening their children with beatings. It was part of the fabric of our upbringing, woven into the very essence of how we were taught to behave.

Daddy was the Pastor Gino of my upbringing. If I had the urge to laugh, I had to pause and check first—was what I wanted to laugh at something he would find funny? Even something as simple as farting was considered against God's will, and we'd often tattle on each other just to see his reaction. Nearly everything, in his view, was dirty. The way people dressed? A reflection of their dirty minds. If we even thought about or witnessed something remotely related to sex, it was because *we* had dirty minds. It seemed that every rite of passage or step toward maturity was, to him, a ploy by the Devil to keep us from going to heaven.

Conversations about the birds and the bees? Those were out of the question. Such talks were viewed as conversations filled with filth. We never broached those topics—there was no room for them in a world where morality was defined by strict boundaries and fear of sin.

Daddy had one brother and one sister. His sister, though poor, was full of love and lived on a farm. His brother, however, was the J. Paul Getty of the family, the wealthy one. We, on the other hand, were more like the hired hands, responsible for doing things his children were either too old or too important to do themselves. I noticed early on how there was a distinction between the people he loved and others—everyone who wasn't a member of our denomination was seen as a sinner. My cousins, for instance, ate pork, which made them sinners in his eyes. But we were never to call them that, because they were family, and love seemed to offer a form of protection from criticism. I learned quickly that being critical was different when it involved people you knew, or when they held a title or position of honor.

In our household, pork was forbidden, along with black pepper—yes, black pepper. Consuming it, like eating pork, was considered sinful. The Bible, as Daddy interpreted it, also taught us that drinking Coca-Cola was wrong. If we found out that a product was made by the Coca-Cola company, or even if it was just rumored to be, we weren't allowed to buy or use it. Coffee was equally sinful, though I remember the daily smell of coffee brewing in my grandmother's percolator—such a rich, memorable aroma. But bacon? Bacon was an outright abomination because it came from the pig, and we were taught never to touch or eat anything unclean, as God commanded.

Anything he didn't like or couldn't afford was a sin. That was just the way it was. We didn't celebrate Christmas, and as a child, I had to contend with that reality. There were no festive decorations, no presents under a tree. Halloween was another forbidden holiday, but ironically, it felt like Daddy thought he was the Motel 6 guy because we were forced to keep the lights on. Our home had to stay brightly lit to attract the 'Trick-or-Treaters,' even though we didn't participate. When the kids, many of them my schoolmates, came knocking at the door, they were greeted not with candy but with Daddy's rehearsed speech: 'Sorry, but we don't believe in Halloween.' It was important for him to make sure the world knew that.

My oldest brother, bless him, was one hell of a coward. He had no interest in thinking deeply about anything. Cause and effect often blindsided him, and he nearly ended up serving in the Adventist Medical Cadets because, as Adventists, we were supposed to be conscientious objectors. The rule was simple: even if we were drafted, we weren't to pick up arms. We were taught to be patriotic, of course, but it seemed like it was the responsibility of non-believers to actually fight and die for our nation. Our part? Standing for the Pledge of Allegiance and the National Anthem. If we found ourselves on a battlefield, we were to give our lives for God and country, but never through violence.

Modern gospel music was another no-no in our home. It was too 'jazzed up,' and therefore sinful. But I remember Daddy recalling, with a bit of fondness, how much he enjoyed the music of Cab Calloway, Nat King Cole, Count Basie, Ella Fitzgerald, and Duke Ellington—true legends of his era. They were the music masters of his youth, though in his mind, those memories were of a time when he 'didn't know better.' He spoke with admiration of Lionel Hampton on the drums and xylophone, and Benny Goodman on the clarinet. These were productions of his past, from his coming-of-age years. But as for us? We were forbidden from enjoying the music of *our* time. The sounds of our generation, the popular music we were drawn to, were labeled as 'end-time music,' signaling the moral decline of the world. If we were caught listening to it, that was a sin.

In fact, it seemed like anything we enjoyed or that didn't sit well with him became a sin, particularly if it had a cost beyond his comfort zone. Every rule, every restriction, was backed by the Bible—or at least, by his interpretation of it.

Now, I write all of this, and it may seem as though I am identifying my dad as a violent or deeply flawed man. But that's not my intent. Many of the behaviors that spooked me, or prompted me to stand up for the one who was getting the short end of the stick, were more common than I once thought. The key to understanding this commonality is to look at the culture. I'll expand on this in an upcoming chapter, but for now, it's important to note that much of his behavior wasn't driven by a desire to cause harm or perpetuate cynicism. Rather, it was the outgrowth of the culture in which he lived and was raised.

Consider this: my dad, born in 1922, was only two generational steps removed from slavery. He grew up in a world where the remnants of that brutal system were still very much alive. The stories and attitudes that shaped his environment were often about control, subjugation, and survival within the harsh realities of a racial caste system. For people like my father, the stories that passed through the community often included harsh truths about how Black bodies were controlled and disciplined, not only by legal systems but by extralegal methods of violence and terror.

A significant portion of this cultural inheritance was rooted in narratives of human brutality—where those on the darker end of the American caste system were frequently subjected to severe punishment, and often, death. My father grew up in what I would call a 'police state,' where the sight of a badge carried vastly different connotations depending on the color of your skin. For many non-Black people, the badge represented protection or order. But for the Black community in which my father lived, it represented authority that could, at any moment, turn violent.

Death was not just an abstract fear in these stories; it was an all-too-real consequence, wielded as a tool of control. These stories weren't just about punishment—they were about deterrence. The violence inflicted on Black bodies served as a warning to others: any act of rebellion or deviation from the established order would be met with swift, unrelenting, and often lethal force.

What strikes me as fascinating—and deeply unsettling—is how this brutal logic was mirrored in the religious teachings of my youth. The early concept of God I received was in lockstep with the logic of that historical reasoning. It wasn't just the Seventh-day Adventists; many Christian denominations and sects promoted a similar narrative. In these teachings, God's wrath was not only justified but glorified. The threat of God's anger was depicted as unhinged and all-consuming. His wrath was not only inevitable for the disobedient but intentionally cruel, serving as an eternal example to the so-called 'saved.' Should they ever, throughout the ceaseless ages of eternity, even *think* of stepping out of line, they would face annihilation at the hands of a vengeful God—one who would not hesitate to punish in the most agonizing and wretched of ways.

In my community, I've had countless conversations where people share odd or even painful stories about how they were raised. What's striking is that a lot of the behaviors were rooted in control—controlling the lives of children and, in many cases, people of color. It's important to understand that much of this comes from a holdover of America's dark history. Our parents, guardians, and even law enforcement learned from a culture where power and control were essential for survival, especially for African Americans.

Today, it seems like we're seeing that same pattern plays out in politics. Some of the more conservative voices don't want us to talk about race at all. In fact, in some states, they've passed laws to shut down Black History courses and erase these conversations. The people pushing for this feel like they have the right to control others—just like my father and many from his generation thought they had control over their families and communities.

These political leaders believe they have the authority to decide what women can do with their bodies, who you should love, and what it means to be a part of the human family. It's like they're trying to hold on to the same old power structures that my dad's generation was taught to respect. And what's even more interesting is how some claim America was founded on Christian principles, yet had no problem with slavery or other acts of cruelty.

So, as we look at today's world, we need to ask ourselves: What are we teaching the next generation? What's really being passed down through homeschooling and conservative social values? These are the kinds of questions I'm tackling based on my own experiences with control and authority.

Understanding the Impact of Control on Human Potential

The behaviors I described, like those I experienced with my father, often have deep and lasting impacts on the lives of children and future generations. When these actions are severe or irrational, they can stifle creativity and discourage the development of new ideas—ideas that might otherwise advance humanity. History has shown us that innovation and progress come when people are encouraged to think freely, ask questions, and develop solutions to life's challenges. What is truly needed is an environment that nurtures self-worth in a respectful and unselfish way, grounded in love as a powerful, kinetic force for good.

It is through love and mutual respect that we teach future generations the value of our differences. It is these differences, when embraced, that reveal our shared humanity and stir our curiosity. This curiosity, in turn, fuels the growth of human potential and helps expand our understanding of life.

However, in today's society, we're seeing a rise in behaviors that run counter to these values. For example, there's an alarming increase in Antisemitism and the demonization of Muslims. We see efforts to delegitimize the rights of atheists, agnostics, and other groups. Hatred toward migrants and immigrants is also on the rise, often fueled by xenophobia—an attitude rooted deep in America's past, even before it became an independent nation.

A striking observation is how many of these prejudices are linked to control. Whether through religion, politics, or culture, control seems to be a driving force behind much of the discrimination we witness today.

Reflecting on My Father's Influence

Now, to be clear, I'm not suggesting my father was a bad man. Quite the opposite—he was a man of strong convictions and great intentions. The reason I use his example is that it helped me learn the importance of observing and questioning. The controlling behaviors I saw in him didn't originate with him. He was influenced by the societal norms and religious doctrines of his time. He believed that his actions were in line with his duty to both God and country.

Many of these influences came from Christian churches, particularly those with more conservative leanings. My father's worldview was very much shaped by an "Us vs. Them" mentality, which has its roots in the power structures of America's past. It's the old 'slave-master' routine—those in control decide the fate of others. And this mindset is not just found in religious circles; it's visible in today's political discourse as well.

The Broader Religious and Political Context

What's fascinating is how many Christian denominations, especially those that emerged in the mid-1800s, contributed to these beliefs. Groups like the Mormons, Jehovah's Witnesses, and other conservative Christian sects played a significant role in shaping these ideas. Even non-denominational churches often carry forward elements of this worldview. For anyone interested in understanding more about how these religious movements developed, I recommend a great read: *On the Margins of Empires: A History of Seventh-day Adventists* by Ciro Sepulveda. The book offers a deep dive into how some of these churches, like the Seventh-day Adventists, were shaped by the social and political forces of their time—many of which still echo today.

There is a reason for the story of Chicken Little. That story was a product of the 1800's. Listen to the ongoing megaphone blasts today signaling 'the sky is falling – the sky is falling'. Consider doing a 'Chicken Little Podcast.' I'm telling you; I hear it. The sky is falling. There is a reason for us who can to step back and once again review the book that became a movie and Broadway play by author L. Frank Baum 'the Wizard of Oz.' Who is behind the curtain? Who stands to gain?

In considering human potential, it is essential to understand that it is not merely a latent force to be recognized but a kinetic one that, when activated, becomes a powerful tool for progress. This potential is far-reaching and transcends boundaries of nationality, race, or creed. Humanity's ability to collaborate, innovate, and transform its environment is rooted in its evolutionary history—one that has led to exponential advances in healthcare, technology, and environmental stewardship.

Our journey from primitive survival to the vast medical advancements of today demonstrates that human evolution, both biological and cultural, is ongoing. The challenge we face now is whether we can channel this potential into solving the most pressing global issues. These include environmental sustainability, social inequities, and the pressing need for collective intelligence that rises above divisive rhetoric.

What we need now, more than ever, is the courage to embrace education and innovation on a global scale. As educators, scientists, and policymakers, it is our responsibility to foster environments where creativity flourishes and boundaries dissolve. The future lies in uniting minds from different cultures, races, and disciplines to address challenges like waste management, environmental degradation, and technological advancements with a shared sense of purpose.

The potential of humanity is vast, but it becomes truly impactful when transformed into kinetic action—when ideas are implemented, innovations are made, and societies are built on respect and inclusion. This is the essence of progress. This is how we collectively evolve.

Summary:

Human potential is not just a dormant force but one that, when activated, becomes a driving power for societal progress. From advancements in healthcare to technological breakthroughs, our evolution as a species is demonstrated through our ability to innovate and address global challenges. The future of human progress relies on harnessing collective intelligence, crossing boundaries of race, nationality, and belief, and fostering an environment where creativity and education are prioritized. Our true potential becomes kinetic when we focus on building inclusive societies, promoting respect, and collaborating on solutions that benefit the all of humanity.

Questions for Further Understanding:

1. How can we create educational environments that encourage the transformation of human potential into actionable, innovative solutions that benefit society on a global scale?

2. What are some examples of global collaborations that have successfully harnessed human potential to solve major challenges, and what lessons can we learn from them to apply to future issues?

The past generations have taught so many lessons guided by fear.

It brings me to this subject, POTENTIAL.

Fear is respect – Greatest fear is fear of God

Fear of other religions – going to church on the wrong day or worshiping the wrong God

Fear of other people

Fear of various therapies and mental health care

Fear of education

Fear of sex

Fear of hell – Which translates not as worship by choice but, worship by coercion.

Fear of love

Fear of losing respect

2 CENTS OF REASON   A DEEP DIVE INTO WHAT SHAPES US

Fear of death

Fear of being wrong

Fear of not being accepted

PAYING IT FORWARD

The importance of sharing wisdom and experiences for the greater good, without imposing it on others.

These are my lessons from the road. I call this: Paying It Forward

As I reflect on the journey that has brought me to this point, I realize how much I've learned from life's experiences—the good, the challenging, and even the unexpected. These experiences have offered me not just lessons, but realizations and revelations that I now understand are meant to be shared. I've come to see that everything we go through has a purpose, and that purpose often extends beyond ourselves.

I've learned that we are more than just observers of life. We are participants in a vast, interconnected world where each of us has the power to influence the course of the future. Whether through small actions or grand gestures, we all contribute to the collective story we're writing for tomorrow. My experiences have taught me that it's not enough to simply absorb wisdom or knowledge. We must act on it. We must "pay it forward."

These are the lessons I carry with me, and they've reshaped the way I see the world and my place within it. The roads I've traveled have made one thing clear: we are responsible for the imprints and impact we leave on the generations that follow. And that impact can either contribute to the world's progress or its stagnation. I choose progress, and I invite you to join me in that choice.

Here's what I've come to understand:

1. Perspective Is Power: Our ability to see beyond our

own experiences—to consider the perspectives of others—enriches our understanding of the world. It's easy to remain confined to our bubbles, but real growth happens when we step outside of them, engaging with the diversity of thought and experience around us. This shift in perspective isn't just enlightening, it's necessary for building bridges across divisions.

2. Imagination Shapes Reality: Everything we see in the world today—the good and the bad—was once imagined. From groundbreaking innovations to destructive ideologies, it all began as a thought. What we imagine, we create. The lesson here is to use our imagination wisely, consciously directing it toward a vision of progress, inclusion, and kindness. What you choose to focus your imagination on today will manifest in the world tomorrow.

3. Action Is the Catalyst for Change: Thought without action is simply a dream. We all have the ability to imagine better futures, but it's our actions that bring those futures into being. I've learned that it's not enough to hold a vision of a more just and equitable world. We must *act* in ways that reflect that vision, even if those actions are small steps taken in our daily lives. Change starts with the smallest gesture, and it grows from there.

4. We Are All Part of Something Bigger: There's a profound connection between us all. Our lives are intertwined, and what we do, or fail to do, affects not just ourselves but everyone around us. This is why it's so important to pay it forward. The kindness, wisdom, and generosity we offer to others today will ripple

outward, influencing the course of events far beyond what we can see.

5. Hope Is a Revolutionary Act: In times of uncertainty, maintaining hope is itself an act of courage. I've realized that hope is not passive; it is active. It propels us forward, inspiring us to take the steps necessary to create the world we want to live in. It's not about ignoring the difficulties we face, but about believing that through our collective efforts, we can overcome them.

What Does This Mean for You?

You hold immense power in your hands. The power to imagine a better world, the power to act on that vision, and the power to inspire others to do the same. This is not just about my story or my lessons from the road. This is about *your* story and the journey you are on right now. The decisions you make, the kindness you offer, the courage you muster to step into your potential—all of it matters.

I challenge you to take the lessons life has given you and put them to work. Use your imagination to dream big, use your perspective to understand the world more deeply, and use your actions to shape a future you'll be proud of.

We are writing the future together, and every small step counts. The road ahead is long, but it is full of possibility. Let's walk it with purpose. Let's pay it forward. Because tomorrow depends on the choices we make today.

The Importance of Sharing Wisdom and Experiences

As I reflect on the chapters of this journey, I am reminded of why sharing our wisdom, insights, and experiences is so vital. It's not about imposing our views on others; rather, it's about offering the fruits of what life has taught us, with humility and respect, so that those who come after us might benefit. Each of us walks a unique path, but there are lessons universal enough that they can illuminate the way for others. That is why I've chosen to share my story and reflections with you.

Why Share at All?

I believe there is tremendous value in passing along the knowledge gained from our struggles, triumphs, and observations. It's not an attempt to dictate the lives of others or to force anyone down a specific path. Instead, it's an invitation to consider alternative perspectives, to take what resonates and discard what doesn't, all while respecting that everyone's journey is their own.

However, it is important to acknowledge that choice is sacred. It's one of the most fundamental rights we possess. But just as essential as the freedom to choose is the responsibility that comes with it. The choices we make must never encroach upon the freedoms of others. Each person is entitled to their autonomy, and yet we must all coexist within the shared space of this world. This balance is delicate, and it demands that we exercise our freedoms with a sense of collective responsibility.

The Power of Choice

Choice, when rooted in respect for others, becomes a force for good. But when wielded carelessly or selfishly, it can cause harm. This is why it's critical that we remain aware of the impact our choices have on those around us. We live on this planet together. Our fates are intertwined, and what we decide to pay forward—whether kindness or cruelty—inevitably shapes the world we all inhabit. The ripple effect of one person's actions can influence the lives of many.

Imagination: A Double-Edged Sword

This is where imagination comes into play. Imagination is the storehouse of created possibilities, the birthplace of progress, and the canvas where we sketch our hopes and dreams. But it is also where disaster can take root. Imagination doesn't discriminate between good and evil; it's a tool that can be used to envision a future filled with hope, or one filled with destruction.

What we choose to nurture in our imagination matters. We must watch what we pay forward, for it will define the legacy we leave behind. Are we cultivating thoughts that will help to heal, to unite, to build up? Or are we allowing our minds to entertain ideas that divide, destroy, or demean others?

Paying It Forward with Humanity

At the heart of everything we do, we must be mindful of one simple truth: we are all connected by our shared humanity. And because of that, the most valuable thing we can pay forward is love—humane, unconditional love. Love, that respects others, that honors their freedom, that sees their value regardless of differences. We must pay forward generosity, understanding, and respect for all. It is not enough to offer these gifts to those who think like us or live like us. We must offer them freely to everyone.

This is why I see the importance of sharing what I've learned. The wisdom I've gathered is not meant to serve me alone; it's meant to serve a greater good. And I believe that each of us has a duty to contribute to the well-being of the world by passing along what we've learned, in a way that uplifts rather than imposes.

An Invitation to You

So, I invite you to reflect on what you carry forward. What lessons, what insights, what dreams do you wish to pass along to the next generation? How can you pay forward the best of what you've gained? In doing so, we create a cycle of progress, where each new generation builds upon the wisdom of those who came before, while making their own unique contributions.

We are each a steward of the future, and our choices, guided by love and respect, are the building blocks of what's to come. Let's pay it forward, generously, with humane love, respect, and a deep commitment to the common good.

A MODERN UNDERSTANDING / OPENING NEW DOORS

Revisiting age-old concepts with a fresh, modern perspective, tailored to today's challenges and complexities.

We stand at the crossroads of history, carrying the weight of the past while glimpsing the potential of the future. Revisiting age-old concepts with fresh, modern perspectives is no longer a luxury; it is a necessity tailored to today's challenges and complexities.

Some claim things don't change. To that, I ask: have you seen any new cars lately? What about GPS, guiding us turn by turn in real time? I think of a famous political leader who once asked, "You think you just fell out of a coconut tree?" As Vice President Kamala Harris wisely put it, "You exist in the context of all that came before you." Each of us carries the imprint of time, shaped by the choices, systems, and ideas that preceded us.

It wasn't so long ago that my classmates and I watched with wide-eyed excitement as a child rode on the back of a slow-moving turtle at the National Zoo in Washington. Hopscotch, jump ropes, and Etch-A-Sketches filled our days, and games like Monopoly and Candyland fired up our imaginations. Things have changed since then, haven't they? Outdoor fun has evolved into digital distractions; muscle memory from childhood games has transferred to the precision of fingers tapping on screens. We've come a long way from CB radios to Zoom meetings, from horsedrawn carriages to Teslas and beyond.

But here's the truth: the only thing that doesn't change is

history. In a moment, something happens, and in the next moment, it's locked in time forever. We cannot rewrite history, but we can chart new paths forward. The distance we've traveled since the dawn of humanity is monumental—from the invention of clothing to automatic washing machines, from clotheslines to all-fabric dryers, from wrinkled shirts to permanent press. Humanity's journey has been one of relentless progress.

History, however, is more than just the record of technological advancements. It's the story of courage and cowardice, of war and peace. It tells us about the exploitation of peoples and the suppression of women, stories often glossed over by those seeking personal gain. History is unchangeable, but it is always truthful in its lessons. And its lessons are clear: we must learn from the past but, also vow never to repeat its idiocies and blunders.

Today is a new day. Time marches on—never backward, always forward. As we step into this new moment, we must ask ourselves: what story will we write for future generations? The old doors are rusting. It is time to open new ones.

Once, left-handed children were forced to be right-handed, their natural tendencies considered "wrong" and corrected through punishment. History tells of such misconceptions. We also remember when children were expected to be silent, and education was seen as weak. But those barriers broke down—remember 'Rosie the Riveter,' the iconic image of women stepping into men's jobs during WWII? It's a perfect example of history's corrective power.

We have seen the ebb and flow of social orders, the tightening and loosening of oppressive norms. We've been punished for our shortsightedness—Mother Nature herself has delivered harsh lessons. Yet today, in this moment, we have the chance to build something better, something brighter.

It is our time. *Our time to open new doors.*

In 1865, as the bloodshed of the Civil War neared its end, President Abraham Lincoln spoke of a future that transcended division. His words still ring true today: "With malice toward none; with charity for all… let us strive on to finish the work we are in, to bind up the nation's wounds." But today, America is once again divided. Or maybe the wounds of that long-ago war never fully healed. The racial strife, the inequalities—they linger.

Yet, despite the weight of history, *there is hope*. There is still time to build. There is still time to imagine a future where we act with purpose, kindness, and respect. The cost of repairing the past is high, but the price of moving forward together is far less expensive—and infinitely more rewarding.

When we care—truly care—we come together. We bridge divides. We create. We inspire the next generation and the generation after that. The power to change tomorrow lies in what we build today. We must inspire innovation, development, and invention—looking at today's challenges not as obstacles but as opportunities to produce what the world has never seen.

Let's remember: imagination is the storehouse of possibilities. But it is also the stockpile of disasters waiting to happen if left unchecked. What we envision, we often manifest. So, let's watch what we pay forward. Let's pay it forward with love, with generosity, and with respect for all humanity.

Let us open new doors—together.

BREAKING FREE FROM THE JONESES

Shedding societal pressures to conform and finding true freedom in living authentically.

I shared with you earlier; I met Mr. Jones. It is true; I've visited with the Jones family. I slept in the Jones' beds. I ate their food. I slowly sipped their wine. I sat on their extravagant furniture. I tell you what I concluded. Now some will say I'm going against what I've shared so far. But, hang in here with me. I want you to know, I finally met the Jones'. And you know what . . .?

Mr. Jones was not that bright. Mr. Jones could not see my imagination born of my bubble. Mr. Jones did not share my life experience. Mr. Jones did not hear through my ears the words of Bobby Kennedy, "Some men see things as they are and ask, 'Why'? I dream things that are not and ask, 'Why not'? America needs you. Indeed, the world needs you. I started with 100 things that don't exist that should exist. It is time to dream. It is time to grow. It is time to say good-bye to the gate keepers. It is time to break free of the lie. The lie is the only weapon used to confine us. We are not safe under the care of the misguided and sometime intentional guard, we are bound by our inadequate self-images, the mask the guarders of our divided cultures demanded we wear.

Mr. and Mrs. Jones' beliefs won't save you from the often-grueling challenges of life. If you look behind the scenes, you will find they have their own container of challenges. We may see the surface of their lives; the veneer that they choose to present – often worn like makeup on a filthy hog. The Jones have learned in their bubble not to share the back-story. They are fighting to maintain their theatrics telling the world that may observe them that everything is alright. The daily sun sets for them as it sets for each and every soul that exist in this moment. As the world turns our bubbles, our perspectives miss vital information in the depictions, the scrips of performances played out on the stages of other lives. We have but this one moment to play our act in a carnival of time.

When we decide who is afforded salvation, as we often do in so very many of the cultural prison encampments, the addiction to apply our standards and beliefs on others can at times bring horrific consequences. The quiet son or daughter, rejected by parents and the parents circle of over-valued influence, has often decided to jump from the train we call life. Some were pushed from the train. Others were forced murderously to the tracks of an oncoming train for no other reason than they did not buy into the belief systems of the assailant.

When do we decide to let freedom ring? The prison guards are those who fight to maintain control. They know the cell doors are open. The know that the cellblocks are unlocked. The wardens know that the confinement of fear is the tool to maintain the mentally and culturally incarcerated. They write the headlines of lies. Mr. and Mrs. Jones want your admiration and respect. You are so fearful that you pay them time and money The cultural encampment has guided too many of us to study them feverishly trying to emulate them. It maintains their freedom. They know, by the value of statistics, that even their days are numbered.

I was asked to visit the local hospital. A special friend of mine was nearing her last moments of her train ride. I met her as a patient in that hospital. She, her family, her friends, the many medical teams had gone through so much. She had been in the hospital and out of the hospital so many times. When I met her, the medical team had decided that there was no more reason to keep her on life support. She had been in a coma for more than a month showing no sign of improvement.

I met her in one of the intensive care units. I had been invited as a fresh new Chaplain to talk with her husband. He was not cooperating with the team making the decision to remove all medical and mechanical support. Like was told to her husband, I was informed that once they remove the lines of support she would die in about 48 hours. I visited. I invited her husband to take a walk with me. I had my assignment and I was in the process of executing it. We left the room and entered the elevator. I introduced myself further as we exited the elevator doing all I could to make time and shield his privacy. We were walking through the lobby enroute to the outside of the main entrance. As I spoke with him, I noticed something very soulfully captivating my energy space. My spiritual energy was going through a rapid renovation. We started back towards the elevator. I stopped. He stopped.

I turned to this more than a gentleman. I asked him a very pivotal and transforming question. It was pivotal because it changed the situation and focus. It was transforming because it changed me. I said to him, "Hold up a minute. I'm in the wrong conversation ain't I?"

"Yes," he responded. "No one will listen to me."

"Really?"

"Yes!" he said very emphatically. "She will be alright."

"Are you sure?"

"Yes!" he continued, "No one is listening to me."

After our pause I responded, "I'm listening to you." I noticed a sigh of relief. I saw trust building. He was about to engage in one of my many crazy stories that I find hard to believe. The only reason I believe is because I lived it. I had a front seat to my life that I shared with no one.

"Hey stop for a moment." I told him. "I believe you."

Every bit of my theory on Perspective Thinking was heading back to the ward. The curtain call was being executed for yet another bow. I'm once again on the precipice of gaining more of my mysterious CEU's or better still, my Continuing Education Units. The experiences of life, the surveillances and frequent observations of life are finally sounding in my soul. Do you remember the little boy's prayer?

I don't know much. Especially given those immediate circumstances. I don't know what to do. In those moments I tend to annoy people who are reading from a different page. I have a tendency to annoy people who I see as willful prisoners in an imaginary mental institution a strange prison system with open doors. From my perspective, I see the many cultural buildings of incarceration where the inmates seek the fondness and praise, the reward for good behavior, the constant admiration of the prison guards. The admirers love their uniforms of money, fame, and imagined power. I get it. The confinement is based on the one thing we all, warden and prisoner alike, hold in common – our imaginations.

In this moment, I could have cared less what the Jones family would do. They have their own challenges. I really did not care about the medical team's request for my services. I cared about this one guy who was asking me to step out of my boat. He wasn't asking me to walk on water. He was telling me that it was safe to hear him. I listened. It was quiet. People were all around us, but it was quiet. People were in motion, but it was quiet. For a moment that seemed like forever, it was quiet. He looked at me in that moment. It looked like life had just been a hard day. His energy shifted with a strange sigh of relief. It looked like breath had returned to his body. We both stood in that lobby in a lightning strike of a stare that seemed to last for hours.

In the back of my mind. I recalled other incidents. I was called on at the last minute it seemed for a guy named Otis. I was contacted by a weird group of spiritual provocateurs and instructors that would challenge me to step beyond the cultural confinement. They showed me the possibility of the impossible. They removed me from the imaginary leg-irons that often overloaded my personal power board. It was me. I was responsible for the lights being turned off. I witnessed the closed door that did not exist. I was the one who recklessly from time to time challenged the wardens and guards.

"Okay my friend." This guy was not my friend. I did not know in that moment he would become my friend with so many others who met me because of their relationship with this lady who laid there; swollen up in a coma.

"Okay, I have a plan. We are going back upstairs. We are going into your wife's room. I am going to say a prayer. When I finish, don't talk to me. I want you to go home and get some rest. Will you agree to that? It seems like this ordeal has taken a lot from you and out of you. Will you keep to the deal without any questions?

"Yes"

"I hear you. I'm listening to you."

We enter the ICU area. The nurse assigned to this patient has a very uncomfortable look on her face. Her eyes are locked on me as under an acute examination. Her face is easy to read that something is going on with me and this man, the patient's husband, that I returned to the room with. I slide open the door. The husband and I walk in. We have no further conversation. I stood there.

What do I do now? I keep my word. We had a simple prayer. The hidden prayer was in the hidden pockets of my heart. That was nobody's business. That was my spiritual turf the boy that asked for wisdom never understood. It was a strange place that opened many doors and closed many as well. Those doors that closed were the end of chapters in my life. They were the many chapters where I found the same thread keeping the book on script. Those chapters taught me to observe. If you want the little boy's prayer to be answered watch. Watch the comedies, the mysteries, the dramas. Watch the horror movies that play out in life. Watch the enslavement of ignorance failing to see freedom. Watch the other inmates who decide to teach me to appreciate my confinement.

They, the so-called smart, the self-defined wise, who by birth of their ignorance, encourage me to work with the wardens and guards preaching at me to remember they are on my side. They are not. They are not on my side. In reality, these people who prey upon and hustle those they feel are inferior are enslaved too. They found appreciation from a group of enslavers that would sell them into slavery. They are the mastered of the masters. They are the fools and village idiots who develop in the world to maintain the conservative nonsense that often pits one prisoner against another. In the

United States of America, the fox knows that it's lying, but the sheep are many. They have been trained to graze upon acres and acres devious grift.

Back to my friends to be. The author took you out there for a moment. In this moment he invites you to think. Everything is true to the best of my understanding. You are reading from the guy setting in the front seat in the theater of his life. The stories are true. The stories are significant. The stories are life. The boy continues to reach for his wisdom. However, he has a few more stories to enter. He is in the development process of a little boy's prayer.

I said a prayer. The husband walks out of the room. I did say, "Get some rest." He left. I stood in the room for a moment and decided to address the nurse. I walked out to the nurses' station. I asked, 'What's going on? Why is there such a rush to disconnect this lady?"

"Well, she's been like this for months and she shows no signs of improvement. Nothing is going to change."

"Are you sure?"

"Look at her. She just lays there day after day. She doesn't respond to any commands. We are keeping her alive for nothing."

"Are you sure about that?"

"I know it. How did it go with her husband?"

"He left. He went home."

I decided to go back and visit one more time before leaving the unit. In a moment that thing that I've seen happen in so many different places had revved up again. It was a spark. It was a simple idea. It was safe. I looked at the patient. I don't know. I was feeling something. I've felt this before. In that moment, I could feel it. I could see it. It looked like she trusted me. There was something that gave me a sense of calm. She laid there as if to tell me I knew what to do next. But she was in a coma. I had a schedule ahead of me. She made me calm. Something is happening and I have no clue. Something is happening. I paused. I stared back at this swollen comatose woman. I don't know her. I just met her. I was trying to locate balance for her husband. The dude needed some rest. I stood there. Me and her all alone. I stood there.

The silence broke. I was doing what I do. I talk. I said this, "Renee, if you can hear me, I want you to wink." In that moment, I saw her right eye twitching. There was a command and there was seemingly a response. I followed up, "It's okay," I told her. Then I went on to say, "Listen tomorrow, when you hear my voice, I want you to wink two times. It's okay." Wow! No more movement.

The next day, I walked on to the unit to visit. I saw the nurse that from that moment she was building the necessary energy to either hate or communicate her discomfort with me. I walked onto the unit. We locked eyes. I asked her to come into the room with me. Before we actually stepped in, I said, "You know, when she hears my voice, I think she's going to wink at me two times."

"No, she won't."

"Why is that?"

"She can't."

"We'll see."

I told this nurse to stand by the head of her bed and watch

her face. I waited for the position. I cut the silence, "Hello Renee." Again, she began to twitch two times. The nurse turned to me with a guarded, seemingly fear driven amazement or curiosity asking, "How did you know that?"

"I don't know. Does it matter?" I told her I guess we had to slow down. She responded, "No! That's not enough."

"Why? What else do you guys need?"

"She has to be able to follow commands."

"Okay. No problem."

The nurse left the room. What do I do now? Time is producing nervousness. Nervousness is my human response as I trace the perspectives of my life. Time is vital. They want to disconnect this lady. Her husband says she'll be alright. Oh, silly me. If I could only read a few chapters ahead. This ain't for the Jones family. This is for me. The little boy prayed a prayer. How does the prayer get answered? Perhaps, it's taking so long because there is no God on the other side of my imagined connection. Perhaps, the earth to heaven phone bill hasn't been paid. Perhaps, the phone is dead. Perhaps, the phone service doesn't exist. Perhaps, as reading the life of Solomon over and over I came to realize he was often in strange circumstances and awkward positions like me. Many, maybe most of my experiences I often described as strange circumstances and awkward positions were based on my own doing. I nearly settled to live out my enculturated agreement with the imagined but real staff of the prison house.

Quietly, I placed two fingers into her right palm. "Renee. If you can hear me, I need you to do more. Renee, I need you to squeeze my fingers." She did it with the shyness of two childhood strangers meeting in kindergarten for the first time.

You know, the "Will he or she like me?"

In that moment. She squeezed my fingers as waking from a paralyzing sleep. Oh! But wait! Newsflash! This sister was in a coma. After she squeezed my fingers, I asked her to move her right foot. She did that as well. But she's still sleeping. I purposely held back the excitement. I toned down the energy. I walked out to the nurses' station and invited the nurse to come in. I wanted her to observe what was going on.

For a long time, there was nothing. The machines hummed, her chest rose and fell, and the sterile hospital air felt heavy. But there it was—two deliberate winks, faint but unmistakable.

I froze, a chill running through me. It was as if in that instant, the impossible became possible, the world of science and the spirit within me merged. We were staring down each other at an awkward but obvious intersection. Renee was alive, not just in body but in will. She was still in there, behind the sleep; buried behind the heavy mask of illness, fighting her way out.

I walked out of the room, heading straight for the nurse. She looked at me with that same discomfort. "She's going to make it," I told her.

Her eyes narrowed, skeptical. "That's impossible. The doctors have already prepared the family."

I smiled. "Then it's time to prepare for the impossible."

The days that followed were nothing short of extraordinary. Renee's husband came back the next day, exhausted but holding onto the slim thread of hope I encouraged him to. And slowly, bit by bit, Renee began to respond. First, the twitches. Then, the winks became stronger. She moved her fingers, just slightly at first, but enough to send shockwaves through the medical staff. They didn't believe it. They couldn't believe it. Well, they could if they had utilized their freedom of choice that sidesteps the 'what was' to the 'what is;' holding an imagination, a creative possibilities believer's view.

But belief, I realized, is a fragile thing. Just like the influence of Mr. and Mrs. Jones, the power of belief can shape reality, but it can also confine it. Renee's story wasn't about miraculous recovery; it was about breaking out of the script everyone else had written for her. Just like the Joneses with their gilded prisons, Renee had been written off by the people around her, but she wasn't done living her story.

That's the crux of it, isn't it? The Joneses of the world build their lives around maintaining the illusion of control; the conceit and hallucination of perfection. They're the gatekeepers of conformity, the guards of the status quo. And too often, we allow ourselves to be confined by their invisible walls, bound by the non-existent keys of their expectations, their rules, their myths. We buy into their fabled lies because often we live out our presuppositions and training accepting the idea that it's easier than breaking free.

But we don't have to. The truth is, the doors have always been unlocked. The Joneses don't have the power to hold us captive; we give them that power when we choose to play along with their game. When we choose to see the world through their eyes instead of our own.

Breaking free from the Joneses isn't about rejecting wealth or success. It's about rejecting the idea that we have to define ourselves by someone else's measure of value. It's about reclaiming our power to imagine, to dream, to create lives that reflect who we truly are—not who society says we are or should be.

We all have the potential to be more than the Joneses ever imagined, to live lives that go beyond the limits imposed by others. But first, we have to see the walls for what they are—illusions, distractions from the real task at hand: finding freedom in authenticity.

That's the essence of perspective thinking. It's the ability to see beyond the surface, beyond the masks we wear, and to recognize the vast range of experiences, ideas, and possibilities that exist. It's about being brave enough to ask the hard questions, to challenge the lies we've been told, and to step into the unknown with nothing but the strength of our own truth.

Renee's story wasn't about me or even about her miraculous recovery. It was about perspective, about seeing beyond the limitations imposed by others and trusting in the possibilities of what could be. She reminded me, once again, that we're all capable of more than we realize. But we have to be willing to let go of the Joneses. We have to stop living for the approval of others, stop seeking salvation in their validation.

Because, in the end, their approval doesn't save us from the real challenges of life. Their success, their perfection, their carefully curated lives—they are as flawed and vulnerable as the rest of us. The Joneses don't have the answers. They've simply mastered the art of looking like they do.

But true freedom doesn't come from mastering that art. It comes from rejecting it altogether. It comes from breaking free, from choosing to live on our own terms, from daring to imagine a life that goes beyond the scripts so easily handed to us.

So, ask yourself: Will you keep playing along with the Joneses? Or will you take that step, break the chains, and start living the life you were meant to live? The choice is yours. The doors are open. The only thing standing between you and your freedom is the lie that you're not ready to walk through them.

It's time to break free. FREEDOM! FREEDOM! FREEDOM!

A REASON TO LIVE OUT LOUD

Encouraging readers to embrace their full selves and live boldly in the face of societal expectations.

We all seek purpose—something that drives us beyond mere existence. This calling, this "niche" we find, connects us to something greater, something both invisible and invincible in its essence. But as we seek these truths, we must also examine how we arrive at our beliefs.

I have lived among communities of so-called believers—well-meaning people who had crafted their concept of the Creator without a solid foundation in either science or scripture. In places like that small church in Parole, the congregation, although sincere, was composed of individuals with limited education. They were, in many ways, what we would call "low-information" people, not because of any fault of their own, but because their lives were shaped by a tradition of following rather than questioning.

Before the widespread availability of literacy, people depended on what they were told. Information flowed from the leaders to the followers, often without scrutiny or challenge. The pastor or spiritual leader—seen as the most educated in the group—became the trusted source of knowledge. He was depicted as a man of truth. The people didn't question his words because they believed in him. But here lies the critical issue: often, the leader himself was no more informed than the people he led. He was merely perpetuating an ideology he had accepted, one that lacked critical thought or sound reasoning. He often unknowingly became a guard and gatekeeper.

This seems to happen, not only within the confines of Christianity but, throughout many religious orders. The followers often lack any logical basis for thought. The cover story usually becomes a 'cover-it-all' statement of action. That is, we accept this belief by faith. If a person develops under the control of a religious order, they are too often compelled to go with the flow – even when they find discrepancies and reliable imbalances with their so-ordered faith and reason.

For many so-called Christian or Abrahamic believers, God too often, has been what I call ANTHROPORMORPHIZED. The claim continues to stand that we were made in the image of God. Too often I find that God is made in our image as humans. God is a man. He stepped out on to nothing and made something. From that something, we were created.

I am certain, this anthropomorphizing of God, creating Him in our own human image, has allowed many to justify their actions and beliefs, often without question. When God is seen as a reflection of human traits—good and bad—people can project their own biases, fears, and limitations onto the divine. It becomes easier to claim divine authority over matters that are entirely human in origin. This has been particularly evident in the ways different religious orders and their leaders shape God to fit their interpretations, leading followers to accept those interpretations without critical thought.

The person who forwarded the story of the creation beginning did not appear on the Biblical scene until day six of the creation story. This story was told in much the same fashion that the story of Job was told. The obvious question becomes, who was there to witness the event that by its own convolution had no witnesses. We don't make our creator. Our creator makes us.

It is very interesting, in Christianity, that Jesus is identified as the incarnate son of God. Jesus would know his father. His father was the creator not only of all living things but of all that exists and the space in between all existence. Let me hear from the historical report of what Jesus said to explain the existence of his father. During his conversation with the woman at Jacob's well. According to John 4:24, Jesus explained his father with these words, "God is a Spirit: and they that worship him must worship him in spirit and in truth."

It is interesting many of the hucksters of many different religions that promote God or Jesus, or as they say 'Leaders of faith,' also have a proclivity to deception and are much too often caught in a circus of lies.

One of the main lies led by most European based guidance in Christendom has too often painted God as white. The authority of the whiteness of God's skin is truly incompatible with the description Jesus gave to the woman at the well. That anthropomorphized whiteness alone has been a tremendous deception of superiority that has been used to undermine many who are considered not to be a significant part of Western Civilization.

Trust me, God is not white. I trust the son of God to tell me the more accurate story. According to him, God is not a man. As a matter of fact, handed down in my Christian faith and the Biblical foundation of Judaism, the same book they both use comes from Numbers 23:19. In the King James the Bible reads, "God is not a man, that he should lie; neither the son of man, that he should repent . . ." Even though the Bible makes this declaration in both the Old and New Testaments there will be some angry persons who will fight to the death because they were furnished in their personal bubbles to believe God is a man.

In our social order, which is made up of many cultures, that includes many communities, born of billions of bubbles, religion has become a strong and over-working part of the engine of hate. It generates the power behind most 'us' vs. 'them' scenarios. We have equated religion with genetics as if one's belief can be seen in a strand of DNA. We are not born Baptist. We are not born Methodist. We are not born Pentecostal. We are not born Christian no matter how born again we claim to be.

However, I must make clear a Jew may have a Jewish ancestry but the fundamentals of Judaism, no matter how much of the foreskin of the penis has been removed, the beliefs cannot be found in the DNA. No Muslim, no Hindu, no Buddhist, and consider this fact, no Atheist can be found in the DNA. These are beliefs, and they all are including Atheism who believes there is no God, and the Agnostic are a product of the furnishings contained in the many bubbles on earth. The bubbles were first furnished by control. The bubble went seeking autonomy but did not veer far from home. Some went far to find furniture representative of their understanding. This is where religion comes in. Many have learned to disrespect and devalue those who are not like themselves especially in religion.

My friend MJ often answers the phone. I ask, "How are you doing MJ?" She responds, "I'm alive!" Often, I've listened to that response asking myself that 'should be obvious' question, "Does she believe I may be thinking she is dead as I listen to her voice?" If I am looking a person in the face and they tell me they are alive or that they woke up this morning, would that not be obvious?

Religion, in all its depth and reach, has wielded an undeniable power over human history. But its influence has often been a double-edged sword—capable of inspiring profound good, yet equally guilty of corrupting the social order, igniting disputes that spiral into bloody wars and senseless deaths. Among the most glaring symbols of this manipulation is the image of "White Jesus."

White Jesus is not simply a depiction; it is a construct—a tool of control born from the Westernized imagination. This Americanized Savior, hailed by some as the Redeemer of the universe, is less about divinity and more about dominance. He represents a carefully crafted narrative, one designed to manipulate minds and societies into submission. But I ask you this: if man could step on the moon and leave a footprint, did he also leave a mark of sin? Is the moon now unclean? Must it, too, be sanitized? Must it be destroyed?

History, like the moon, cannot be bleached or scrubbed clean of its blemishes. We are the architects of our stories, the draftsmen of our realities. The lines we draw, however jagged or imperfect, are indelible. Every joy we celebrate, every sorrow we endure, every injustice we perpetuate—all of it becomes the ink with which history writes its unflinching account.

And history is an honest storyteller. It does not flatter us with tales of our greatness while ignoring the darkness. We can twist it, lie about it, or spin it into something more palatable, but truth speaks with its own voice. It is there for those who pause long enough to listen—a voice unshaken by our illusions or our attempts at erasure.

So, why live out loud? Because this moment is ours. This day, unlike any other in history, is fresh with opportunity. "I'm alive," MJ shouts with joy, and her energy is infectious. She marvels at the sheer wonder of seeing a new day, reminding us that today is unlike any day that has come before.

We, too, should raise the decibels of our existence—not out of vanity, but because we have a singular chance to make an impact. To craft our stories with courage and purpose. To ensure that when history speaks of us, it speaks of a truth we can stand by, even if it's imperfect.

This is our moment, fleeting and irretrievable. This is our reason to live out loud. Let us make it count—not for the sake of history's judgment, but for the joy of knowing we lived authentically, fearlessly, and fully. We have a reason to live out loud.

I'VE SEEN A LOT

Pausing to reflect on the journey thus far, with a sense of openness to what remains unseen.

I've seen a lot. It began long before the light touched my eyes, when life stirred within the darkness, held within a world small yet whole. From the very start, my existence was cloaked in shadow, each movement an echo, each growth an unexplainable tension. My bubble, once boundless, began to press upon me, the walls creeping inward with each beat of time. As I stretched, space folded in on itself. Freedom was something I had yet to understand—but, in every push, I sensed it.

Then came a door, tight and hesitant, one that I knew only as resistance. It opened not by intention but necessity, hinting at a world beyond even before I knew what "beyond" meant. The warmth of that space had turned unbearable, confined and thick with expectation. My spirit, unformed but unmistakable, leaned into the passage ahead, sensing a greater expanse. I reached, pushed, and strained; what was once a wall gave way to a corridor, dark yet liberating, an unknown portal of potential.

And with each quaking tremor, each rhythmic pulse, I felt the nudge to move forward. It was a call, a challenge of the walls themselves, daring me to reach. My chest beat faster, filling with an urgency I did not understand but could not ignore. I was pressed, first by doubt and then by will. My senses were alert, primed for something greater. And when the call grew louder, echoing like thunder in the spaces of my mind, I pushed back—knowing that on the other side lay more than freedom; it lay my purpose.

Voices spoke, urging, "Push! Push! Push!" and then, as if from a world just beyond reach, another voice called, "Breathe. Take a breath." The closer I drew to that new reality, the more I felt a resistance that begged to be broken. Darkness turned soft, yielding to light. That first spark grew brighter, and in its warmth, I glimpsed the invitation of freedom, one I had sought unknowingly, that had burned within me even in the smallest, darkest spaces.

Each of us crosses thresholds like this, again and again, reborn to new realities and challenges, and sometimes gifted with golden clouds, other times met with walls we must push through. Some rise holding silver spoons, unaware of the privilege, yet there are others still who arrive with the hardened resolve of those who have known confinement. And for each, the call persists—an invitation to observe the light, a reminder that beyond every doorway lies another journey, another battle for freedom and understanding.

I remember that last obstacle, the veil between the worlds, that thick curtain that had held me back yet taught me strength. It resisted, held tight, but yielded to the drive within. And when I broke free, the struggle itself became a lesson. We are each tested, bent, sometimes bloodied, yet through these trials, we become the masters of our destinies. The artist, the visionary, the fearless soul—they each carve their path with the resolve born only from experience.

It is a daring imagination, unafraid of shadows, that awakens us to freedom. It is the force in every artist's hand, every philosopher's question, the spark in every dreamer's eye. True freedom does not wait for our time but our readiness, calling us to seek, push, and transcend. For in finding freedom within, we claim our place in the grandest story of all—the journey from shadow to light, from confinement to boundless, undeniable purpose.

From the first glimpse of light and that initial stretch toward its warmth, life has been an adventure, layered and relentless. I don't claim to have seen it all, but I've experienced enough to share with you the impressions, the stings, and the quiet triumphs that have shaped my path. My journey has been much—a series of tight spaces and humid chapters, often humbling in ways I never anticipated. Yet amid that tension, there have been rare moments to breathe deeply and savor the exhilarating rush of surprise and discovery.

I come from a past shaped by contrast and complexity, a background woven with the unexpected and the unknown. It is awkward at times, yet I lay it here openly. My words, like footprints, track across the table of time, each one marking the places where meaning took root. This journey, which began with a small boy's prayer, has grown in ways that even he could not have foreseen. Though his answer may still be out there, that boy continues on, drawn toward the soft flicker of distant light. And with every step, the call to freedom grows louder, echoing from that place where light and life converge.

May this story speak not only of my journey but to the fire that lives within every seeker of light, pushing us all forward toward the vast, unwritten chapters of freedom.

We stand at the threshold of an uncharted freedom, a freedom not merely from the constraints of others, but from the veils of perception that have long dictated how we see ourselves, our purpose, and each other. Ours is a freedom that embraces the whole of human experience—a boundless liberation from inherited fears, from collective illusions, and from the tangled roots of obsolete belief.

To the philosopher who quests for knowledge beyond reason alone, who sees truth as a multidimensional reality shaped not just by ideas but by experience: we call upon you to help frame this emerging world, a world that demands we think beyond boundaries, beyond assumptions. The call is to peel back the layers that obscure our vision, to shed light on the truths hidden in shadows of history and within the walls of our own minds.

To the metaphysical realist, who stands grounded in the absoluteness of existence, yet perceives that there are worlds within worlds, dimensions we cannot yet see: it is time to transcend even the confines of logic and sense, to look beyond what is and imagine what could be. The truths you hold are the foundations upon which new understandings will rise, challenging dogma and dismantling the illusions that bind humanity to a singular view of reality.

To those spiritually frustrated but unafraid, the ones who have wandered through the valleys of doubt and surfaced not with answers, but with questions that fuel the soul: let us gather together, to build bridges of understanding, empathy, and wisdom that will endure. Yours is the vision that seeks unity without conformity, transcendence without abandoning the earthly. You are the harbingers of a spirit-led liberation, one that calls humanity not to isolate itself in sanctified spaces but to expand, to integrate, to *become*.

We stand on the edge of this dawning consciousness, an unbroken horizon where thought, spirit, and action merge into something transcendent and unstoppable. Let us cast aside the chains woven from ignorance and fear. Let us draw up a new history to be told in the language of freedom—freedom as deep as the soul, as wide as the universe, as unbreakable as the truth we hold within.

This is our charge: to liberate the human spirit in its entirety. To dismantle the myth of separation. To embrace a future undivided, one that reflects the boundless potential in each of us. We are the ones who will make this mark on freedom—and with it, redefine what it means to be truly human.

2 CENTS OF REASON

A DEEP DIVE INTO WHAT SHAPES US

KEEP UP THE FIGHT

A rallying cry to stand firm in the pursuit of naturally birthed freedoms for all citizens of the world.

My friends, thank you for your patience, your consideration, and your time in reading these pages. I hope they offer you a spark of inspiration worth sharing. Change is rarely easy, but change is our moment. Change is the destiny of time itself, guiding us toward evolution. We are being coached by an energy as ancient as time, urging us forward. This is our moment.

This is our rallying cry to stand firm in pursuit of freedoms born not just for a few, but for all citizens of the world. Many of those fighting today are not driven by malice—they're simply driven by a lifetime of knowing little else. Their understanding of peace is limited. But how do you bring people like this together? It's challenging to cultivate peace when pain and anger are louder than the voices calling for healing.

In mediation, I often witness people quick to list others' faults while avoiding their own. It's human nature to defend ourselves, but growth demands we look deeper. Too often, solutions are imagined only through personal benefit—thinking peace will come if others conform. This outlook ignores the real core of resolution: mutual respect and the readiness to meet halfway. Statements like, *"I'll never speak to him again,"* or *"I don't care about her anymore,"* arise from pain, but these walls only reinforce division. Demonizing the other's perspective while elevating our own is a sure way to halt any hope for peace.

This reminds me of a debate with my friend MJ, rooted in her strong faith as a Seventh-day Adventist, over whether diabetes could one day be cured. While MJ holds that a cure is unlikely, I am open to the possibility, though it's not yet realized. Possibility is vital; it's the door to progress. When she mentioned her belief that a cure isn't feasible, I reminded her of the saying, *"With God, all things are possible."* Limiting ourselves to what is currently true ignores the potential for tomorrow and its giftwrapped opportunity to bring something new. This isn't about who's right or wrong; it's about trusting that change—real change—is possible. Change is always possible. Change is history said out loud. History shouts of change.

Whether in mediation or in life, we need a mindset open to change. Assuming that today's reality is unchangeable closes the door on growth. The path to peace demands setting aside our need to be right. True peace comes not from victory in debate but from a deep respect for each other's humanity, rights, and dignity. Anger is a natural response to discomfort, but growth requires that we turn discomfort into understanding.

The journey toward peace requires embracing *possibility*, *probability*, and *potential*—three related but distinct ideas shaping how we perceive our power to create change.

- **Possibility** forms the foundation of hope and imagination. It's what *can* happen, however improbable it may seem. When we sit at a table to resolve conflict, entertaining the possibility of peace is essential. Without it, any hope for reconciliation fades before it even starts. This is the idea that something different could happen, that we're not stuck.

- **Probability** looks at what's likely based on current realities. It's shaped by today's data, often showing slim chances for peace when pain and history produce a typhoon of opposing forces. Probability can hold us back when we see it as fate rather than a snapshot of the present.

- **Potential**, however, is where real transformation lies. It's the capacity we have within us to bring about change, not passively, but actively choosing to bridge divides and build something new. Potential requires effort and intention; it lives in us but only activates when we choose to embrace it.

The challenge is to move beyond what's probable and invest in what's possible, believing in our potential to change. Looking through the lens of potential means recognizing that every person carries the seed of transformation. Our greatest moments of discovery and growth often appear in our darkest hours. Whether we're striving for peace in our relationships or scientific breakthroughs, potential reminds us that we're never truly stuck; we are capable of growth beyond the limits of today's beliefs.

So, keep up the fight—not a fight against others but within ourselves to raise the visibility; to see possibility where others see impossibility, to believe in potential where others see limits, and to seek peace where others expect conflict. Our most profound progress comes not from accepting things as they are, but from daring to envision what better they could be.

2 MORE CENTS

We made history. We are making history. History will be made. If there is one truth that I am happy to hold as a certainty, it is this: history does not lie. You can review it, spin it to suit your tastes, attempt to doctor it, or dismiss it entirely, but history stands as an unalterable record of what has occurred. What happened yesterday is fact. It cannot be dusted off, bronzed, or polished to fit a more pleasing narrative. What happened—happened.

The challenge lies not in interpreting history but in producing it.

Too often, we are locked into the immediacy of today. We act without fully considering how our deeds will resonate when history records the facts. The real task is to confront the "right now" with an awareness of its lasting implications. In the bubble of the present moment, we are both the artists and the art, shaping the canvas of time. If we could fast-forward into the future, what would history reveal about us? Who were we? What did we do? How did we handle the challenges under our control?

As humans, we are fallible. Our view is frequently narrowed by selfish motives, and we rarely stop to consider the broader context of our actions. Without deliberate reflection, our understanding remains confined to the stained furnishings of our individual bubbles—our personal lives shaped by experiences, beliefs, and biases. These bubbles merge, interact, and inevitably pop, leaving traces that contribute to the historical record.

As I noted earlier, "The Bubble represents the inner self, shaped by a lifetime of experiences, thoughts, and beliefs. It is inherently self-centered, focused on self-preservation, self-interest, and self-protection." This truth is timeless. Throughout history, the bubbles of individuals have coalesced into the collective decisions of societies, empires, and movements. History records not just the moments of triumph or failure, but also the intentions and actions shaped by these bubbles.

History reports what happened—not always why it happened, nor what could have happened. We've seen nations rise and fall, their stories etched in the context of their time. It is the shared furnishings of bubbles—the common ideals, values, and visions—that create the threads of continuity in the human story. Some of these shared elements are so beautiful that they become prized heirlooms, passed from generation to generation, shaping cultures and legacies.

But herein lies the tension: are we intentional about what we contribute to this shared history? Do we understand the weight of our decisions beyond the fleeting moments of now? Or are we content to float along, oblivious to how our actions today will ripple across time, becoming history tomorrow?

Time, the unyielding arbiter, does not negotiate. It captures each moment, weaving it into the unbroken tapestry of history. What we choose to do in a fleeting second has a tendency to ripple into eternity, shaping not only ourselves but those who inherit our actions.

There was a little boy once. He sat at his mother's knee as she sat on that old piano bench. He was captivated by the stories she read to him and his younger brothers. That moment, like countless others, passed. It became history. Yet even as the years rolled forward, the seed of that moment took root within him. The stories inspired a dream; one he continues to chase—a dream both elusive and unrelenting.

His journey, like all journeys, was marked by frustrations, mistakes, and mishaps. There were times when the pressures of his own realities solidified into painful lessons, leaving scars only time could soothe. Yet, there were also joys—unwritten stories hidden in the folds of memory and moments so vivid they still breathe in the fine and hidden print of history.

Through it all, he kept trying. He failed often, but he learned. He reads his own headlines, seeking meaning, uncovering truths, and sometimes merely surviving. His only certainty became his understanding of time—a force that pulls us forward even as we struggle to make sense of the past.

Now grown, sitting at a keyboard, he offers his two cents of reason. Looking at the newer generations, he wonders if they'll listen. He tries to understand, constantly searching for perspectives beyond his own, holding onto a faith—stained and imperfect—that humanity can rise above its perceived limitations.

This reflection reminds him of a simple truth: time is not just a force that carries us forward; it is a mirror reflecting the imprints of our moments. Each action, however small, positions the next, and each next solidifies behind us, etched into the saga of time.

History, after all, is not just a record of events; it is a teacher, relentless in its lessons. It may not always tell the story perfectly, but its imperfections are part of its beauty. Like the little boy who once sat wide-eyed before his mother, sitting on that wooden floor still overly fragrant of its Sabbath pine-washing, his life and every human life is a testament to the tension between hope and failure, between aspiration and reality.

The boy's journey, now the author's, is humanity's story. It is a mosaic of moments—some triumphant, some painful, some yet untold. What we do matters. The challenge is not simply to live but to live with the awareness that our actions today will one day be judged by the lens that gives its focus to history. Who were we? What did we do? How did we handle the moments we were given?

Time is the canvas, and we are the artists. Every stroke—the joys, the mistakes, the lessons, the dreams—is part of the masterpiece we leave behind. And while we may not see the full picture, we continue to paint, guided by the hope that someday, somehow, humanity will do better than its moments lived.

The Power of Persistence and the Gift of Presence

For every moment since our conception, time has woven an intricate tapestry of events that no human hand can unravel. History stands as the unflinching keeper of these moments—solid, unalterable, and immune to our subjective interpretations. What has happened remains fact, static in its existence, even as we attempt to spin it, doctor it, or dismiss it entirely.

I have lived through moments that time has already solidified, and as I write this, I carry the weight of those experiences. Some of them inspire me. Others haunt me. But all of them shape my understanding of humanity, of resilience, and of our interconnectedness.

A couple of weeks ago, my country held an election. The results were not what I had hoped for, and I found myself grappling with disappointment. Yet, as a citizen, I accepted them because I believe in the process, flawed as it may sometimes seem. History, after all, doesn't lie. It records what is, not what we wish had been.

The day after the election, I walked into my home. The energy of that space greeted me like a balm, reminding me of the days when my sons, Jack and Brandon, were young. I have only ever had two children, and they were—and still are—my entire world. Their mother's divorce from me etched grief into my soul, a permanent scar. But history, as always, tells the truth: those boys were my anchor. Their laughter, their presence, gave me purpose.

When COVID-19 swept across the world, I found myself serving others in ways I never anticipated. I stood by hospital beds when even family members couldn't be present. I prayed over strangers and friends alike. I was a pillar of strength when others faltered, but when it was my turn to need support, I found myself alone.

After multiple surgeries and a life-threatening digestive condition, I returned home a changed man. My once-robust 310-pound frame had dwindled to 175 pounds, and my spirit felt equally diminished. The leaders I had served so faithfully during the pandemic offered no thanks, no acknowledgment of my sacrifices. They only voiced complaints about my inability to meet their wants and expectations.

I fell into a deep depression. My days were marked by silence, my nights by the dim, flickering glow of the television. The light in my life felt extinguished.

Then one night, the doorbell rang. I ignored it at first, too weary to move, but the persistent ringing pulled me from my bed. Every step was a battle against pain, both physical and emotional. When I finally opened the door, I found two sisters standing there, their arms full of grocery bags.

One of them, Valery, had become a dear friend. The two women didn't speak my language, and my Spanish was poor at best, but their intentions needed no translation. They moved past me into the kitchen and began preparing a meal. I tried to explain that I could only have broth, but my feeble attempts at communication were drowned out by their determination.

What they prepared wasn't just soup—it was a gift. The broth was rich, the chicken tender, the vegetables hearty. More than its physical nourishment, it was an act of love that reached into the depths of my despair and pulled me back to life.

As I sat there, savoring their offering, I realized something profound: the history being written in that moment was one of connection, of compassion, of humanity at its best. These women, immigrants in a country that often undervalues their contributions, had shown me a kindness I hadn't experienced from those I had once called my community.

Their generosity contrasted sharply with the demands of the church leaders I had once served. Even in my weakened state, they expected me to fulfill my obligations, oblivious to the toll it took on me. Yet here were these two sisters, asking for nothing, giving everything.

History doesn't lie. It remembers both the wounds inflicted and the hands that heal. That night, it recorded a moment of grace that will forever remain etched in my heart.

Back to the Wednesday Evening Children

History continues to speak.

It was a Wednesday evening, the day after the election. I

pulled into the driveway, weary from the day. As was my habit, I sat in the car for a while—my private time. This was when I'd decompress, catch up on current events, brush up on my Spanish, and play a few mind-calming games. If calls needed to be made or accepted, this was often the time.

After some moments, I stepped out of the car and headed toward the door, knocking lightly before it opened. Rapidly. Unusually. The energy on the other side wasn't the welcoming hum I'd grown used to.

"Donnell, sit down. We need to talk to you."

"Okay," I said, taken aback but trying to remain composed. "Let me put these things down first."

Something was off. The atmosphere was thick with a tension I couldn't place, like a storm gathering just out of sight. As I put my belongings away, my mind raced. Was it an accident? Trouble at school? Some kind of family crisis?

"Okay, I'm here," I said, returning to the kitchen. They were standing together; their expressions etched with urgency and worry. A chair was pulled out for me, and they motioned for me to sit.

"Do you know what happened at school today?"

My dry wit rose instinctively, a reflex to lighten the mood. It fell flat. This was no time for humor. I caught myself, leaned in, and listened.

The details tumbled out, fast and chaotic, their voices overlapping. I struggled to catch everything, piecing the story together through the noise of emotion and cultural layers. A few of them spoke almost proficient English, but the excitement and fear robbed them of their confidence, making their words a tangled mess of languages and gestures.

"Slow down," I said gently. "One at a time. I'm listening."

What unfolded hit like a freight train. At school that day, they'd been taunted—mocked by classmates emboldened by the political climate. Words laced with hate and ignorance had spilled from children's mouths, their bubbles filled with the toxic air of learned prejudice. For these kids, the election's aftermath wasn't abstract; it was personal.

They feared deportation. They feared their family being torn apart. Some of them were born here, Americans by birthright, yet even that felt fragile under the weight of cruel taunts and threats.

And then came the question that broke me.

"Donnell, are you going to let something happen to us?"

It was the seven-year-old, the one I lovingly called my shadow. She stood beside me, her small face flushed, her cheeks ruddy with fear, and her eyes pooling with tears she fought to hold back.

Her broken English sliced through the air with the sharpness of pure truth: "Are you going to let something happen to us?"

I froze. Her innocence, her trust, her desperation—it all crashed over me. She wasn't just asking for reassurance; she was demanding an answer. A real answer. Not a platitude. Not a lie. She needed the kind of truth that could calm her trembling world.

I felt the weight of her question. My heart ached at the cruel reality these children were forced to confront. They were innocent, yet they bore the consequences of a society fractured by hate and ignorance.

I looked into her eyes, seeing the reflection of every child in that room—each carrying their own fears, shaped by bubbles of confinement and the venom of inherited prejudice.

In that moment, I realized my response wasn't just about words. It was about action, about presence, about being a shield against the storm for these kids who had no other defense.

I took her hand, meeting her gaze with all the strength I could summon.

"No," I said firmly. "I won't let anything happen to you. We're in this together. Always."

Her tears spilled over, but she nodded, gripping my hand tightly. Around us, the room began to settle, the chaos giving way to something quieter.

But inside, I was far from calm.

The world outside was on fire. The tainted bubbles of hate, stoked by toxic leaders, were expanding, spilling their poison into the minds of the young. Even those who seemed innocent carried the burden of their upbringing, molded by the furnishings of intolerance within their own bubbles.

This wasn't just a clash of cultures or politics. It was a battle for the hearts and minds of the next generation.

And in this battle, the children—both those who taunted and those who suffered—were victims of the same labyrinth. They were trapped in bubbles that confined their humanity, their potential, their capacity to understand one another.

The question now wasn't just what I would do for these

kids. It was what we, as a society, would do to break these cultural bubbles, to pierce the toxic air, to teach our children—*all* our children—to see beyond the walls of fear and hate.

The children are speaking.

Are we listening?

The Bubbles Are Lining Up

Dear Reader,

Thank you for journeying through these pages with me. I appreciate the time and energy you've invested in exploring these ideas. Thanks to you, I've been able to offer my two cents as a sampling of my reasoning, and I truly believe our best days are still ahead. It's not often that an author pauses at the end of a book to extend gratitude, but I feel it's important. I hope that what I've shared has been more than just words. I hope it has been a perspective-shifting experience. My wish is that your bubble now holds furniture of greater value, carefully chosen and meaningful, rather than outdated hand-me-downs passed along without question.

As you continue navigating your own labyrinth, I encourage you to pause and consider the perspectives and positions of others as they make their way through theirs. Each of us carries a unique bubble of experiences, shaped by the lives we've lived, the stories we've been told, and the truths we've embraced or avoided. And yet, within those bubbles lies both the beauty of individuality and the danger of isolation.

Much of what we've been taught—what we've accepted as "truth"—is rooted in myth. These myths persist, ghostly in their nature, feeding off the energies of willing minds. They thrive because we allow them to, offering up belief where skepticism might better serve. And so, myths flourish, casting long shadows over reality.

It's the willing mind, however, that holds the key to both destruction and liberation. A mind willing to confront the faces of truth can recognize deception, challenge it, and ultimately dismantle it. But a mind willing to ignore reality, to trade curiosity for comfort, becomes the soil where falsehoods take root and grow. This is where stagnation begins.

We've all witnessed the dance—the uneducated swaying to the rhythms of deception, responding to the alluring melodies of those who prey on ignorance and fear. The consequences of such dances are dire: lives lost, communities fractured, properties destroyed, and truths buried beneath the weight of purposed manipulation. And yet, the choice remains ours: will we be complicit, or will we seek to understand?

This book isn't just about ideas; it's a call to action. It's about recognizing the responsibility we bear as individuals and as members of a shared world. To dismantle the bubbles that confine us, we must be brave enough to look beyond their walls and question what we've been taught to accept.

Take this journey forward with courage. Be willing to see, to listen, and to grow. The world we leave behind for the next generation depends on it.

As I mentioned earlier, the method I employ to understand complex matters is to examine the macro to understand the micro and vice versa. Sometimes, it's the smallest fragments that illuminate the larger order, while the broader strokes help decode the intricacies of the details.

In this light, I've been observing the intensifying polarizations taking shape across the globe. On the surface, they appear most vividly in politics and religion—arenas that are deeply personal yet universally impactful. These polarizations are like magnetically charged bubbles, separating themselves into culturally polarized zones. On one end, we see micro-cultural clashes over identity, ideology, and belonging. On the other, a cosmic polarization emerges, an existential tug-of-war between humanity's shared future and its fragmented present.

We are, unmistakably, walking headlong into a reactive zone. The signs are everywhere—charged headlines, shock-laden rhetoric, and the visible fractures in communities that once found unity in diversity. These are not random occurrences; they are the intentional release of charged particles, deliberately deployed to stoke division and deepen mistrust.

What lies at stake is nothing short of our shared humanity. We must recognize that polarization thrives on fear, ignorance, and the manipulation of personal and cultural insecurities. The micro-examples—a neighbor turned enemy over a political sign, a family fractured over ideology—mirror the macro-level divisions that paralyze nations and halt progress.

But just as polarization can be charged, it can also be neutralized. It begins with understanding. By acknowledging the forces at play, questioning their origins, and refusing to be complicit in the chaos, we reclaim agency. The antidote to division is deliberate action: bridging gaps, fostering dialogue, and refusing to let fear dictate the terms of our relationships.

This journey forward is not easy. It demands courage, humility, and an unwavering commitment to growth. Yet, it is a journey we must take—not just for ourselves, but for the generations who will inherit the world we create.

Let us not walk blindly into the reactive zone. Let us face it with eyes wide open, ready to transform charged bubbles of division into spheres of shared understanding. The potential is within us; the question is whether we will act on it.

A Critical Warning: The Polarization of Our Time

Here is the matter that concerns me deeply, and I urge you to grasp this fully if nothing else: It is not the fear of some hypothetical asteroid collision that should ignite urgency in us. Instead, it is the light—subtle yet persistent—that trolls the darkness of our collective ignorance, pulling us further into the void of division and polarization.

Something profound has been happening, an unsettling shift that we can no longer afford to ignore. This is not about religion. It's not Catholic versus Protestant, Christian versus Muslim, or any other binary opposition of faiths or philosophies. It's not even about ideological battles—right versus left, liberal versus conservative, or science versus religion.

No, the real issue lies in the dangerous magnetic pull of polarization, a force that has been quietly gathering strength over generations. This force works not through thoughtful dialogue but through fear, misinformation, and manipulation, fracturing societies into opposing camps. People are being drawn into extreme positions, abandoning critical thinking for reactive certainty.

The Roots of Polarization

Throughout history, during times of confusion and uncertainty, people have often sought the safety of tribal consensus. They were guided—sometimes deceived—by leaders of church and state to believe that conformity would bring stability. But this coalescence came at a price. It nurtured intolerance, sowed division, and fed into the hypocrisies we see today.

Consider the contradictions of modern Western Christianity: preaching love while practicing exclusion, proclaiming tolerance while harboring disdain for those who reject its dogmas. Or the politician who promises salvation from societal woes, only to exploit the vulnerable for power. Both pull at the fragile threads of our humanity, tightening the knots of polarization.

The energy fueling these divides is real, and it has been building for a long time. It manifests not only in political arenas but also in religious fervor and cultural clashes. It is the same energy that gave rise to Jonestown, Waco, and countless other tragedies born of extremes. These are not just isolated events; they are warning signs—fragments of supercharged bubbles bursting under the pressure of accumulated radioactive polarization.

The Dangers of Extremes

These polarizations are more dangerous than we often realize. When the critical mass of these ideological bubbles is released, the consequences can be catastrophic. They produce not just violence and upheaval but a deeper erosion of trust, compassion, and reason.

The most troubling aspect of this phenomenon is that those caught in its grip are often unaware. Like a child endlessly asking "Why?" without ever understanding the answer, they follow the loudest voices, the most compelling narratives, without question. They act—not out of informed conviction but out of conditioned reflex.

History is rife with examples of where this stuff leads. Leaders like Hitler and Mussolini capitalized on these divisions, offering poisoned wells as solutions to complex problems. Their promises of restoration and greatness were mere bait for destruction. And today, we see echoes of these tactics—leaders who peddle nostalgia for a painful past as if it were a golden age, leading us toward dangerous repetitions.

A Call to Critical Engagement

The curves of polarization—both in the West and globally—are sharper and more perilous than ever before. We are at a crossroads where our collective trajectory could either deepen these divides or steer us toward understanding and unity. The choice is ours, but it requires courage, self-awareness, and a willingness to confront uncomfortable truths.

Take this warning seriously. Recognize the patterns of division and manipulation, and resist their pull. Engage critically with the world around you, not just as a passive observer but as an active participant in shaping a better future.

The stakes are high, and the time to act is now.

As I close, let's slow drive back to the prophets.

I hold a viewpoint that's uniquely mine. Some may appreciate it, some may not, and others might not care at all—and that's okay. I am who I am, no more and no less, as my creator intended. Like every bubble in the great sea of existence, I am here to live out this one fleeting moment in time (**One Moment in Time** – Whitney Houston). But in this moment, I see something that I must speak about.

I come to this from my background, shaped by teachings from the Old Testament and the New Testament—two volumes of human history written in ink that has long since dried. The Old Testament tells us of a God deeply intertwined with the struggles of specific tribes, navigating a world teeming with untold stories of other peoples and places. And yet, these stories of creation, destruction, exile, and deliverance form the bedrock of our spiritual imagination.

Then came the New Testament, a profound shift in tone and purpose. The vengeful God became the embodiment of love, hope, and mercy (***Mercy Mercy Me*** – Marvin Gaye). A servant leader emerged, offering not wrath but grace, and through his story, we glimpsed the possibility of redemption and renewal for even the most broken among us. He was called a prophet by some, a savior by others, but in every interpretation, his life was a testament to the transformative power of compassion (***Change is Gonna Come*** – Sam Cooke).

Now, here we are, living in what I call ***Our Testament***. We are the authors of this chapter of human existence, just as those before us penned theirs. The prophets of old, though flawed and human, served as beacons, offering guidance and warnings in the many languages of their time. Today, I believe we are surrounded by modern prophets—voices crying out in songs, poems, speeches, and actions.

Some of these prophets come in the form of artists who, like the psalmists of old, give us melodies of hope, warning, and reflection. They ask us to imagine a better world (***Imagine*** – John Lennon), to find strength within ourselves (***Eye of the Tiger*** – Survivor), and to confront the man in the mirror (***Man in the Mirror*** – Michael Jackson). Their words and notes are not just entertainment; they are calls to action, reminders that we are all part of something greater (***We Are the World*** – USA for Africa).

But too often, like those who ignored the prophets of old, we fail to heed these messages. We become consumed by the noise of division—political polarization, religious strife, cultural clashes—until the music fades into the background. The world begins to break apart at its most fragile seams (***Eve of Destruction*** – Barry McGuire).

This is where my concern lies. It's not the asteroid that should ignite fear and urgency among us; it's the light that is trolling the darkness, slowly dimming our sound understanding. The danger is not religion vs. science, right vs. left, or any of the other battles we so often rage against. The danger is in the polarization itself, the magnetic pull of extremes that drives us further apart.

From time to time, fragments of these polarized bubbles break, releasing supercharged energy with devastating force. Whether it's the tragedies of Jonestown, Waco, the World Trade Center, Mother Emmanuel Church, Tree of Life Synagogue, the Sikh Temple of Wisconsin, one of the many mass shootings beyond, or the shadows of totalitarian regimes, these moments are not just accidents of history—they are the outcomes of unchecked polarizations. They are reminders that when we fail to listen, fail to see, and fail to grow, we place ourselves on a collision course with destruction (***Blowin' in the Wind*** – Bob Dylan).

Yet, amidst the chaos, there remains a choice. We can write a new verse in *Our Testament,* one that doesn't replay the comforts of a painful past but charts a path toward a brighter, more united future (***Here Comes the Sun*** – The Beatles). That's what this oration is about. It's about paying attention, listening to the songs that guide us, and finding the courage to build a better world.

Let's turn the page and begin.

Here is a sharing of words—timeless, profound, and alive with meaning—that we can choose to heed. These are not just melodies but messages, not just entertainment but echoes of the prophets before us. They call us to reflection, to action, and above all, to understanding. May we seek the wisdom woven within them or at least consider the guidance they offer.

(**Respect** – Aretha Franklin) reminds us of the foundational human need to see and be seen, to honor one another's worth, and to stand firm in our shared dignity. It is the cornerstone of every just society, the seed from which harmony grows.

(**Say it Loud, Say it Clear** – Mike and the Mechanics) speaks to the courage required to voice our truths, even when the world prefers silence. It urges us to move beyond whispers and fears, to articulate the hopes and fears that bind us all.

(**Give Peace a Chance** – Plastic Ono Band) When someone dies, we say, "Rest in Peace." Can we at least try to encourage each other to, "Live in Peace?" This song pleads for a pause in our endless conflicts, an opportunity to imagine a world where peace is more than a fleeting hope, but a living, breathing reality.

(**We Got to Have Peace** – Curtis Mayfield) emphasizes the urgency of our collective mission. Peace is not just a lofty ideal; it is the essential framework upon which justice and equality can thrive.

(**The Way it Is** – Bruce Hornsby) reminds us of the stark realities we face—the divides that persist, the struggles that endure. Yet, it also carries the subtle truth that change is possible, even if the way things are now seems immovable.

(**Ordinary People** – John Legend) shines a light on the beauty and strength found in everyday humanity. It is not the extraordinary alone who shape the future but the collective will of ordinary people refusing to surrender to despair.

(*I Want to Know What Love Is* – Foreigner) echoes the deepest longing of the human soul—a desire for connection, understanding, and an abiding sense of belonging that transcends fear and division. It's about value. It is about being valued and an honest act of valuing the positives seeded in the heart.

(*I've Got Dreams to Remember* – Otis Redding) reminds us that even amidst loss and hardship, our dreams are worth holding onto. They tether us to hope and inspire us to move forward, no matter how dark the road may seem.

(**Unforgettable** – Nat King Cole) celebrates the enduring power of memory and legacy, urging us to honor the voices and visions that have shaped us, even as we create new ones.

(*I Made it Through the Rain* – Barry Manilow) testifies to the resilience of the human spirit. It speaks to the storms we endure and the strength we find in ourselves and one another to keep going.

(**Hold Fast to Dreams** – Florence Price) and its instrumental counterpart by (Dave Brubeck) carry a universal truth: dreams are the lifeblood of progress. When we cling to them, we safeguard the hope of a better tomorrow.

(**Keep on Pushing** – The Impressions) reminds us that change is not instantaneous. It demands persistence, resilience, and the willingness to push forward even when the weight of the world presses back.

(***In the Morning When I Rise*** – Joan Baez) is a quiet but powerful declaration of renewal, the promise of a new day where hope and possibility rise with the sun.

These songs, like the prophets of old, offer us anthems for our testament. They guide us through moments of uncertainty, urging us to look inward, outward, and upward. Together, they remind us of the power we hold to shape our shared story, a song still unfolding.

These pages have woven a story, a mosaic shaped by the bubble's viewpoint of **My Life** (Billy Joel). It is a testament to the journey—complex, unfiltered, and uniquely human. Along the way, I've come to understand that sometimes, **No One is to Blame** (Howard Jones) for the twists and turns that shape our paths. Yet, life has its moments, burning like **Paper in Fire** (John Mellencamp), when the chaos feels unrelenting, and the world itself seems to smolder.

Through it all, I've sought the solace of **Wide Open Spaces** (The Chicks), a yearning for freedom, for room to breathe, to exist fully and freely. But there have been times, too, when I've felt the weight of solitude, the echo of being **So Alone All My Life** (Kenny Rankin). It is in those moments that an unsettling truth reveals itself: we are all caught in **An Unsettling Force** (Luke Nephew), pulled between the familiar and the unknown, between comfort and the call to grow.

In those moments, my mind could only **Turn, Turn, Turn** (Pete Seeger), caught in the cycles of time and reflection. But turning wasn't enough. I had to learn to embrace **Thinking Outside the Box** (George Wallace & Leonard Lehrman), to reject the confines of what was handed to me and seek new truths. Only then could I see **The Bigger Picture** (Lil Baby)—a broader, more connected vision of humanity and its endless potential.

But the road to understanding is not paved with ease. **Freedom Ain't Free** (Brother Ali). It demands struggle, sacrifice, and a relentless push against the tides that seek to pull us back. And yet, even in the struggle, I have found a rhythm, a reminder that **Freedom is a Constant Song** (Si Kahn), one we must sing together if we hope to harmonize in this dissonant world.

So, I guess by now, you may understand my reverence for music as the voice of the prophets in our testament; the story of our time. These artists paid close attention to the pulse of their times, crafting songs that spoke directly to the hearts of those who listened. They lifted us *Higher and Higher* (Jackie Wilson). They challenged us to *Reach Out and Touch Somebody's Hand,* urging us to make the world a better place if we could (Diana Ross).

And, oh, how those **memories light the corners of my mind.** Misty, watercolor memories of *The Way We Were.* Scattered pictures of the smiles we left behind, the smiles we gave to one another for the way we were. *Can it be that it was all so simple then? Or has time re-written every line? If we had the chance to do it all again, tell me, would we? Could we?* (Barbra Streisand).

I hope that the man I am today—the guy who once was that little boy staying awake long enough to pray—has learned enough, seen enough, and grown enough to open his eyes to the truths that were always there. I hope I've heard the words that remind us life is fleeting, the bubbles we live in are fragile, the labyrinths we navigate are complex, and the perspectives we build are both our freedom and our responsibility. Together, they lead us to a higher place—a place where our legacy may one day be celebrated as the time when we finally got it right. May **Love Lift Us Up Where We Belong** (Jennifer Warnes and Joe Cocker).

Listen to the music. ***What the people need is a way to make 'em smile. It ain't so hard to do if you know how. Gotta get a message, get it on through. Oh, now mama, don't you ask me why*** (The Doobie Brothers).

Someone told me long ago, there's a calm before the storm. I know, it's been coming for some time. Have you ever seen the rain? (Creedence Clearwater Revival). **Gone are the days of youthful ignorance I never knew how to cherish. Gone are the days of naivety I never put to good use.** ***The rain keeps falling*** (Micah P. Hinson). ***Feels like it's raining all over the world*** (Brooke Benton). Yes, **Rainy Days and Mondays Always Get Me Down** (The Carpenters).

But even on those rainy days, ***the sun will come out tomorrow. Bet your bottom dollar that tomorrow there'll be sun*** (Martin Charnin). ***Hello, hello sunshine. It's mighty good to see you, bright sunshine. Hello, hello sunshine. It's been dark for such a long time. It's been dark for such a long time*** (Rev. Maceo Woods and The Christian Tabernacle Baptist Church Choir).

So, **Get up. Stand up** (Bob Marley). The challenge is on we're **Living for the city** (Stevie Wonder). They told us about **Ohio** (Crosby, Stills, Nash, and Young). We know ***they're coming to America*** (Neil Diamond). They told us about **The Border** (Willie Nelson). They gave us the **Border Song** (Elton John). They sang about **the Streets of Philadelphia** (Bruce Springsteen). We were reminded **In the Middle of the Night** (Billy Joel). From the dream, to the blessing some so willing to share ***Living in the Promised Land*** (Willie Nelson).

I know that there are those ***They smile in your face***, we call them ***Backstabbers*** (The O'Jays). Only ***If I had a hammer*** (Peter, Paul, and Mary). I would ***Fight the power*** (The Isley Brothers / Public Enemy). Politically, ***I'm a street fighting man*** (Rolling Stones), ***a fortunate son*** (Creedence Clearwater Revival). ***I just want to live*** (Keedron Bryant). ***Sometimes you just can't make it on your own*** (U2). I hear her sing ***Give me on reason to stay here*** (Traci Chapman). Sometimes, ***A house is not a home*** (Luther Vandross). But ***The times they are a changing*** (Bob Dylan).

Freedom is a constant struggle (Roberta Slavitt). History displays some ***strange fruit*** (Billie Holiday). ***Precious Lord, take my hand*** (Thomas A. Dorsey). ***Gonna break these chains around me. Gonna learn to fly again. May be hard, may be hard, but I'll do it; when I'm back on my feet again*** (Michael Bolton). There may be ***Tears in heaven*** (Eric Clapton) but, ***Don't stop believin*** (Journey). ***Ain't no mountain high enough*** (Diana Ross). ***There's a moral revolution going on*** (Ruth MacKinze). ***Somebody's hurting my brother, my people, our people*** (Yara Allen). ***Everyday people*** (Sly Stone), ***They don't care about us*** (Michael Jackson). ***It's a ball of confusion*** (The Temptations).

All you fascists bound to lose (Woody Guthrie). ***Oh Freedom*** (Negro Spiritual) cries from the graves of those who only saw the dream of freedom. ***They killed him*** (Kris Kristofferson). It was ***the Death of Emmett Till*** (Bob Dylan), ***Goodman, Swerner, and Chaney*** (Tom Paxton), ***Abraham, Martin, and John*** (Dick Holler), they too were ***American skin*** (Bruce Springsteen).

From the ***Scottsboro Boys*** (Lead Belly), to the

Exonerated 5 (Adrian Dunn), We *Bleed the same* (Mandisa). *White privilege* (Macklemore & Ryan Lewis)? *Just another day* (Queen Latifa). *People get ready* (Curtis Mayfield / Rod Stewart). *Someday we'll all be free* (Donny Hathaway).

We are the ones (Melissa Ethridge). *The people will rise* (Nelini Stamp). It's *Spiritual* (Jay-Z). *People gonna rise like water* (Peace Poets). *We will rise together* ((Hali Hammer). *Let's stay together* (Al Green). *Stand by me* (Ben E. King). *Lean on me* (Bill Withers). *I'll take you there* (The Staple Singers). *It's Our turn now* (Len Seligman). *No justice, no peace* (Z-ro). We must *Rise up* (Andra Day). *Be the change* (Arlon Bennett).

Oh, Mary don't you weep (Aretha Franklin). *Vote 'em out* (Willie Nelson). *Hearts ain't gonna lie* (Alisa). *Sittin' on the dock of the bay* (Otis Redding). *Thinking Out Loud* (Ed Sheeran). *I love everybody* (Lyle Lovett). *Lead with love* (Melanie DeMore). *A lot of love* (Chris Brown). *Oh freedom* (African American Spiritual)! *Freedom! Freedom! Where are you? 'Cause I need freedom, too. I break chains all by myself. Won't let my freedom rot in hell. Hey! I'ma keep running - 'Cause a winner don't quit on themselves* (Beyoncè).

Here in my hands (Amy Wadge). *Tear down that wall* (Bright Light Social Hour). *Ten thousand bridges* (Greg Artzner & Terry Leonino). *That's what friends are for* (Dionne Warwick & Friends). *Our God is watching us from a distance* (Bette Midler).

Wow! *I love music, sweet sweet music. I love music. Just as long as it's groovy. Makes me laugh. Makes me smile for the world* (O'Jays). I did it! I'm excited. In closing, I strung together more than a hundred songs.

This completed project began as a thought I carried with a dear friend, Linda Harris. She resides in Massachusetts, but I first met her during my early college years. Over the past several years, Linda and I have engaged in numerous conversations about reality and the social impacts of irresponsible religion and politics.

Many of our basic presuppositions about life were formed during our earliest stages, long before we had the capacity to push back or question the information given to us. We accepted it because we had no other choice. For most of us, these early impressions became the anchors of our reasoning and understanding—the grounding point for countless opinions in the ever-present debates of "Right" versus "Wrong."

As adults, we often become fierce defenders of these early faiths and understandings, clinging to them as though they were immutable truths. Many of us are easily triggered, reactive, and defensive when those deeply rooted, childlike beliefs are questioned. Linda and I often spoke about the challenges of illiteracy, and while society has made great strides in improving literacy rates, we also coined a term—*Functional Illiteracy*.

Functional illiteracy highlights the lack of skills necessary to cope with most jobs and everyday situations. It's more than an inability to read or write; it reflects a gap in critical skill sets essential for managing daily life. According to the National Center for Educational Statistics (NCES), 21 percent of adults in the United States—around 43 million people—fall into the illiterate or functionally illiterate category.

Yet, there is another form of illiteracy that remains understudied: *Cultural Illiteracy*. Across the globe, there is a profound lack of understanding of cultures outside our own "bubbles." These collective bubbles—communities of shared experiences and beliefs—often foster ignorance toward other perspectives.

In our carelessness, we dismiss and delegitimize cultures and subcultures that we refuse to understand. When faced with gaps in knowledge, we too often rely on the selfishness of our imaginations to fill in the blanks of someone else's story. This default response, rooted in presuppositions and limited perspectives, is a grave disservice to the pluralistic world we live in today.

In such a society, where selfish reasoning and unreal logic often dominate, those who exist beyond our narrow worldviews are marginalized or even destroyed. This cultural illiteracy undermines our collective potential, making it harder to build bridges between communities and individuals.

As I reflected on these conversations and paid closer attention, I found myself returning to a lonesome stage of life. Linda was the only one who attended my mental and spiritual events, and together, we explored countless topics. Those discussions fueled a profound growth spurt in my thinking, pushing me beyond the limits of that little boy's prayer for *Wisdom! Wisdom!*

Wisdom became the rallying cry of my soul as I began to see the world more clearly. I realized that many teachers of the so-called "Word" had never truly been students of it. They were, often unknowingly, charlatans vending hand-me-down teachings from cultures long past. These peddlers perpetuated superstitions and "old wives' tales," catering to audiences whose own basic presuppositions anchored them to unexamined traditions.

This project is my offering, a culmination of years of conversations, reflections, and prayers for wisdom. It is my hope that these words inspire readers to challenge their own presuppositions, question the stories they've been told, and seek a deeper understanding of the world and the people within it.

There was a Bible text that came to mind as we talked one weekend. It resonated deeply with our discussions, and I think it is fitting to share it with you at this moment. To appreciate its depth, I'll present it in three translations: the King James Version (KJV), the New International Version (NIV), and the Amplified Bible (AMP).

King James Version (KJV):

"Wisdom is the principal thing; therefore get wisdom: and with all thy getting get understanding." – Proverbs 4:7

New International Version (NIV):

"The beginning of wisdom is this: Get wisdom. Though it cost all you have, get understanding." – Proverbs 4:7

Amplified Bible (AMP):

"The beginning of wisdom is: Get [skillful and godly] wisdom [it is preeminent]! And with all your acquiring, get understanding [actively seek spiritual discernment, mature comprehension, and logical interpretation]." – Proverbs 4:7

Each version shines a unique light on the value of wisdom and understanding. The KJV, with its poetic brevity, emphasizes wisdom as a priority. The NIV highlights the costliness of wisdom, suggesting its pursuit is worth any price. The AMP enriches the concept further, expanding wisdom to include spiritual discernment and mature comprehension.

This text reflects the essence of what Linda and I often discussed: the relentless pursuit of wisdom and understanding, not as static possessions, but as dynamic forces that guide our lives. It challenges us to seek not just knowledge, but the discernment and depth to apply it in meaningful ways.

I would like to share these verses with you as well. **1 Timothy 1:5-7** shines a powerful light on a tragic portion of teachings that often distort and disorient the teacher/student relationship in reasoning. Again, I'll present it in three translations: the King James Version (KJV), the New International Version (NIV), and the Amplified Bible (AMP).

King James Version (KJV):

"Now the end of the commandment is charity out of a pure heart, and of a good conscience, and of faith unfeigned: from which some having swerved have turned aside unto vain jangling; desiring to be teachers of the law; understanding neither what they say, nor whereof they affirm."

New International Version (NIV):

"The goal of this command is love, which comes from a pure heart and a good conscience and a sincere faith. Some have departed from these and have turned to meaningless talk. They want to be teachers of the law, but they do not know what they are talking about or what they so confidently affirm."

Amplified Bible (AMP):

"But the goal of our instruction is love [which springs] from a pure heart and a good conscience and a sincere faith. Some individuals have wandered away from these things into empty arguments and useless discussions, wanting to be teachers of the Law [of Moses], even though they do not understand the terms they use or the subjects about which they make [such] confident declarations."

These verses offer profound insight into the nature of true teaching and the responsibility of those who guide others. At its core, the passage calls for love—born of a pure heart, good conscience, and sincere faith—to be the foundation of instruction. However, it also warns of those who stray into "vain jangling" (as the KJV vividly puts it), indulging in meaningless talk and confident assertions without understanding the weight of their words.

This caution speaks directly to the distortion that can occur when teachings are unanchored from truth and love, serving as a reminder for teachers and learners alike to remain rooted in sincerity and purpose.

Linda and I had very long conversations. During which, we began to examine the rhetoric of careless, uncontrolled, and uncensored hate. We listened to the often promotion of various superstitions. I joked, *"As the Prophet Stevie Wonder said,* **'When you believe in things that you don't understand; then you suffer. Superstition ain't the way.'"**

We started to examine the many superstitions that are exacted at our presuppositions for pecuniary gain and ongoing control. The traditional impress of both the political world and the role religion has been—and is becoming—more and more destructive when left in the hands of the ignorant and irresponsible.

Our conversations had an amazing impact on me. I was given a judgment-free space to think out loud. It was in this space that I could reflect on the many ways in which personal beliefs, societal structures, and cultural blind spots intersected to shape not only our lives but the very fabric of our collective humanity.

A couple of months ago, my dad gave me a challenge to write another book. He, having turned 102 yesterday, pushed me. I wondered, *'How much time do I have'?* The question wasn't merely about hours or days but about the urgency of sharing, creating, and contributing before the final curtain call.

I went to work immediately. These words are now in your hands. It is not a complete thought, but it does contain some ideas that I thought would add my two cents to the conversation for times to come.

Just as an added act of heart and humor, I thought of the many songs I have appreciated over the 62 years of my life. These songs gave me the challenge to think—sometimes, to think out loud. But what you read are the inner voicings of a guy who listens as he hopes to develop a greater cultural literacy that participates in the bridging developments of peace.

I heard the challenge of the '60s: *"**All we are saying is give peace a chance**"* (John Lennon and Yoko Ono). Those words, though born in another era, still echo with relevance today. They remind us that the call for peace and understanding is timeless, an ever-present need in our world.

There are two songs I want to close with. One, I will share the title and summation of my ongoing thought. The second is an ongoing struggle for a dream to live. It represents an enduring heart.

The first says, *"**I'd like to see the world for once all standing hand in hand, and hear them echo through the hills for peace throughout the land. I'd like to teach the world to sing, in perfect harmony . . . that's the song I hear**"* (The New Seekers). It is a vision—a possibility—that can only become reality if each of us commits to being the change we long to see.

Secondly, I close with the poetry of James Weldon Johnson. I encourage you to stay vigilant. The road is long. We all will see the ending someday. But for now:

Lift every voice and sing,
Till earth and heaven ring,
Ring with the harmonies of Liberty;
Let our rejoicing rise
High as the list'ning skies,
Let it resound loud as the rolling sea.

Sing a song full of the faith that the dark past has taught us,
Sing a song full of the hope that the present has brought us;
Facing the rising sun of our new day begun,
Let us march on till victory is won.

Stony the road we trod,
Bitter the chast'ning rod,
Felt in the days when hope unborn had died;
Yet with a steady beat,
Have not our weary feet
Come to the place for which our fathers sighed?

We have come over a way that with tears has been watered.
We have come, treading our path through the blood of the slaughtered,
Out from the gloomy past,
Till now we stand at last
Where the white gleam of our bright star is cast.

God of our weary years,
God of our silent tears,
Thou who hast brought us thus far on the way;
Thou who hast by Thy might,
Led us into the light,
Keep us forever in the path, we pray.

Lest our feet stray from the places, our God, where we met Thee,
Lest our hearts, drunk with the wine of the world, we forget Thee;

2 CENTS OF REASON A DEEP DIVE INTO WHAT SHAPES US

Shadowed beneath Thy hand,
May we forever stand,
True to our God,
True to our native land.

A BONUS 2 CENTS OF REASONING

Allow me please to take this a little further before I leave

Well now, I've shared my two cents—not a piece of my mind, for I'm mindful of how precious and finite those pieces are. We are living in strange and unsettling times, yes, but also in a moment ripe with extraordinary opportunity. This is a now moment—a crossroads where we, as individuals, nations, and a global family, can rise above the shadows and live out the best of what our Creator endowed us to achieve.

We are not confined to darkness. We are the children of light—progeny of the divine spark that compels us to illuminate every corner where darkness, stubborn and deceptive, persists. It is time to reclaim that light, to let it shine boldly into every crack and crevice where ignorance and injustice have taken root.

For too long, social wardens and cultural prison guards have perpetuated a blackout—an artificial confinement designed to control and divide. In the United States, those who claim to hold the keys to freedom have twisted righteousness into a deceptive weapon, cloaked in religious fervor and manipulated for power. This control thrives on superstition, religious hypocrisy, and a toxic stoicism that feeds on fear and ignorance.

This system does not liberate; it binds. It robs the vulnerable of dignity and humanity while enriching those who profit from division. It silences those who dare to speak truth, using social insanity to uphold lies. But truth cannot be silenced forever.

The United States of America was not founded as a

Christian nation. If it were, there would have been no need for abolitionists to rise, no need for women to demand suffrage, no need for Civil Rights or Voting Rights movements. Such struggles for justice and equality would not exist in a truly righteous society, for the natural rights of dignity and respect belong to all—not as gifts to be bestowed, but as inherent freedoms.

These rights are the supreme law of humanity. They transcend courts and legislation because they are written into the very essence of our being. To those who recognize the chains of cultural incarceration and confinement: you have the power to walk free. Break the mental barriers that divide us and reclaim your rightful place in the light.

Only then, when we refuse to be bound by darkness, can we move toward a world where justice truly is for all.

January 21, 2025

Yesterday was a day like no other—a paradox of extremes where the shadows of history mingled with the glimmers of hope. Darkness and light met at an intersection so profound that it left no room for neutrality. It was the place where optimism and pessimism stood face to face, each vying for dominion over our collective future. A stage was set where clarity wrestled with blindness, and the battle lines between progress and regression were drawn for all to see.

Yesterday's juxtaposition was stark: a national commemoration of Dr. Martin Luther King Jr., a man who envisioned a future of freedom and unity, alongside the ongoing rumblings of cultural and systemic forces seeking to drag us back into the grips of division and oppression. On one side stood the dreamers, armed with hope and the belief that humanity is capable of evolving toward a just and equitable tomorrow. On the other side, those clinging to the past—a past steeped in manifest destiny, systemic domination, and the coercive expansion that justified the subjugation of sovereign peoples.

The narrative of manifest destiny was not just an expansionist agenda; it was a moral contract devised by those who claimed divine endorsement. It snowballed into a destructive ideology: the belief that a white, anthropomorphized God sanctioned the domination and annihilation of native tribes. This version of God, a deliberate fabrication of supremacy, was wielded as a weapon to justify conquest, abuse, and death. By this logic, righteousness was reserved for the conquerors, while the oppressed were stripped not only of their lands but also of their humanity.

Where, then, can we find a righteous God in this narrative? Can such a God exist in a system designed to undermine the natural law of human freedom? The marketers of enslavement and institutional fear have constructed a prison of the mind—a prison without locks, guarded only by the illusions they perpetuate. These self-appointed wardens and guards of cultural imprisonment have sold us a lie: that freedom is theirs to grant, that dignity is theirs to dictate.

Yesterday was more than a memory; it was a confrontation. It was the dungeon of faith—a prison built on lies—positioned against the dream of liberation. It was the legacy of those who weaponize religion to control, juxtaposed with the words of a dreamer who spoke of justice, love, and the mountaintop experience.

Dr. King's vision was not one of conquest or domination, but of a shared humanity. His dream challenged the very fabric of the structures that imprison us, urging us to see the divine spark in every human being. His words reminded us of the possibility of breaking free from the chains of fear and division, of rising above the darkness to create a world where freedom is not a privilege, but a birthright.

Yesterday, as we remembered the dreamer, we also faced the reality of our present. The volcanic rumblings of destruction—fueled by those who violate the natural order of freedom and equality—were on full display. Yet, within this tension lies an opportunity: the chance to reclaim our humanity, to reject the lies that have enslaved us, and to rise as a global body dedicated to justice, compassion, and light.

Willful Blindness and the Weight of Supremacy

The question before us now is glaring: will we be chained to the misconceptions of our past, or will we seize the light of clarity to guide us into a better tomorrow? Do we even care anymore? Whether or not we care, time marches on, pulling us forward, leaving the past behind. The real question is whether we will rise together, evolving toward a higher understanding of our shared humanity, or surrender to the trash heaps of history, consumed by the destructive delusions of selfish pride and false superiority.

Do we care enough to confront our reality? Or will we let profound apathy write the script of our future—a deceitful promissory note bouncing with empty promises to generations yet unborn? Has our faith in weakness grown so strong that we've become blind—willing prey for those with malicious intent?

Blindness is devastating, especially for those with the ability to see. It is not only the inability to perceive but also the lack of willingness to recognize. Some forms of blindness are so severe that even the perception of light is lost, robbing the individual of the natural distinction between day and night. To choose blindness, especially willful blindness, over clarity and vision is a demoralizing act that harms not only the individual but everyone forced to navigate their darkness.

Years ago, I spent my first night at my future in-laws' home. If you haven't picked up on it by now, I am a Black man. My mother-in-law, by contrast, was white—both by DNA and culture. She held beliefs that were deeply entrenched in a supremacist framework, though she likely didn't see herself that way. Was she a white supremacist in the organized sense? No. She had no robes hidden in her closet or secret memberships in extremist groups. But she was, in her worldview, a supremacist—unaware of how her ingrained cultural attitudes perpetuated a sense of superiority.

This lack of self-awareness is critical to understanding supremacy. It doesn't require overt affiliations with hate groups. Supremacy operates quietly, even within seemingly harmless environments like a white church or a rigid religious upbringing.

I know this firsthand because I was raised in a home where a different kind of supremacy reigned. My family's religious orthodoxy convinced us we were members of God's "true church." That identity justified looking down on everyone else, regardless of their wealth, education, or prominence. Supremacy wasn't limited to race or gender—it extended to all dimensions of life. We were taught to see others as less, no matter their achievements, because they weren't part of "us."

This is the essence of supremacy: the belief that our way, our identity, and our understanding are inherently superior, and therefore, we have the authority to dismiss or diminish others. Supremacy insists on controlling not just our own lives but the lives of others, demanding they conform to our views simply because we claim the right to dictate their path.

But the truth is, our willful blindness to our ignorance can be our most avoidable failure. When I, as an untrained observer, assume my ideas about flight—based on watching geese at a pond—are equal or superior to the expertise of a seasoned aviator, I am practicing a dangerous form of false superiority. I am willfully blind to my lack of knowledge, dismissing the hard-earned expertise of another simply to affirm my own imagined dominance.

To live this way is to perpetuate a false and destructive narrative. Supremacy, in all its forms, is not a strength; it is a profound weakness. If we are to rise beyond the dark confines of ignorance, we must first open our eyes—truly open them—and confront the illusions we hold about ourselves and the world around us. Only then can we move forward, free of the chains of willful blindness and toward the light of collective progress.

The Colorblind Declaration

It was my first morning in what would later become my in-laws' home. I had walked into the kitchen and taken a seat at the glass table just off the deck, overlooking the backyard. As I sat there, soaking in the unfamiliar surroundings, Kathleen—my soon-to-be wife—joined me. After preparing breakfast, she sat down, and we began talking, enjoying the quiet of the morning.

We had just started eating when her mother entered the room. She didn't greet us or ease into our conversation.

Instead, she walked directly over to me and stood there, hovering like she had something important to say. I looked up, curious.

"Donnell," she began, "I want you to know something."

She had my attention. After all, I had just met her in person the evening before. "I want you to know," she said, "I am colorblind."

Now, let me tell you—I've been Black all my life. I know that statement. I know its rhythm, its intent, its place in the catalog of well-meaning declarations meant to assure Black people of something vaguely comforting. But I also knew what lay behind it: a careful but misguided dodge of reality.

Rather than take offense, I decided to have a little fun.

"Wow," I said, feigning concern, "I'm so sorry to hear that."

She looked puzzled. My words hung there for a moment, and I could see her trying to process them. I leaned in. "You know, I've been reading about these new glasses doctors have developed—they can actually correct colorblindness. They're supposed to be amazing."

"No, no," she stammered, "that's not what I mean. I mean, we don't see color in this house."

Ah, there it was.

What she couldn't see—what she was blind to—was the history behind her words. To her, this was a virtuous proclamation, a statement of good intentions. To me, it was a dismissive attempt to sidestep the reality of my Blackness and what it means to live in this world as a Black man.

She didn't see her own contradiction. If she truly didn't see color, why was I the only person in the house who needed to hear this announcement? She hadn't felt the need to explain her "colorblindness" to anyone else. Her urgency to tell me—her decision to start this conversation uninvited—was proof that she absolutely saw my color.

Kathleen sat quietly as her mother continued her impromptu TED Talk on post-racial harmony. I sat back, letting her finish, watching her build a castle of good intentions on a foundation of misunderstanding.

When she finally stopped, she gave me a look—a look that said she thought I just didn't get it. Maybe I wasn't bright enough to understand her magnanimity. She turned and walked away, satisfied that she had done her part to enlighten me.

As the door swung shut behind her, Kathleen turned to me, her voice tinged with frustration. "Why did you do that?" she asked. "She meant well. She just wanted you to know she's not prejudiced."

I sighed. "Kathleen," I said, "she's not colorblind. She's blind to the fact that she sees color and doesn't know what to do with it."

You see, her mother's words were born out of something deeper—a cultural form of supremacy that isn't overt but is just as impactful. Supremacy isn't always a loud, violent declaration of superiority. Sometimes, it's as subtle as assuming you have the right to define someone else's experience. It's deciding, uninvited, to be the spokesperson for harmony while dismissing the complexities of someone else's reality.

Supremacy doesn't always come dressed as hate. Often, it's

dressed as paternalism, as a well-meaning hand that assumes the right to steer the ship without ever asking for permission. It's the same instinct that compels someone to run their fingers through another person's hair without consent, or to loudly declare that they lost a job to someone "less qualified" without ever seeing that person's résumé.

It's the belief—conscious or not—that your perspective is the default, that your intentions excuse the impact of your actions.

As I sat at that table, smiling to myself at the absurdity of the moment, I realized this wasn't about intent. It was about result. She had entered the room to tell me how she thought the world should work, without any regard for how I actually experience it. That's the heart of supremacy—not hate, but control.

And as her footsteps faded down the hallway, I was left to marvel at the irony of it all.

The Supremacy of Ignorance

This week, we climbed a little higher on the chart of moronic ignorance. They fought the words *Affirmative Action* into hiding, but that wasn't enough. I listened to the long, enduring eulogy for DEI. And then it arrived—the proclamation of a "colorblind society."

In this picture-perfect delusion, white men are handed their unearned star on the self-curated tour of the elite "Walk of Fame." It is theirs to take. And isn't this, after all, the essence of supremacy?

Let me pause here and recall the words attributed to Albert Einstein:

"The world is in greater peril from those who tolerate or encourage evil than from those who actually commit it."

I will not debate the invisibility of my skin, nor will I apologize for it. I am reminded, time and again, of my *guilty until proven innocent* status. I am reminded of the culinary skills I am assumed to lack before I've ever been given a chance to boil an egg. I am reminded every time an unarmed brother or sister is shot, their only "crime" being that they were born into the "costume" of their skin.

I will not engage in debate with the colorblind ignorant whose eyes fail to see and whose minds fail to comprehend. Nor will I entertain the self-centered fables of those who use their racist soapboxes to justify the worlds they've built for themselves, free from accountability.

I am who I am, and I am proud of it. I don't need permission from anyone to exist as I was born.

The Face of Supremacy

Supremacy is a terrible thing. It is insidious, seeking to dictate what I can see and what I am forbidden to see. It looks back into what it calls *prophetic books* and demands I hold to its definitions of prophecy. It builds systems requiring payment for the simple right to dream. It censors, determines, and controls—deciding what I should read, think, or consider.

Supremacy insists I define myself on its terms. It demands allegiance to its religion, its rules, and its worldview. It tells me what art to value, what music to love, and even what thermostat setting should make me comfortable. It presumes the right to dictate my worth and my values without ever consulting me.

And let's be clear: supremacy is not just white. Supremacy is the voice that shouts from one church pulpit to another, proclaiming salvation only through affiliation. It's the audacity to define for me what Catholics and Jews think without understanding their beliefs. It's the presumption to decide my sexual identity or determine who I am allowed to love, even in the innocence and ignorance of my heart.

The Many Masks of Supremacy

Supremacy is a chameleon, cloaking itself in attitudes, assumptions, and actions that often go unnoticed, even by the one acting from its influence. It is not always loud or violent. Often, it is subtle, creeping in like a shadow, whispered in the tone of a refusal, or veiled in polite dismissals. Supremacy doesn't need a manifesto; it thrives in the quiet assurance of superiority.

It may sound like the quiet confidence of someone refusing to acknowledge another's authority, as in, "I can't work under Marsha." The discomfort isn't rooted in Marsha's ability or achievements but in the existence of an internal hierarchy that dismisses her merit. Supremacy's voice says, "Respect is given, not earned, and I am the one who decides whether you qualify."

Supremacy in Everyday Exchanges

Supremacy often hides in the mundane. It sits in the awkward refusal of help from someone presumed incapable for no reason beyond prejudice. It finds its voice in the casual dismissal of a person's presence, as if their very being is an affront to an unspoken rule. "I'll come back later" may seem innocuous, but beneath the surface, it speaks volumes about perceived worthiness and belonging.

It thrives in the "us versus them" narratives:

- "Don't eat with those people."
- "They worship idols."
- "I don't need to learn your language."

These statements do more than draw lines—they build walls. Supremacy constructs barriers that isolate, separate, and divide, all while feeding on fear and ignorance. It does not seek understanding; it demands conformity or erasure.

The Poison of Supremacy

Supremacy poisons the mind of its bearer as much as it harms its victims. It blinds the individual to the richness of shared humanity, replacing curiosity with suspicion and compassion with arrogance. It imagines the worst in others to justify its stance, relying not on evidence but on stereotypes and hearsay.

Supremacy does not ask, "What can I learn from you?" Instead, it declares, "There is nothing you can teach me." It refuses reciprocity, as in the case of trying ethnic foods but dismissing others' culinary traditions. It sees no value in exchange—only in control.

Supremacy as a Revealing Mirror

What is most revealing about supremacy is not what it says about the object of its disdain but what it exposes about the person harboring it. Supremacy is a confession, an unwitting admission of insecurity, ignorance, and fear.

- It reveals a mind shackled by stereotypes, unable to engage with nuance or complexity.
- It reveals a heart closed to connection, clinging to

imagined superiority to shield itself from vulnerability.

- It reveals a perspective so self-centered that it cannot fathom a world where others' experiences hold equal value.

Supremacy is not power; it is a defense mechanism. It is the voice of a fragile ego, desperately holding onto imagined hierarchies to avoid confronting its own inadequacies.

Moving Beyond Supremacy

To dismantle supremacy is to challenge the narratives it builds. It begins with questioning:

- Why do I believe this?
- Where did this assumption come from?
- What would happen if I engaged rather than avoided?

It requires courage—the courage to confront biases, to admit ignorance, and to embrace the vulnerability of learning. It demands an openness to experiences outside one's own, an acknowledgment that superiority is not strength but limitation.

Supremacy cannot thrive in the presence of humility, empathy, and curiosity. It withers when faced with the light of honest self-examination and the warmth of genuine human connection.

A Final Thought

Supremacy may wear many masks, but its essence is always the same: fear disguised as power, ignorance masquerading as certainty. When we recognize it for what it is, we gain the power to dismantle it—not only in others but within ourselves.

Supremacy is the demand to root for *its* team, to pledge allegiance to *its* cause, or to vote for *its* party under the guise of patriotism. Supremacy, in all its forms, is the theft of personal agency cloaked in false authority.

The Deep Dive

It's easy to recognize supremacy when it wears the colors of white versus Black, but how do we understand the political supremacy that seeks to dictate my party affiliation to qualify me as a "good American"?

We've dived into the depths of ignorance without first learning how to swim. And now we're seeing the cost. The careless investments of supremacy are yielding devastating returns. The surging waters are claiming casualties.

Lady Liberty, once a symbol of hope, stands neglected in New York's harbor. Lady Justice, who once held the scales with dignity, has become a peeping Tom, blindfold askew. The promises that once made America the envy of the world are now punchlines in a global comedy.

We've worshipped at the altar of supremacy for far too long. It's time for us—not just as Americans, but as a collective humanity—to reevaluate the platforms on which we stand. It's time to reclaim reason, rebuild our values, and choose humanity over hegemony.

The Supremacist's War on Reason

The supremacist needs no facts. His supreme imagination dictates the story, bending reality to the will of his convenience. Science? An unnecessary obstacle. If he declares, "Gravity is not a thing," then in his mind, the gravitational pull of the earth ceases to exist.

With a bullhorn in hand, he preaches his doctrines to an eager audience: *"The world is flat!"* The need for evidence evaporates under the weight of his conviction. Education? He brags about dismissing it, declaring proudly that he's teaching his *young'uns* at home, despite barely being able to count himself.

To him, the moon landing is a hoax—a fabrication spun by a conspiracy of intellects who dare challenge his common sense. After all, *"If people were on the other side of the earth, commonsense tells you they'd just fall off."*

The supremacist thrives in the absence of scrutiny, demanding unwavering acceptance of his untamed reasoning. He presents doctrines and beliefs devoid of foundation, other than the unchallenged traditions of his own voice.

The Commandments of Supremacy

The supremacist's reach extends far beyond the realm of ideas. He presumes the authority to govern the minutiae of your life:

- What to eat and what not to eat.
- How to dress and how not to dress.
- Where to sleep and where not to sleep.
- Who to like and who to dislike.

His rules are arbitrary, born not of logic but of control. It's not enough for him to live within his self-imposed constraints—he must impose them on you as well. To the supremacist, your autonomy is a threat to his imagined dominion.

The Power of Reasoning

My friend, I'm genuinely glad you picked up this book. It tells me you're willing to lean into the discomfort of thought, to sift through the complexities of human existence, and perhaps even challenge your own assumptions. I hope my pitching in my two cents has sparked something in you—a spark that can grow into a fire of understanding.

This volume is a glimpse, a snapshot, a fragment of my thoughts, but not the whole picture. Thought is fluid, and reasoning is its vessel. It carries us to places unimaginable, often lifting humanity to remarkable heights, but at times, dragging us to the darkest depths.

Reasoning is a powerful thing. It's what we do, all of us. It is the spark that has ignited every step of progress, every leap of innovation. Reasoning is the fertilized seed of imagination, and imagination is what births the impossible into the possible. Together, they have carried us through the long journey of evolution, pushing the boundaries of what it means to be human.

The Duality of Reason

But reason is a double-edged sword. It has been the destruction and the backbone of our survival. It is as much the architect of creation as it is the destroyer of worlds. Reason has ignited wars, fueling the fires of conquest, power, and greed. Yet, paradoxically, reason has also been the examiner of war, the cool-headed mediator, and the relentless extinguisher of conflict.

Reason builds bridges between divided lands and walls within unified hearts. It can be used to justify atrocity or to champion justice. In its purest form, it is neutral—a tool, neither good nor evil. Its outcome depends on the hands that wield it and the minds that direct it.

So, as you turn these pages, consider the reasoning that

shapes your own life. Is it building or tearing down? Is it a bridge or a barricade? Is it bringing humanity closer to its potential or dragging it further away?

The Responsibility of Reason

Reasoning, my friend, is more than an ability; it is a responsibility. To reason is to wield influence—not only over your own life but over the world around you. When reason is abandoned or misused, it becomes a weapon, wielded carelessly in the hands of the ignorant or malicious. It is not enough to reason; we must reason well.

Reason must be paired with accountability. Like a river carving its way through the earth, reason shapes the landscape of humanity. Left unchecked, it floods, destroying everything in its path. But when guided—when tempered with wisdom and compassion—it irrigates fields, sustains life, and nurtures growth.

The Danger of Lazy Thinking

There is a plague far more dangerous than ignorance, and it is lazy thinking. The refusal to reason, the acceptance of shallow conclusions, and the blind following of voices louder than our own—these are the diseases of progress. They fester in the complacency of comfort and the ease of conformity.

Lazy thinking does not challenge, does not question, does not seek. It clings to the familiar, even when the familiar is harmful. It repeats the mistakes of the past, disguised as tradition, and calls it wisdom. It trades critical thought for convenience and imagination for apathy.

The Call to Reason

This is why I write, why I speak, why I share these words with you. Not to preach or to impose, but to provoke. To prod the sleeping giant of thought within you and remind you that your reason matters.

Your reason is your compass, your guide through the chaos of existence. It is the lens through which you perceive the world and the tool with which you shape it. Without it, you are adrift, carried by the currents of others' ambitions, their fears, their supremacy.

To reason is to reclaim your agency. It is to stand tall in the face of manipulation and declare, "I will think for myself." It is to examine the stories you've been told and decide which ones to keep, which ones to challenge, and which ones to discard.

The Evolution of Humanity

Humanity is at its best when we reason together—when we bring our diverse perspectives to the table and allow them to sharpen one another. This is the evolution of humankind, not through conquest or domination, but through understanding. Through the fertile exchange of ideas, we rise.

And yet, the opposite is also true. When reason is silenced, when dialogue is suppressed, when minds are closed—the descent begins. Progress stalls, walls go up, and the seeds of division take root.

The Question for You

So, here's the question, my friend: How will you use your reason? Will you let it lie dormant, or will you cultivate it? Will you wield it carelessly, or will you refine it?

This world doesn't need more noise. It needs clarity. It needs thoughtfulness. It needs the kind of reasoning that builds, that heals, that inspires. It needs you—not just your voice but your mind, your heart, your imagination.

So, what will you do with the gift of reason? That is the question I leave in your hands.

I shared my 2 Cents of Reason.

Can we at least make some change?

ONE LAST CALL

My Final 2 Cents: A Call to Courage

This is the end of this book, but I do have some afterthoughts.

As a child, I was told never to talk about religion and politics. I was to have no right to my own point of view. I became one of the many—**culturally confined.** I thought I was right because what I was taught was the only truth and the only way to live. We were right, I was told, and we were not to listen to those who did not support our beliefs.

Today, I see a **merger of religion and politics.** The prison wardens and guards have taken their positions to shut down dissent. The first step was to silence factual news as being unreliable. We were told all other news beyond the chosen echo chambers was fake. The Constitution of the United States of America may no longer protect us. Ideologues have hijacked the freedoms we once boasted of having.

The lady in New York Harbor once lifted her light to welcome **"the tired, the poor, the huddled masses yearning to breathe free, the wretched refuse of the teeming shores."** She stood, asking for the world to send these—the homeless, the tempest-tossed—so they could find refuge in a nation still working toward its promise. That promise is written in the very **Preamble of our Constitution:**

"We the People of the United States, in Order to form a more perfect Union, establish Justice, insure domestic Tranquility, provide for the common defense, promote the general Welfare, and secure the Blessings of Liberty to ourselves and our Posterity..."

The Lady's poem at her base represents her. It speaks loudly for her, telling the world that **she lifts her lamp beside the golden door!** But today, that door has closed for many who came with a dream. They were not living under our laws; they were living in places where the great colossus seemed to offer them a chance—a hope for something better. They heard the invitation. **They came.**

Yet a segment of the religious community has cohabitated with a political scheme and **produced a bastard child of hate and extremism.** This tornadic disaster of the selfish narcissistic brain trust promotes the idea of becoming a welcomed immigrant to his nation can be welcomed at the cost of 5,000,000 dollars for a gold card.

I have been watching. That young boy—who once prayed for wisdom—has grown into an adult. He doesn't know everything, but he is **attentive.** He hears the construction teams—not of bridges, but of walls, both **invisible and literal.**

They don't seek peace. They don't seek progress. They don't seek righteousness.

They are **purveyors of conflict.**

They fear the future and seek instead to **recreate the past.** But if those who truly have a heart for righteousness remain confined by fear—especially the fear of change—this will be our historic end.

We are living in a **Constitutional crisis.**

The President of the United States took a solemn oath:

"**I do solemnly swear (or affirm) that I will faithfully execute the Office of President of the United States, and will to the best of my Ability, preserve, protect and defend the Constitution of the United States.**"

Yet, our current president, much of Congress, and even the Supreme Court have bent their knees—not to justice, not to righteousness, not to the people—but to **themselves** and those who feed them a putrid plate of shared wealth and dishonesty.

Our national ship is not perfect. As of this writing, many can see the current peril. The indicators, the alarms are warning us that it is signaling that it may be capsizing. Do you, can you, get that? **The nation is capsizing. Water is rushing in. But there are lifeboats.**

When fair and honest opposition is shut down, when only one point of view is allowed, when truth is silenced and propaganda reigns, the people become ever more **culturally confined.**

They shrink their reality to the size of their inferior **bubbles.**

They ignore the vastness of the universe—the limitless scope of possibility.

But I cannot leave you without telling you this:

Life has no prison bars.

It confines no person. **You need no key.**

There is light.

There is darkness.

There is truth.

I have shared my **two cents of reason.** Now, I invite you to **reach.**

Reach for the best in your life.

Reach beyond your bubble.

Don't be afraid. **Live.**

Be **alive.**

Stand for **truth.**

Stand for **mercy.**

Be the **image of love.**

It isn't hard to do when you consider the **payoff.**

The choice is yours: **Stand or surrender. Live or fade.**

The world is watching.

I can't write 'The End' because this may not be the end. For many who resonate with these thoughts, I welcome you to discover your beginning. What I've offered here is my humble contribution—a 2-cent investment in the fertile soil of our shared evolution, with hopes of planting seeds that will grow into something impactful for the world to come.

Some may say, 'We are living in the last days.' My friend, that may be true. But I choose to live in the first day of the rest of my life. I invite you to embrace that same charge—to see each new day as a beginning, full of possibility and purpose.

CULTURAL ILLITERACY: THE CONTROLLED SUPREMACY OF TASTE

When Preference Becomes Power and Division Masquerades as Identity

When I consider the lessons, I've learned from my personal experiences and testimonies that I've shared with you previously, I am drawn to many ideas. Among them are culture ideas and issues, that if left unchecked can cause clashes, social neglect and disorders. Here are some subjects to give some thought to:

- Cultural Security
- Cultural Insecurity
- Cultural Sensitivity
- Cultural Insensitivity
- Cultural Warfare
- Cultural Neglect
- Cultural Isolation
- Cultural Terrorism
- The Chemistry of Culture
- Cultural Denialism
- Cultural Maturity
- Cultural Immaturity
- Cultural Infiltration

- Cultural Assassination
- Cultural Appropriation
- Cultural Exploitation
- Cultural Welfare
- Cultural Intimacy

This well alone runs deep. I encourage those who can, with the dignity of curiosity, to take on these cultural issues and matters. Don't be afraid to go into a deep dive and help humanity to understand those stories and lessons that both expose who we are and how humanity can discover new pathways to our better selves; not only as a nation, but as a global community.

In this bonus chapter, I want to use what I've shared with you to explain my views on a limited aspect of the cultural dynamic. As I observed my connections with both side of the cultural divide I realized: this wasn't just about rudeness or personality. This was about **Cultural Illiteracy** — the entitlement to decide which ways of being are valid… and which are not. This is not a blame game. As I observe the behaviors of my Honduran family, I can expose their constant failures as well as the failures of my own. In doing so I can also provide limited understanding guiding the current social order in the United States. The issue has so much to do with literacy.

Now, my 2 cents of reasoning concerning "Cultural Illiteracy" and The Controlled Supremacy of Taste.

Cultural illiteracy is not merely a lack of knowledge — it is often a deliberate resistance to shared understanding, where personal preferences evolve into tools of exclusion,

reinforcing invisible walls that divide communities, relationships, and nations.

Here it is. I asked the weekly Bible Study class a very simple question.

I never expected the response to hit so fast. It came like a reflex—hands flying up, fingers stretching like antennae trying to catch a signal from heaven. They weren't waiting to learn; they were racing to confirm what they already knew. The question I asked was this: *"Who can tell me what sin is?"*

It was the kind of question that felt safe in the room we were in. A room filled with polished believers, many of them steeped in what they were taught was "the truth." These were students molded by the voices of the KJV, EGW, GC, and BC—the full alphabet of authority in their world. They were also familiar with three other sets of letters they didn't claim but used frequently: LGBTQIA. And they knew what to do with BLM and DEI. Those were labels for "the other"—terms spoken often, but rarely understood.

The enthusiasm in their response was almost childlike. I hadn't even finished the question before the oohs and ahhs, the bouncing bodies, and the "Pick me! Pick me!" chorused through the room like a Sunday School revival. I chose one. She smiled with a kind of self-righteousness that made me wonder if she had personally shaken hands with Jesus over breakfast.

Her answer: "First John, chapter three, verse four: *'Sin is the transgression of the law.'"*

It was technically correct—Biblically precise, even. And everyone in the room nodded as if we had just unlocked the secrets of the universe. But then, I shifted.

I asked again: *"Who can tell me **what sin really is?**"*

This time, silence fell like snow in a graveyard. Heads didn't nod. Hands didn't wave. And somewhere in the back, someone probably prayed I had misspoken. The air went still. I offered my answer: *"Sin is what the other person does."*

That's when one woman burst out laughing. She got it. She caught the mirror I had held up—saw her own reflection and grinned with recognition. The rest were still looking for the frame.

The Walls We Build Without Knowing

Cultural illiteracy doesn't arrive in our lives like a parade. It doesn't announce itself. It doesn't wear the robe of a villain or storm the gates. Instead, it comes in quietly — tucked inside preferences, passed down through dinner tables, hidden in polite refusals and exaggerated stares. It thrives in our assumptions. It is made strong by our comforts.

You don't have to burn a cross to be culturally illiterate. You just have to believe that your taste is the natural taste, your customs the proper ones, your humor the intelligent kind. And if someone doesn't laugh, doesn't agree, or doesn't eat what you eat? Then it's their fault — their failure to assimilate. They're the foreigner. The outsider. The other.

What begins as a "preference" can grow into a supremacy — not the violent kind that riots or marches with flags, but the quieter kind that believes itself to be neutral. Cultural illiteracy is often not fueled by hatred. It is powered by disinterest. Disinterest in others' foods. Others' languages. Others' ways of mourning, loving, dressing, or worshipping. It is the act of never asking, *Why do you do it that way?* — because deep down, the answer might challenge the belief that our way is the only right way.

I once invited a friend to a community gathering — nothing extravagant, just food, music, and faces she hadn't met before. I knew it could be meaningful. But I watched her shrink back like I was offering poison. "No, thank you," she said with a smile that didn't reach her eyes. "I'm not really into that stuff." That stuff. That's what she called it. A world. A people. A culture reduced to *stuff*.

And yet, in the same breath, she'd proudly invite me to her own cultural events, expecting my full participation and cheerful taste-testing of dishes I didn't grow up with — dishes I've learned to politely decline after enough episodes of pressure and protest.

This isn't about food. This is about control. This is about who gets to decide what is considered "normal." It's about how the rejection of difference is masked as good manners, and how hospitality turns into hierarchy.

The Fine Print of Familiarity

The harm of cultural illiteracy rarely announces itself in cruelty. More often, it drips slowly through the faucet of familiarity — one quiet preference at a time. It's the shrug that says "not my thing," the laugh that dismisses a name as "too hard to pronounce," the dinner invitation that only includes dishes someone's palate already knows.

It is in the quiet exclusions — unspoken, but loud in their effect.

Sometimes, cultural illiteracy looks like kindness. It wears a smile, even as it closes doors. It says, "You're welcome here," but adds a silent *so long as you act like us*. It tolerates difference the way a museum tolerates noise — temporarily, and only if it doesn't disrupt the tour.

And when someone dares to offer a piece of themselves — their flavor, their rhythm, their heritage — it's often met with a gentle but firm "No, thank you." Not because it's bad. But because it's *unfamiliar.* And unfamiliar feels like a risk to the one who has never had to adjust, adapt, or explain their own culture in the first place. Often, it is the unfamiliar that rapidly becomes unacceptable.

I have lived in that risk. I've sat across tables where my presence was tolerated but my culture was not tasted. I've seen the eyes that scan my plate with curiosity but hold their fork with refusal. And I've learned that the deeper hurt isn't rejection — it's the assumption that what I bring is optional, while what others bring is expected.

We don't always name this for what it is. But it is not neutrality. It is not harmless. It is not a minor gap in taste. It is a silent shaping of what is allowed to belong.

And somewhere, in a thousand living rooms and shared meals, this unspoken power begins to write the story of who gets to feel "normal" — and who will always be a guest.

When the Unseen Becomes the Unspoken

Cultural illiteracy is not just a lack of knowledge — it is a disinterest in acquiring it. It is the comfort of staying within one's own taste, perspective, and assumptions while disregarding or dismissing the richness others may carry.

It is not simply ignorance. It is a choice — sometimes quiet, sometimes loud — to elevate one way of being as *normal* and regard the rest as *other.*

Cultural illiteracy often hides behind politeness. It does not storm into rooms with fists. Instead, it decorates walls with the art of one people and calls it "neutral." It fills menus, music stages and stations, school curriculums, newsrooms, and dinner conversations with the familiar and insists: *This is just how things are.*

But what it really says is: *We don't need to know about you to live our lives. But you must know about us to survive yours.*

In its most everyday form, cultural illiteracy is a kind of quiet supremacy — the supremacy of taste, of comfort, of assumed relevance. It controls the dial of whose stories matter. It is the shrug that makes the unfamiliar invisible. And invisibility, over time, becomes silence.

When preference becomes power, culture becomes hierarchy.

And while many who live in cultural comfort may not intend harm, intention does not equal impact. The harm still lands. It lands in children who never see their names on book covers. In neighbors who must code-switch to be heard. In communities who are invited to participate, but only if they conform.

Cultural illiteracy, left unexamined, ensures that empathy is optional — and that bridges never have to be built.

The Unreciprocated Table

I have always believed that food could be a language of peace. That maybe if we break bread together, we might also break down a few barriers. I've extended invitations with this hope — to dinners, to community events, to spaces where the flavors may not be familiar but the welcome is genuine.

But time after time, I've found myself on one side of a locked gate.

One friend in particular stands out. She came into my life at a time when trust was growing roots, when mutual respect felt possible. She asked for my help navigating the systems she didn't understand — immigration forms, community engagement, civic expectations. I offered my knowledge without hesitation. I shared my connections. I opened my world.

But when I asked her to step into my circle — to meet my friends, to share a meal outside her comfort zone — I was met not with curiosity, but with resistance. Her anger wasn't just a wall; it became a weapon. Voice raised. Arms crossed. Accusations hurled. And over what? A hamburger. A gathering. A gentle suggestion that she try something — someone — new.

I've sat across the table from a bowl of tripe, honoring her culinary traditions. But that grace has not been returned. I've tasted her culture. She has rejected mine.

And I ask myself — how many people live this imbalance every day? How many bridges remain uncrossed because only one side is expected to build?

This is not a story of blame. This is a story of pain. Of the exhaustion that comes when you are always the one doing the stretching, the folding, the bending to fit.

It is not cultural difference that wounds. It is the refusal to meet difference with dignity.

When Taste Becomes Territory

What I've come to understand is this: we are not simply

dealing with matters of preference — we are navigating power.

This isn't just about food, or friendship, or whether someone chooses to step into a space that is unfamiliar. These are signals. Indicators of something deeper. Of what's valued, of who is welcomed, of who is expected to change and who is allowed to stay the same.

This is where cultural illiteracy begins to take root.

Cultural illiteracy is not just a lack of exposure; it is the refusal to recognize or engage with a world beyond one's own cultural borders. It can be passive — a quiet ignorance. But more often, it is active. A deliberate avoidance. A choice masked as tradition, or faith, or comfort. A subtle enforcement of dominance where only one set of tastes, norms, and expressions are considered "right," while all others are either tolerated, exoticized, or rejected outright.

It becomes clear in those small, everyday interactions: who gets to define the menu, who gets to speak their native tongue without being corrected, who gets the benefit of interpretation — and who doesn't.

When someone insists that only their food matters, their language dominates, their holidays are honored, their way of living remains centered — they are not merely being "proud of their heritage." They are participating in a quiet supremacy of taste. One that doesn't burn crosses or shout slogans, but one that still divides, still wounds, still decides who belongs and who must prove their right to be there.

This is what I mean by **"the controlled supremacy of taste."** It is the idea that what is familiar is superior. That what is different must justify its presence. It creates a cultural caste system — subtle, polite, often unspoken, but deeply felt.

And it is here, in this very space, that we must learn to see clearly. Not just for what offends us, but for what blinds us.

The Quiet Architecture of Exclusion

Cultural illiteracy isn't always loud. It rarely wears a name tag. It doesn't usually storm into a room with fists clenched or voices raised. More often, it slips through unnoticed — embedded in our habits, inherited through rituals, passed down through what we *don't* say. It reveals itself when someone winces at a different accent, when a child's lunch is mocked at school, when a hiring manager "just doesn't see the right fit," though qualifications are met. It shows up when "diversity" is celebrated on paper but resisted in practice.

It hides inside assumptions:

- "They don't want to integrate."
- "They should learn our way."
- "They're too sensitive."
- "This is just how we've always done it."

But cultural illiteracy isn't just about misunderstanding others — it's a fundamental misunderstanding of *self*. It is believing that the way you see the world *is* the world. That your preferences are neutral. That your discomfort is evidence of someone else's error. It creates a one-way street where empathy is demanded from others but rarely returned.

This is why raising cultural literacy is not just a social courtesy — it is a civic and moral responsibility. In an age where communities are increasingly diverse, where borders are porous, where global problems demand cooperative solutions, cultural illiteracy is not just a blind spot. It is a liability.

And like any form of illiteracy, it can be addressed. But only when we name it.

Defining Cultural Illiteracy

Cultural illiteracy is not merely a lack of knowledge. It is the active inability—or in many cases, the refusal—to engage with, acknowledge, or even recognize the customs, values, expressions, or lived experiences of others outside one's immediate cultural comfort zone. It is the unseen wall that separates "us" from "them," built not only by unfamiliarity but by assumptions, fear, pride, and sometimes an unconscious entitlement to remain unchallenged.

Where cultural literacy opens doors, cultural illiteracy locks them. It creates echo chambers where a single narrative dominates and anything unfamiliar is labeled as strange, threatening, or irrelevant. Left unchecked, it becomes a form of the *controlled supremacy of taste* — a quiet insistence that one's preferences, language, food, traditions, and values are the default or the superior.

Cultural illiteracy does not always come dressed in hostility. It may arrive cloaked in politeness, hidden behind preferences or "traditions." But it still marginalizes. It still isolates. And in its most dangerous form, it gives rise to policy, prejudice, and public behavior that builds social structures around exclusion.

The Cost of Cultural Illiteracy

Cultural illiteracy is not just a personal blind spot — it is a collective liability. It impairs our ability to work together, solve shared problems, and grow as a society. Whether in schools, workplaces, hospitals, in governance, or places of worship, it shows up as miscommunication, mistrust, avoidance, and sometimes overt hostility. It distorts judgment. It shapes who is heard and who is dismissed.

In civic spaces, cultural illiteracy breeds reactionary politics. It fuels policies shaped by fear rather than understanding. A culturally illiterate society resists multicultural education, questions bilingual signage, and views inclusion as dilution. It does not recognize difference as enrichment — only as deviation. And when leadership echoes those views, entire populations may be led to believe that knowing "the other" is unnecessary, or even dangerous.

In personal relationships, cultural illiteracy is the reason friendships fracture over assumed offense. It's why invitations go unanswered, why someone's food is "weird" but not yours, and why extending a hand across a cultural line is sometimes met with confusion or resistance. It creates emotional minefields where curiosity is mistaken for criticism, and suggestion is heard as shame.

But this doesn't have to be our fate. Recognizing cultural illiteracy is not a call to guilt — it is a call to growth.

A Walk Through the Fizz: The Neighborhood of Bubbles

We don't live in isolation — we live in what you call "The Fizz," a community of individual Bubbles. Each person walks around encased in one. That Bubble is made of experience, upbringing, tradition, bias, trauma, joy, and language — and, most dangerously, it is transparent only to the person inside. To others, it can look like resistance. To ourselves, it looks like reality.

Some people never leave their Bubble. Not once. And because they've mistaken the inside of it for the whole of the world, anything outside feels foreign, threatening, or unnecessary. They believe their taste is the taste, their norms are the norms, their faith is the truth, and their language is what God speaks. They have become trapped by what is rightly called **Cultural Incarceration** — a confinement that masquerades as comfort.

But it's not always malicious. Sometimes it's just a failure to observe. This is where *Perspective Thinking* becomes the antidote.

When a person begins to recognize that others also have Bubbles — that their views are shaped by their own environments, histories, and daily negotiations with the world — something miraculous happens. Judgment turns into inquiry. Reactions slow down into reflection. That is the beginning of cultural literacy.

Cultural Literacy: A Third Pillar of Human Intelligence

If IQ measures our cognitive abilities, and EQ measures our emotional intelligence, then Cultural Literacy — Cultural Intelligence, or CQ — must be elevated as the third foundational dimension of our cognitive or rational selves. It is not a soft skill. It is a survival skill. It is not extra credit. It is core curriculum for human coexistence.

Cultural Literacy is the capacity to recognize, understand, and respectfully engage with the full spectrum of human cultural expression. It goes far beyond knowing a few facts about different holidays or being able to name a few dishes from another cuisine. It is the deep, calibrated ability to decode how values, customs, language, symbols, and behaviors are shaped by molding of cultural context — and how they shape individuals in return.

Cultural Literacy does not require you to agree. It requires you to *observe*. And through observation, it invites humility. It teaches that your lens is not the only lens — and that others are not simply wrong, but rather, they are right in a way you may not yet understand.

This is where the often-annoying example of the well-meaning Liberal comes in. A person may study inner-city culture from the outside and speak eloquently on its challenges — but they may still speak through the filter of their own assumptions, never truly shedding their own Bubble. Their words might land not as solidarity, but as condescension. This isn't always a problem of prejudice; sometimes, it's a problem of *perspective illiteracy*.

Without Cultural Literacy, good intentions can miss the mark — or worse, cause harm. With it, we move from performance to presence. From speaking about communities to standing *with* them.

The Three Core Dimensions of Cultural Literacy (CQ)

1. Awareness: The Opening of the Eye

Cultural Awareness is the first threshold. It is the *realization* that cultures other than your own are not just different — they are internally coherent systems of meaning, value, and logic. Awareness means noticing how your own background, upbringing, and environment have silently shaped your personal sense of "normal." It's the moment the fish becomes aware of the water it swims in.

Without awareness, we cannot recognize our own assumptions. Without recognizing our assumptions, we mistake our preferences for universal truth. And that mistake is the seed of cultural arrogance.

Awareness asks us to see what we have been trained not to see. It is not guilt. It is *vision*.

2. Adaptability: The Willingness to Shift

Awareness without adaptability is like seeing a storm and refusing to take cover. Cultural Adaptability is the ability to flex — to change your approach, your communication, even your expectations, depending on the cultural context you're in. It's not performative; it's *responsive*.

Adaptability doesn't mean abandoning your identity. It means holding space for others to exist fully in theirs. It means being willing to learn a new tone, a different pace, an unfamiliar etiquette — not for show, but for real connection.

This is where many fail, especially institutions and governments: they want the presence of diversity without the discomfort of change. But without adaptability, diversity remains isolated as decoration.

3. Appreciation: The Respect That Transcends Tolerance

Cultural Appreciation is not just liking someone's food, music, or clothing. It is the *humble reverence* for the roots from which these things grow. Appreciation says: "You do not need to become like me to be valid. I want to understand you — not consume you."

This dimension guards against appropriation, which takes without context. It also guards against tokenism, which showcases without commitment.

Appreciation is what happens when curiosity matures into respect. It asks nothing in return — and in doing so, earns trust.

Why Cultural Literacy Is Urgent in the 21st Century

We are no longer *becoming* a global society — we *are* one. Cultures no longer exist in tidy, separated corners. They are overlapping, migrating, merging, colliding. Whether across borders or neighborhoods, people are in closer contact than ever before — and closer conflict.

Without Cultural Literacy, we default to fear, stereotypes, and dominance. We fight over who gets to define the "right" way. We protect our bubbles instead of building bridges.

With Cultural Literacy, we gain the ability to negotiate difference with dignity. We unlock cooperation where there was the confinement of conflict. We design policies that serve people *as they are*, not as we imagine them to be.

Perspective Thinking: The Multiplier of Cultural Literacy

If Cultural Literacy is the body, then *Perspective Thinking* is the breath. It animates awareness, adaptability, and appreciation with depth, movement, and choice. It is the cultivated capacity to pause — to wonder: "What might this moment look like through their eyes?"

Perspective Thinking is not just imagining someone else's shoes. It is acknowledging that *you do, in fact, have shoes* — and that they've shaped how you walk the world.

It pushes beyond sympathy into empathy, beyond empathy into analysis, and beyond analysis into *agency*. You begin to notice how your inherited values — your notions of time, decorum, worth, and even politeness — are not natural laws, but cultural agreements.

And that's where growth begins.

The Bubble Theory: Understanding Resistance

But why is this so hard? Why do so many — even those who are well-meaning — fail to engage?

Enter *The Bubble Theory*.

Every person is encased in a cultural bubble — invisible, insulating, and reinforced by repeated comforts. These bubbles are filled with affirming feedback loops: media we agree with, communities that reflect us, traditions we never question. Bubbles aren't always malicious; many are inherited with love. But their comfort breeds blindness.

And when someone outside the bubble knocks — when they challenge its limits, or suggest that the world is far bigger than the view inside — the instinct is defense. The air gets tight. The pressure builds. The person inside may lash out or retreat, convinced that their way of being is under attack.

They are not evil. They are afraid. Not just of others — but of the unknown inside themselves.

Remember, the bubble is the container of our perception. A person's understanding of the external world is a reflection of the inner self. Our self-developed / self-driven descriptions are living mirrors of our evolving social development. The personal bubble produces limitations on how we view the world around us. Remember, positive or negative, bubbles can be infected.

The "Fizz" of Cultural Conflict

Now, imagine a society made of these bubbles. Different groups, side by side, but sealed off. Each with their own language, logic, and lived truths. When these bubbles bump into each other — especially when one is larger, louder, or more politically empowered — they create friction. Foam. Static. What I've identified as the *Fizz*.

In the Fizz, people mistake difference for danger. They collapse nuance into stereotype. They flatten stories into slogans.

And that's where Cultural Illiteracy thrives.

But when one bubble opens — even a crack — to curiosity, to discomfort, to Perspective Thinking, something radical happens: the Fizz calms. The static begins to clear. A bridge begins to build.

And that is the moment we must seize.

Cultural Incarceration & Confinement: The Invisible Cell

Imagine a prison with no bars, no warden, no locked doors — only stories. Stories repeated so often they calcify into "truth." Stories that define who you are, where you belong, what you're worth, and how far you're allowed to reach. This is *Cultural Incarceration*.

It is not enforced by iron, but by assumption. Not guarded by guards, but by *myths*.

For some, this incarceration is inherited. They're born into a narrative of inferiority or danger, shaped by historic bias or generational trauma. For others, the confinement is more subtle — they live within a dominant culture that rewards sameness, and quietly punishes those who challenge it. Even the "free" are confined by their belief that they already see clearly.

Cultural Confinement is its close cousin — not just who

you *believe* you are, but where you're *permitted* to go. It is the internal voice that says, *"That's not for people like us,"* or, *"They wouldn't understand you anyway."*

It is the child told to quiet their language at school.

The elder mocked for their accent.

The artist told their truth is "too niche."

The immigrant laughed at for their dreams.

These are walls you can't always see, but you *feel* them when you walk up to the edge of someone else's comfort.

The Reactive Mind: Reflex Before Reflection

And here lies the mechanism that keeps these walls in place: *the Reactive Mind.*

The Reactive Mind is the part of us that flinches when we hear something new. It recoils when a worldview is questioned. It fires off defensiveness before discernment. It is the brain on auto-pilot, trained by habit, fear, and social approval.

This is not a flaw of intelligence — it's a byproduct of survival. Humans are pattern-seekers. But when those patterns go unexamined, we mistake familiarity for truth, and discomfort for danger.

This is why even *well-meaning people* react with outrage or mockery when challenged on race, faith, gender, politics, or nationhood. They are not debating *the idea* — they are defending *the identity* they've constructed around it.

And in this reaction, the walls of Cultural Confinement are quietly reinforced.

Myth-Conceptions: The Stories That Keep Us Stuck

Now bring in the myths — those inherited beliefs that are rarely questioned, because they are *soaked in the sacred*. Myths like:

- "They don't want to work; they just want handouts."
- "Our way is the best way — they're just backwards."
- "If they would just act right, they'd be treated right."
- "We're all the same — I don't see color."
- "Their culture is just too different."

These *Myth-Conceptions* serve as emotional shortcuts — quick ways to judge, dismiss, or feel superior. They relieve people from the burden of learning. They provide a false sense of clarity. And they inoculate communities against the very discomfort that is *required* for cultural growth.

Left unchallenged, Myth-Conceptions become walls. But when exposed, they become doors.

CULTURAL LITERACY: THE POWER TO SEE, FEEL, AND NAVIGATE DIFFERENCE

Cultural Literacy is more than knowledge — it is *navigation*. It is the ability to recognize, respect, and respond meaningfully to cultural difference without collapsing into fear or superiority. It is not merely the study of "the other," but the ability to *stand with* the other, without losing yourself.

It is *vision*.

It is *voice*.

It is *vital*.

In a world increasingly bound together but emotionally torn apart, Cultural Literacy is no longer optional. It is essential — as foundational as reading and writing, as necessary as emotional intelligence. Without it, misunderstanding flourishes. Polarization hardens. And those with the least understanding hold the loudest microphones.

But Cultural Literacy changes the dynamic. It teaches us how to move from:

- **Assumption to Awareness**
- **Fear to Flexibility**
- **Pity to Partnership**
- **Curiosity to Connection**

It prepares a person not just to *know* about cultures, but to *engage* across them. To enter unfamiliar rooms with humility. To exit with new understanding. And to return to their own community with the wisdom to lead.

Cultural Literacy is not just knowing the right vocabulary.

It is knowing how not to use your lens as law.

It is knowing when to speak, and when to listen.

It is asking, *"What am I missing?"*

And meaning it.

The Final 50 Feet

I don't have all the answers. What I offer is what I've seen, what I've gathered by intentionally — and sometimes accidentally — being *in the picture*.

Much of what I've learned came not from classrooms or pulpits, but from moments — seismic dashes in time that quietly became history. I've lived in the cracks and margins, observing culture through personal case studies in real time. Not from the outside looking in, but from the inside — surrounded, affected, transformed.

We're not all at the same place on the road to understanding. Some are a few baby steps away. Others are still navigating corners they didn't know existed. I've come to believe the real question isn't just *What is important?* but *Who?*

For me, it was the lady who became my friend — a woman who, against the odds, woke from a comatic state. By medical standards, she was meant to die in days. But she didn't. She lived. She laughed. She lingered. And in the sacred geography of her hospital room, we formed a friendship that bypassed small talk and wandered instead into soul talk.

We were within 50 feet of our final conversation. I was asked to visit her. Her doctor, one of many who'd become more like family, met me in the hallway after exiting her room.

His white coat couldn't hide the burden on his shoulders.

"There's nothing else we can do," he told me. And in that moment, his professional armor cracked just enough to reveal the humanity beneath.

He didn't know she was why I'd come.

As I continued, a nurse thanked me. Her eyes — tired but tender — carried the same weight. I opened the door, stepped in, and there she was. Weak but awake. Surrounded by tubes and monitors. She reached for me — a crooked, clumsy hug made powerful by proximity.

"Sit down," she said.

I moved toward the chair. But she stopped me.

"No. Sit here with me." She patted the bed.

We sat. Legs dangling. The weight of eternity brushing our feet.

"Mr. Harris," she said softly, "I'm scared."

I didn't speak. I let her have her moment.

"What are you scared of?"

Her voice was low but sharp.

"I'm scared because I don't know what happens when you die."

She was the daughter of a preacher — raised on sermons about death, heaven, salvation.

But her honesty was naked. Real.

"Those who know all about dying… those who preach and teach it…" she paused. "They've never died."

That moment wasn't just a conversation. It was a confession. A torch passed in the last stretch of her journey. And that torch — her curiosity, her courage, her uncertainty — burned through me.

What you've read in this book is not the fullness of anyone's culture. I didn't attempt to capture that. No one can. What I *did* offer was a way to see. A lens to hold. A path forward.

Because Cultural Literacy isn't a subject — it's a survival skill. It's not about memorizing customs or cuisines. It's about resisting the myth that your world *is* the world.

Cultural Illiteracy exists wherever controlled taste becomes unearned power. Wherever "my way" becomes the only way. Wherever identity is weaponized into superiority.

I believe in the power of Cultural Literacy — Cultural Intelligence, or CQ. I believe it must grow. It must expand. Not as a trend. Not as a badge. But as a compass in our collective hand.

To know each other deeply.

To sit in rooms dimly lit by truth.

To ask, "What are you scared of?"

And really mean it.

Okay, this time I'm done. Seriously.

This book is complete.

Now it's your turn. Sit here with me. Let's talk. Let's grow. Let's listen before we lead.

I've said my part. Now I leave you with yours. Read the room. Read the world. Read each other — not just to decode, but to understand. That is Cultural Literacy. And it starts with presence. The rest is your story.

To the only world I'm learning to know, Best of Hope & Blessings

DONNELL L. HARRIS

ABOUT THE AUTHOR

Donnell Harris is an author, chaplain, and cultural observer whose life has placed him at the crossroads of education, ministry, government, and global engagement. He has taught in Japan, served in government at city, county, and state levels, ministered across denominations, and worked as a hospital chaplain in North Alabama's largest healthcare system. Harris is also a charter member of *Unity Now*, a grassroots movement that rose against division and hate in Maryland's state capital.

In *2 Cents of Reason*, Harris draws on personal stories and decades of service to introduce bold frameworks such as *The Bubble Theory*, *Cultural Incarceration and Cultural Confinement*, and *Perspective Thinking*. He challenges the reality of *Cultural Illiteracy* while inviting readers into conversations that are both deeply personal and globally relevant.

With over forty years of ministry and public service, Harris writes with the conviction that humanity's differences are not barriers, but building blocks. His message is simple yet urgent: in a world of polarization, each of us must choose whether to build walls—or join the construction team of building bridges.

DONNELL L. HARRIS

"Building bridges of reason where conflict builds walls."

www.ingramcontent.com/pod-product-compliance
Lightning Source LLC
Chambersburg PA
CBHW050512170426
43201CB00013B/1923